Cultural and Critical Perspectives on Human Development

Cultural and Critical Perspectives on Human Development

EDITED BY

Martin J. Packer
and
Mark B. Tappan

State University of New York Press

Published by
State University of New York Press, Albany

For information, address State University of New York Press,
90 State Street, Suite 700, Albany, NY 12207

Production by Diane Ganeles
Marketing by Michael Campochiaro

Library of Congress Cataloging-in-Publication Data

Cultural and critical perspectives on human development / edited by
Martin J. Packer and Mark B. Tappan.
    p. cm.
    Includes bibliographical references and index.
    ISBN 0-7914-5179-8 (alk. paper)—ISBN 0-7914-5180-1 (pbk. : alk. paper)
    1. Developmental psychology—Congresses. 2. Developmental psychology—
Social aspects—Congresses. I. Packer, Martin J. II. Tappan, Mark B.
BF712.5 .C85 2001
155—dc21
                                         2001020009
                                             CIP

10   9   8   7   6   5   4   3   2   1

Contents

Acknowledgments

We would like to take this opportunity to thank those who have, in various ways, contributed to this book. The authors included in this volume all began their involvement in this project by participating in two linked symposia on Critical and Cultural Perspectives on Human Development held at the Annual Meeting of the American Educational Research Association in 1995. Since that time they have been very generous and very patient with us as this project has come to fruition.

We would also like to thank the following for permission to reprint material that was originally published elsewhere:
- Chapter 3 contains material from *Welcome to middle age!: (and other cultural fictions)*, edited by Richard Shweder. © Copyright 1998 by the University of Chicago Press. Reprinted by permission of the University of Chicago Press.
- Chapter 8 contains material from *Raising their voices: The politics of girls' anger* by Lyn Mikel Brown. © Copyright 1998 by Lyn Mikel Brown. Reprinted by permission of Harvard University Press.
- Chapter 10 contains material from "Deconstructing surveillance pedagogy: 'Dead Poets Society'" by Peter McLaren and Zeus Leonardo. This article was originally published in *Studies in the Literary Imagination*, vol 31(1), pp. 127-147, © Copyright 1999, Department of English, Georgia State University. Reprinted by permission.

Colby College provided critical financial and administrative support that enabled us to complete this project. We particularly appreciate the work of Grace von Tobel and her capable office staff, who helped us prepare the final manuscript. Grateful thanks also goes to the staff at the State University of New York Press, particularly Priscilla Ross, Diane Ganeles, and Marilyn Semerad, for their professionalism, perseverance, and patience.

Finally, Martin Packer wishes to acknowledge Tamara Massimi, for demonstrating development in a different cultural context. Mark Tappan thanks Lyn Mikel Brown and Maya Tappan Brown for their unwavering love, support, and good humor.

CHAPTER 1

Introduction

Martin J. Packer
Mark B. Tappan

Anyone who has recently attended the biennial meetings of the Society for Research in Child Development or the annual meetings of the American Educational Research Association knows that the terms in which, and methods with which, human development are understood and investigated are changing rapidly, as are the aims of such investigation. These are mainstream North American organizations, yet after spending a few days at either conference it would be hard to identify a mainstream position. Instead one can sample a delightful plurality of approaches to children's (and adults') learning and development. What has happened is that the cognitive-developmental paradigm that for the past four decades defined developmental research (not to mention practices like teacher education and counseling) has lost its sway. No longer is it assumed without question that development is solely a process of cognitive reorganization, directed toward a single, universal end point, and accomplished within the individual child. This paradigm of inquiry was so hegemonic that even when new domains such as the social or the emotional were opened up for examination, they were construed in purely cognitive terms. Of course this cognitive-developmental interpretation has never gone completely unchallenged, but these days it is no longer clearly the norm to be challenged. The centrality of the autonomous, individual subject has been called into question.

Instead we have a situation of flux in which the theoretical presuppositions and the research methods of cognitive-developmentalism have been swept away and a variety of alternatives are being explored. The very nature of "learning" and "development" have become called into question (cf. Donmeyer, 1996; Salomon, 1995; Kessel, 1981). New attention to social relationships, emotions, and context, goes hand in hand with a movement of inquiry from the laboratory and the natural experiment to include ethological and ethnographic approaches, interpretive analysis, and with the exploration of biography, narrative, and other new genres of writing. Increasingly psychologists now mingle with anthropologists, linguists and psycholinguists, sociologists, historians, political scientists, psychoanalysts, kinesiologists, pediatricians, and others. Interpretations of the passage from childhood to adulthood are offered in which the possibility of multiple developmental pathways is admitted, the role of social and historical context is appreciated, and the value-judgment involved in calling a change "development" is acknowledged.

One sign of all this is the new attention to *cultural* and *critical* considerations in scholarship concerning human development. Cultural considerations include not simply the investigation of differences in the ways in which children develop in different cultures and subcultures, but cultural variation in the ends toward which development moves, as well as attention to the cultural work that children and adults are engaged in when learning and development occur. No longer is "culture" simply an independent variable in analyses of variance. Critical considerations include a growing reflective awareness on the part of researchers and theorists of their social positions and responsibilities, and of the values in terms of which they evaluate what they investigate, as well as a critical stance toward the societal institutions in which children become adults.

This new attention to culture and critique has brought new voices into academic departments, and it is beginning to transform academic institutions: journals, programs, and faculty. At the same time, there has not been a great deal of communication between, for example, cultural psychologists and critical pedagogists. There are some concerns clearly shared by those who attend to culture and those who engage in critique (increased reflexivity on the part of the investigator, to pick just one example), some interesting differences, and not much occasion of comparing notes.

This book had its origins in two linked symposia we organized at the annual meetings of the American Educational Research Association (AERA) in 1995, in San Francisco. The other presenters were Michael Cole, Peter McLaren, Lyn Brown, Robin Leavitt, Elizabeth Debold, Linda Rogers, and Frank Kessel. We sought to bring together people "doing cultural work" and those "doing critique," in the hope that some cross-pollination (if that is the apt metaphor) would occur. In many respects our expectations were exceeded. For one thing, the person we had invited to represent cultural psychology spoke of critique, while the person invited to speak of critical pedagogy undertook a cultural analysis! The sessions overflowed the room they were held in, with an engaged and enthusiastic audience. This, and the fact that

AERA reviewers had rated the theoretical significance of the symposia "excellent," encouraged us to develop a book based on these papers. We hope and believe the book makes a timely contribution to the reformulation of the study of human development, and we think it is unique in its attention to both cultural and critical perspectives and the opportunity it consequently provides to explore how these perspectives can inform one another. The chapters in this volume explore many of the implications for the study of human development and of an awareness of culture and the adoption of a critical stance. They bring insights from critical pedagogy, cultural psychology, feminism, postmodernism, critical theory, semiotics, and other approaches into dialogue, presenting studies of developmental change at various points across the life span, and also presenting reflections on the changing character of inquiry. They illustrate disparate ways in which the complexities of human development can be grasped and comprehended, while avoiding the reductionisms of cognitivism.

In this introductory chapter we first raise the questions, What is culture? and What is critique? Our intention here is not to provide an exhaustive survey, a grand review of the intellectual landscape in which these two topics have been explored, but more modestly to provide a preview of the approaches to cultural analysis and critique that are employed by the authors in this volume. We want to give the reader some sense of the range of options available and their relation to one another. In part this is to remind the reader that the authors have not, considered together, exhausted all the possibilities for approaching culture and undertaking critique.

Next we provide a brief description of each chapter in turn, again showing how culture and critique have been taken up in each particular case.

Finally we suggest that the work represented in this volume contributes in three main ways to our understanding of human development. First, making us more aware of what the researcher brings to inquiry; second, showing how closely human development is linked to human history; and third, reminding us that development is the creation of a human being.

What is Culture?

cul_ture 1 : CULTIVATION, TILLAGE 2 : the act of developing the intellectual and moral faculties esp. by education 3 : expert care and training <beauty ~> 4 : enlightenment and excellence of taste acquired by intellectual and aesthetic training 5 a : a particular stage of advancement in civilization b : the characteristic features of such a stage or state c : behavior typical of a group or class 6 : cultivation of living material in prepared nutrient media; also a product of such cultivation. (Webster's Seventh New Collegiate Dictionary)

The creation and use of culture is a biological characteristic of our species (Cole, 1996, p. 8), and it is equally true that our species has become a creation of culture. Bruner says of the "culturalist" approach to the nature of mind that it

> takes its inspiration from the evolutionary fact that mind could not exist save for culture. For the evolution of the hominid mind is linked to the development of a way of life where "reality" is represented by a symbolism shared by members of a cultural community in which a technical-social way of life is both organized and construed in terms of that symbolism. This symbolic mode is not only shared by a community, but conserved, elaborated, and passed on to succeeding generations who, by virtue of this transmission, continue to maintain the culture's identity and way of life. (1996, p. 3)

Culture, then, is that wherein we dwell. Culture is for humans what water is for fish—without it we would cease to exist, or certainly we would not have become what we are. The difficulty is that, just as fish would presumably give no thought to water were they able to give thought to anything, culture is so much part of our lives, so much part of who and what we are, that it is hard to get it clearly enough into our sights to ascertain just what kind of thing it is. Indeed it's really no kind of thing at all—culture is what makes it possible for something to be a thing, and for a human being to be a person.

How best to conceptualize the pervasive yet evasive nothing that is culture? One set of possibilities that is quite evident in this book is drawn from the "cultural psychology" whose influence on developmental psychology is being strongly felt. The growing influence of cultural psychology and its cousins, such as sociocultural theory and cultural historical analysis (e.g., Bruner, 1996; Cole, 1995; Shweder, 1989; Valsiner, 1987, 1995; Lave, 1988; Rogoff, 1991; Engestrom, Miettinen, & Punamaki, 1999) resonates with a growing realization among developmental psychologists that the assumption that human development is a movement of irreversible progress toward a universal end point is no longer tenable, and itself is a historical and cultural construction (cf. Kessen, 1990). The past several years have seen the publication of two new journals in cultural psychology: *Mind, Culture and Activity* (edited by Cole, Engestrom, Star, & Wertsch) and *Culture and Psychology* (edited by Valsiner).

Cole (1996), drawing from the work of Vygotsky (1986), Leont'ev, and Luria has identified as a central notion in cultural psychology the focus on cultural artifacts and the role they play mediating person-environment interaction. Cole proposes this as a "psychologically relevant" concept of culture. (Other central notions that Cole describes are an interest in cross-cultural variation, especially in the different "designs for living" that a culture hands down to its junior members, and an insistence that adults are active agents in the developmental process, in addition to the active child that Piagetians have emphasized.)

In such a conceptualization, culture is viewed as "a medium of mediational means." (It is such a conceptualization that underlies the design of an environment such as the Fifth Dimension, described in chapter 2 by Brown and Cole.) Culture is a medium in which biology and environment interact, a medium composed of "historically accumulated systems of artifacts." Artifacts are "simultaneously ideal (conceptual) and material," (Cole, 1995, p. 32) organized, not randomly assembled. Context is not just that which surrounds; it is a qualitative relationship that weaves together structure and function. Artifacts' ideal form stems from the fact that they, as Cole puts it, "contain in coded form the interactions of which they were previously a part and that they mediate in the present." An ax, for example, has a "subjective component," which is a "concept or attitude." Cole feels that "human beings live in a 'double' world, simultaneously 'natural' and 'artificial'" (p. 10). The "first world," the "external" world, is that of "direct" unmediated, sensory contact of subject and objects; the "second world" is mediated by artifacts; this is the "world of ideas and philosophies." (1995, p. 32)

Like Bruner, Cole sees the mind as the product of an interaction between the child and an environment that can be partitioned into universal features (e.g., gravitation) and historically specific features (e.g., knife and fork). And "because what we call *mind* works through artifacts, it cannot be unconditionally bounded by the head or even by the body but must be seen as distributed in the artifacts that are *woven together* and which weave together individual human actions in concert with and as part of the permeable, changing events of life" (1996, pp. 136–137). It is logical, then, to seek to influence learning and development by designing new webs of artifacts, such as the Fifth Dimension.

A related conceptualization also represented here is to see culture as the "intentional worlds" in which we live. This approach is central to Shweder's formulation of cultural psychology. (This is the basis for the study of Hindu women reported by Menon and Shweder in chapter 3.) Shweder sees human experience and subjectivity as grounded in intentional worlds that consist of artifacts and events whose "existence is real, factual and forceful, but only so long as there exists a community of persons whose beliefs, desires, emotions, purposes and other mental representations are directed at it, and are, thereby, influenced by it" (1989, p. 2; cf. 1991). Shweder has offered the example of "the 20th century intentional world of American baseball." The objects, artifacts, and events that populate an intentional world cannot be adequately described by an objective, neutral scientific language. Just as it is true of a "weed" that it is defined by human interests and involvements, so this is true of what is "true" or "good" or "beautiful." In line with this, Menon and Shweder in their chapter define culture as "a reality lit up by a morally enforceable conceptual scheme or subset of meanings instantiated in practice."

This strand of cultural psychology starts in anthropology, though Shweder considers cultural psychology "an interdisciplinary human science." He acknowledges that it has "many ancestral lines" and invites other tellings of the story of its lineage: his own narrative invokes the figures of Levy-Bruhl; Wittgenstein; Cicourel and the ethnomethodologists, D'Andrade, Geertz, Kleinman, and Sapir (Shweder, 1991, p. 40); and even "Abelard, Herder, Hegel, Heidegger, Brentano" (p. 72). As Shweder tells it, the origins myth of cultural psychology is a narrative that begins with the failure of the cognitive revolution to "develop an adequate theory of the 'person'" (p. 1).

> Cultural psychology is the study of the way cultural traditions and social practices regulate, express, transform and permute the human psyche, resulting less in psychic unity than in ethnic divergences in mind, self and emotion.

> Cultural psychology is the study of the ways subject and object, self and other, psyche and culture, person and context, figure and ground, practitioner and practice live together, require each other, and dynamically, dialectically and jointly make each other up.

> Cultural psychology is premised on human existential uncertainty (the search for meaning) and on a (so-called) "intentional" conception of "constituted" worlds. (1989, p. 1)

So understood, according to Shweder, cultural psychology differs from general psychology, cross-cultural psychology, and psychological anthropology in not engaging in the search for Platonic general, transcendent structures of mind, and in dismissing the belief in a psychic unity to humanity, typically assumed to take the form of a standard "central processing mechanism." Psychology has for some time generally viewed the person as merely an embodied, ahistorical, and universal general computational device. And anthropology has complimented this conceit by viewing culture as something exterior, arbitrary, socially sanctioned, and historically in flux, and so as having nothing essential to do with psyches or persons. "The 'person' disappeared from ethnography" (p. 38).

Cross-cultural psychology has extended the error by assuming that such a universal competence is simply manifest differently in different cultures, or in different tasks in a single culture. Shweder considers cross-cultural psychology "not heretical enough, even as it raises its serious concerns" (p. 22) to the presumption of psychic unity. And psychological anthropology took just a small step forward by viewing sociocultural environments as adapted to, and hence expressive of, the general central processing mechanism.

Cultural psychology, in contrast, rejects the distinctions between intrinsic and extrinsic properties of mind, between form and content, between deep and surface structure, and instead sees the mind as "content-driven, domain specific and constructively stimulus-bound" (pp. 23–24); as showing "local response patterns" (p. 24).

Shweder aims with this conceptualization of culture to capture the dynamic interrelationship of subject and social structure. Just as Cole sees the mind as "distributed in . . . artifacts," Shweder views thinking not as the process of a general-purpose conceptual device, but as an extension of, or an analogue to, the artifacts of a specific culture. The mind, according to Shweder, is to be understood as "embodied in concrete representations, in so-called 'mediating schemata,' 'scripts' and well-practiced 'tools for thought'" (p. 43). This version of cultural psychology might be described in a nutshell as anthropology with the person put back in, with a conception of the person drawn from sources other than mainstream psychology. Persons are understood as intentional—as "responding to, and directing their action at, their own mental objects or representations" (p. 41); as "directing their behavior with respect to their own descriptions and mental representations of things" (p. 44). The "central theme" of such a cultural psychology is that "you can't take the stuff out of the psyche and you can't take the psyche out of the stuff" (p. 40).

If culture is viewed as made up of the mediating artifacts of an intentional world, it follows that development is a matter of becoming adept at handling the cultural tools and signs that mediate human action; becoming skilled in employing the "toolbox" a culture provides. These tools are typically viewed as internalized or appropriated by the learner (but cf. Packer, 1993).

The tool metaphor is an apt one: a tool embodies, both formally and informally, clues to its appropriate use. A mark that has been scratched on the blade of an awl by a previous owner, for example, may show us how deep a hole to bore. And tools provide their user with a sense of the world; using a file on aluminum feels quite different from using it on steel—the character of the material becomes sensible (cf. Shotter, 1993). But material implements are not the only tools: language, too, can be thought of as a tool, or perhaps more adequately as a set of tools. The spoken utterances we produce can be understood as mediating our contact with the world. Utterances are artifacts and, human creations, shaping the material medium of the air around us. Because this medium is so plastic they dissipate rapidly and vanish, unlike artifacts like digging tools or pottery that can be excavated hundreds of years later. Nonetheless, utterances mediate our interaction with, and our knowledge of, other people.

One might extend the tool metaphor still further: for example, Jaan Valsiner has considered marriage forms such as monogamy and polygamy as "social devices that organize life in family units in ways that satisfy the multitude tasks of family members," and so provide a "social structural context within which child development takes place."

Adults play a crucial role assisting this growing expertise with, appropriation of, and internalization of artifacts. As Newman, Griffin, and Cole point out,

> the objects in the child's world have a social history and functions that are not discovered through the child's unaided explorations. The usual function of a hammer, for example, is not understood by exploring the hammer itself (although the child may discover some facts about weight and balance). The child's appropriation of culturally devised "tools" comes about through involvement in culturally organized activities in which the tool plays a role. . . .

> Children . . . cannot and need not reinvent the artifacts that have taken millennia to evolve in order to appropriate such objects into their own system of activity. The child has only to come to an understanding that is adequate for using the culturally elaborated object in the novel life circumstances he encounters. The appropriation process is always a two-way one. The tool may also be transformed, as it is used by a new member of the culture; some of these changes may be encoded in the culturally elaborated tool, as the current sociohistorical developments allow. (Newman, Griffin, & Cole, 1989, pp. 62–63)

This "scaffolding" by adults and by other expert members of a community is one form of interaction that results in the handing of increasing responsibility for social activities to the child, such that children's development can be seen as changing participation in cultural practices (e.g., Miller & Goodnow, 1995). It is "guided participation," both tacit and explicit, which includes both adults and children in a type of involvement that makes the child an apprentice learning the ways of their culture (Rogoff, 1990).

A "reciprocal causal system," as Valsiner puts it, is at work in development, guiding children to competent adult functioning in their society, where "children's developmental trajectories are guided by cultural organization of the environment. . . . At the same time, children are active in modifying the cultural environment in which they live" (1989a,

p. 4). The result is that "development can take place along a multiplicity of pathways, each (or at least many) of which are equally adequate for arriving at the desired outcome" (1989b, p. 74).

Cultural psychology is not the only source of an interpretive framework with which to examine the role of culture in human development at work in this volume. A somewhat different approach of culture is drawn from the work of Foucault. Although his vocabulary is different, Foucault was also exploring developmental issues. He described "the goal of my work during the last twenty years" as being "to create a history of the different modes by which, in our culture, human beings are made subjects" (1982, p. 208). Central to these modes are the "power relations" in which people are placed, but, unlike the case with relations of production and relations of signification and communication, the tools for studying power have been largely lacking. Seeking to forge the appropriate analytic devices, Foucault proposed that what is central to power is not actual or threatened violence, or acquiescence and consent. Rather, he suggested that "what defines a relationship of power is that it is a mode of action which does not act directly and immediately on others. Instead it acts upon their actions: an action upon an action, on existing actions or on those which may arise in the present or future." As a consequence it is necessary "that 'the other' (the one over whom power is exercised) be thoroughly recognized and maintained to the very end as a person who acts; and that, faced with a relationship of power, a whole field of responses, reactions, results and possible inventions may open up" (p. 220).

This description of Foucault's approach makes it clear that when cultural psychologists consider ways in which adults influence the action, and so guide the development, of children, they are addressing a concern that was also considered central by Foucault. There is thus a certain convergence between those chapters in this volume that focus on the "medium" of development (including Brown & Cole, chapter 2; Menon & Shweder, chapter 3) and those that focus on power (including Leavitt, chapter 5; Debold, chapter 6). When Debold writes that "[d]evelopment, then, can be considered as the process by which we become drenched in and shaped by culture-bound assumptions of power/knowledge," her position can be related to that of Rogoff when the latter insists that "it is incomplete to focus only on the relationship of individual development and social interaction without concern for the cultural activity in which personal and interpersonal actions take place" (1995, p. 141).

At the same time, this convergence should not obscure important differences in the way in which Foucault's "archaeology" and cultural psychology conceptualize and investigate culture. For, as Debold points out, many developmental theories, including those that have otherwise broken with cognitive-developmentalism, have assumed "that the child's construction of knowledge is politically neutral." Cultural psychology has only just begun to extend its analysis into the political dimension of everyday life and children's development. But attention to power surely leads quickly to the consideration of such phenomena as social status and social division, and such issues as identity and inequality. How to conceptualize these? How to understand the place and role of power in culture? How to grasp the ways in which the child develops within a "socio-politico-cultural context"?

The problem to be overcome is that psychology typically "posits a functioning social order in equilibrium, and individuals molded and shaped through socialization into performers of normatively governed social roles and practices" (Lave, 1988, p. 87). Even in cultural psychology there is often a presumption of "holism": the thesis that a social order has an overall systemic pattern that gives definition to its parts and to their interrelations. The metaphor of culture as a set of tools or a toolkit is holist, and this unitary and unproblematic conception of culture can lead us to assume, erroneously, that cognition and ways of knowing, too, are unitary, fixed, and unchanging, and unaffected by the situations in which they are employed.

> "Warehouse" and "toolkit" metaphors for the location of culture in memory make it possible to abnegate the investigation of relations between cognition and culture by, in effect, defining culture as "what people have acquired, and carry around in their heads," rather than as an immediate relation between individuals and the sociocultural order within which they live their lives. (Lave, 1988, p. 91)

The view that development is a matter of internalization or appropriation of cultural tools can turn into a simple enculturation model: a picture of the individual acquiring knowledge and values rather than as engaged in an ongoing process of interaction, negotiation, and cultural production (Willis, 1977/1981). Against such an interpretation, Rogoff insists that "it is incomplete to assume that development occurs in one plane and not in others (e.g., that children develop but that their partners or their cultural communities do not) or that influence can be ascribed in one direction or another or that relative contributions can be counted (e.g., parent to child, child to parent, culture to individual)" (1995, p. 141).

One source of this tendency toward holism is the fact that the paradigmatic community studied by classical anthropologists was the small village society. But such societies are clearly no longer the norm, and if society is now far more complex, the same must surely be said about culture. And division is a crucial social activity. Human groups are differentiated by practices, beliefs, and institutions (Lamont &

Fournier, 1992). Mauss declared that "The domain of social life is essentially a domain of differences" and Bourdieu (1979/1984) has said that if there is a principle of organization to all forms of social life, it is the logic of distinction. Boundaries and differences separate members of a group from others. These distinctions are symbolic but also political: they "freeze a particular state of the social struggle, i.e. a given state of the distribution of advantages and obligations." And domination and authority require legitimation, so that culture can become, as both Marx and Weber saw, an ideology at the service of the dominant classes. It follows that power relations between groups can be read through their relations with culture.

This implies that cultural artifacts need not form a unitary, organic whole, but instead formations that are differentiated by social position and social group. Culture is a "labyrinth," as Debold says. "Let us assume that there is no socially constructed objective reality. . . . This is not to deny that there are socially constructed real conditions and distinctions, but these conditions and distinctions are manifold and situational and cannot necessarily be reduced to a single, ordered objective matrix" (Hall, 1992, p. 276).

> Viewed at the surface, the cultural objects of this world have no apparent order to them. They appear everywhere, diverse, often in a jumble. Similarly, to look at how each individual acts is to see cultural practices that form a unique and shifting array. Nevertheless, the dazzling variety and endless differences of culture obtain surprising coherence when we look at them through the lens of social stratification. People prepare and consume food in distinctive ways. . . . Such stances toward culture differ by social position and group, there can be no doubt. . . .

> Such a model recognizes the existence of heterologous, relatively coherent cultural objects, texts, and audiences external to any individual whose actions may be structured in terms of them. However, the multiple and overlapping institutionalized cultures described as cultural structures do not have the character of a single, encompassing objective field of distinction, and heterologous "markets" and "currencies" of cultural capital interfigure with one another in ways that do not reduce to a single calculus of distinction." (pp. 257, 260)

In market societies, communities interpenetrate so that individuals participate in more than one, with the result that enforcing an overarching status order is both more problematic and less relevant. In such societies, culture provides the structured categories by which we organize

our actions, and cultural symbols are mobilized in exclusionary practices that result in the creation of status groups, positioning individuals socially and defining social identities. Competing definitions of what
counts as "legitimate" culture get mobilized in group conflict, and various types of inequality are reproduced in the process. In such a conceptualization, culture consists of "institutionalized repertoires that have
as powerful an effect on the structuration of everyday life as do economic
forces" (Lamont & Fournier, 1992, p. 7).

There are two directions one can go from here. One is to move outward to the larger political and economic systems in which power and
money circulate in ways that seem to be autonomous of human agency, in
order to locate their influence on culture and development. The other is to
move inward to study the play of power and influence in the intricacies of
human interaction.

The first move entails drawing a distinction between two aspects
of society, as lived by its members and as an objectified dynamic structure—call them "lifeworld" and "system" perspectives respectively—in
order to comprehend their interrelation. Habermas (1981/1984,
1981/1989) has argued for the importance of drawing such a distinction,
and proposed that over historical time these two aspects become increasingly differentiated both internally and from each other. Lifeworld, "the
intersubjective, sociocultural field of social relations," is

> the province of reality in which man continuously participates
> in ways which are at once inevitable and patterned. The every-
> day life-world is the region of reality in which man can engage
> himself and which he can change while he operates in it by
> means of his animate organism. . . . Furthermore, only within
> this realm can one be understood by his fellow-men, and only in
> it can he work together with them. Only in the world of every-
> day life can a common, communicative, surrounding world be
> constituted." (Schutz & Luckmann, 1974, p. 3)

The "system" is the apparatus of political and economic factors,
processes, and institutions that complex modern society requires for its
continued operation.

Viewed in such terms it is evident that cultural psychology, with
its conceptions of culture as intentional world, as mediational means,
focuses on lifeworld. Such conceptions need to be complemented and
extended by paying attention to the institutional apparatus in which
the lifeworld is embedded (and that it in turn grounds).

The second move entails focusing in on the details of human relationship. Foucault has pointed out the influence of "three types of relationships which in fact always overlap one another, support one another

reciprocally, and use each other mutually as means to an end" (1982, p. 218): relations of instrumental action, communication, and power. To the first belong "things, . . . perfected technique, and the transformation of the real," to the second "signs, communication, reciprocity, and the production of meaning," and to the last "the domination of the means of constraint, of inequality, and the action of men upon other men" (pp. 217-218).

Evidently Piagetian genetic epistemology, with its emphasis on logico-mathematical knowledge, has attended solely to the first type of relationship. Developmental psychologists have begun to correct this by paying attention to the second, and now the third. One way to do this is to extend the notion of cultural tools to include "cultural forms." (The chapters by Tappan, Brown, Rogers, and McLaren & Leonardo do this.) Culture can be viewed as a source of messages that young children—along with the rest of us—are always receiving and passing along to others. Such an approach to culture focuses not so much on setting or context as on the semiotics of symbolic artifacts (cf. Thompson, 1990; Eagleton, 1991). We can view attention to "voice," as Gilligan (1977, 1982) has done, as a version of this. Such an approach is likely to employ close textual reading, though this can draw for its techniques and logic on a whole range of interpretive approaches, including semiotics, psychoanalysis, deconstruction, and hermeneutics. The role of interpretation becomes central, starting with the "preinterpreted" character of what is investigated—for texts and messages are already understood by participants, before the researcher comes along. This is culture now viewed not so much as a whole way of life but as the bits and pieces with which we weave a way of living. Attention is directed to the performative aspects of everyday action, to the ideological role and effects of the metaphors and messages whose sources range from the commercial media to casual gossip.

It may be useful to draw a rough-and-ready distinction among three conceptions of culture. The first views culture as mediational means, as the arrangements of artifacts, practices, and events that make up an intentional world. The second views culture as the play of power, as a place and process of division, exclusion, and domination. And the third finds culture in the semiotic forms of messages and texts in human communication. These three are by no means mutually exclusive: one could conceivably draw on all of them, and consider the influence on children as power is enacted in messages circulating through one or more forms of life.

But the threefold division is a helpful one, in part because parallel to these conceptions of culture we can anticipate three broad strategies of critique. After all, "every theory of criticism is implicitly a theory of culture" (Gunn, 1987, p. 5). The first seeks to disclose how culture provides conditions for a possible way of life. The second diagnoses the operation of power and its consequent exploitations and coercions. And the third aims to read critically, to disclose the operation of subtexts.

What is Critique?

> cri.tique : an act of criticizing; *esp* : a critical estimate or discussion
>
> crit.i.cism 1 a : the act or criticizing usu. unfavorably b : a critical observation or remark c : CRITIQUE 2 : the art of evaluating or analyzing with knowledge and propriety works of art or literature 3 : the scientific investigation of literary documents (as the Bible) in regard to such matters as origin, text, composition, character, or history. (Webster's New Collegiate Dictionary)

Whether one starts to attend to the impact of the larger societal system of people's lives and communities, or to the role of power and ideology in people's everyday mundane interaction, one has begun to invoke something of a critical perspective in one's work. But what range of forms can this critical perspective take in developmental psychology, and how might it be combined with an exploration of the role of culture?

Two senses of the term *critical* are frequently confused, and sometimes combined. "Critique" has, since Kant at least, signified the examination of the *conditions of the possibility* of some phenomenon; Kant's *Critique of Pure Reason* (1787/1965) considered the epistemological conditions necessary for human perception and reasoning to be possible. But "critique" has, especially in the United States, also come to be understood as a politically slanted identification of forms of exploitation and the criticism of those considered responsible. The conflation of these two senses of "critique" can probably be placed at the Marx's doorstep, since he considered exploitation of wage laborers to be a condition for the possibility of a capitalist economy. Within critical pedagogy, for instance, both of these senses of critique are still operative, linked in the way Marx linked them, though popular perception of critical pedagogy sometimes notes only what is taken as a fondness for complaint. To many people who wish not to practice it and who are uncomfortable with those who do, critique seems to be simply the habit of criticism, of carping. We hope to make it clear that this is a mistaken view. On the contrary, cultural analysis and critique are intimately linked.

When culture is conceptualized as a medium, as an intentional world, critique in the first sense, that of uncovering the conditions for the possibility of a particular form of life, is readily invoked, for this critique is simply a matter of articulating the context this culture provides for a specific way of living.

Such a strategy of critique requires researchers to be both engaged and reflective. In this regard cultural psychology already, despite the absence of an explicit political stance, involves critique. This can be seen in the reflective awareness it encourages on the part of the psychologist, as theorist, researcher, and practitioner, that he or she is also a member of a culture—of various cultures, in fact, from the professional to the local to the national and beyond. And one impetus for cultural psychology has been dissatisfaction with the questionable value-judgments flowing from traditional cross-cultural research, with its characterizations of "primitive" thinking. Criticism of the hidden cultural basis of such prejudiced cultural comparisons has motivated aims to reconstruct the methodology and aims of psychology.

One larger issue here is the political role and responsibilities of the scholar, theorist, and researcher, relatively privileged, and involved in the production of knowledge. For example, Valsiner has argued that developmental psychology has remained intellectually indebted to the traditions and social expectations of the Western societies in which it emerged. Children in these societies (one might add, typically white, middle-class, male children) have provided the unquestioned norms that have oriented psychologists in their investigations. As psychologists have increasingly come to see development as an interaction between organism and its environment, interest in cross-cultural research should have increased, but this has not been the case. And an emphasis has largely been lacking "on culture as an *organizer* of an individual child's development." The result is that "the core of contemporary developmental psychology . . . remains remarkably separate from issues of cultural organization of childhood in different societies" (1989a, p. 3).

If one adopts the second conception of culture, as practices of division, exclusion, and domination, the critical strategy of diagnosing these practices of power, and seeking to undo their effects, is an evident one. To the extent that critique is concerned with understanding and combating oppression focused on gender, race, class, and sexual orientation, the common moral objective is "to empower the powerless and transform existing social inequalities and injustices" (McLaren, 1995, p. 168). To the extent that critique is concerned with the dynamics, contradictions, and asymmetries of power and privilege in human experience, researchers must understand that knowledge is always a social and ideological construction tied to particular interests, relationships, and discursive practices. Feminist critique (e.g., Walkerdine, 1988, 1997) and critical theory, for example, evidently take such an approach; both seek to draw attention to forms of systematic oppression.

This kind of critique can take the form of a challenge to the culture of one's own discipline. Several chapters in this book (and in a sense the book as a whole) challenge in fundamental ways the positivist, decontextual, ahistorical, and purportedly value-neutral analysis employed by most traditional developmental inquiry among psychologists, anthropologists, and educational researchers and practitioners. The assertion that these are sciences that seek and can achieve objective, context-free knowledge is denied by efforts to apply research findings, as well as theories and methods, to non-Western cultural contexts. "At a minimum, such applications overlook important areas of psychological phenomenology that are relevant in those cultures but absent in Western ones, such as children's development in polygamic families" (Valsiner, 1989a, p. 4). Ostensibly "objective" knowledge turns out to be culture-specific, inapplicable to other cultural conditions.

A researcher's interpretation is always shaped by the culture, the tradition, from which they come. And this means in turn that the legitimacy and authority of that tradition must be questioned. This raises complex issues concerning the nature of the relationship between critique and culture. Does criticism require somehow standing outside the traditional practices, the culture, of a community, in order to evaluate it? But how is such a stance possible?

One possible resolution to this issue is found in "positional epistemology," the view that those who are oppressed are better able to discern the forms and forces of power than those who employ them. One root of this is Hegel's depiction of the "master-slave dialectic," where since the slave must grapple with the exigencies of life in order to meet the demands of the master, who remains dependent, it is the former rather than the latter who comes to see things clearly. Feminist "consciousness raising" has a similar basis, as does Lukács's (1923/1988) depiction of "class consciousness": the interpretive frame the working class develops as a result of their position in the economic class-structure of society. To speak of only one of the chapters in this volume, Menon and Shweder effectively turn the strategies of positional epistemology back on those who would utilize them too quickly and formulaically.

And, third, if one conceives of culture as manifest in semiotic forms, critique can logically take on the task of the appraisal of the ideology of these forms, and the effort to diagnose their latent operation, the hidden interests at work in messages and texts. The analysis of cultural forms and the ways in which they are produced and received in social interaction and human relationship comes in many shapes and sizes—narrative analysis, conversation analysis, argument analysis, reader response theory, and so forth—with as many nuances in their critical stance. But in general they can be subsumed within a hermeneutical logic of inquiry, and entail a "depth hermeneutics," a "hermeneutics of suspicion" (cf. Thompson, 1990; Ricoeur, 1973/1990; Packer & Addison, 1989; and Packer, 1999).

Hermeneutics has advanced from the study of religious and literary texts to the examination of human action (Packer, 1985). Texts, messages, signs, gestures, and utterances have a *performative* character; they don't merely convey sense; they are ways of acting on people—moves in a language game. But censorship, displacement, and substitution conceal the operative principles; hence analysis takes a critical turn. Unmasking ideology is necessary when what is said denies and disguises what is being done; when communication and metacommunication clash; when interpersonal knots are being tied.

Overview of the Chapters

These three forms of critique certainly don't exhaust all the possibilities; again, our intention has been to preview the approaches to culture and critique explored by the authors of the chapters that follow. Now that we've completed this preview we can offer the reader a succinct overview of each of these chapters, with an ear to the types of discourse in which cultural and critical considerations make their appearance. Then we shall consider some broader considerations they raise. We have divided the chapters into three sections on the basis of the *primary* way in which they deal with culture, though as we've noted there is much overlap.

Culture as the ground for a form of life

Brown and Cole, in chapter 2, "A utopian methodology as a tool for cultural and critical psychologies: Toward a positive critical theory," draw upon and extend their conception of cultural psychology. They describe a program of research for the study of development in the context of a community, one that involves distinct phases of involvement of the researcher with the community of people who constitute the subject of the research.

In order to develop what they call a "positive critical theory," Brown and Cole locate their work in relation to the discourses of critical theory, critical communication studies, feminism, and critical pedagogy. They reject the pessimism they associate especially with the critical theorist Adorno, the view that all efforts at radical change are "doomed to fail." Brown and Cole argue that failure is not inevitable, and they also point out that even when it does happen, we can still learn something valuable.

Their "utopian methodology" typically involves four phases. In the first of these, issues are identified that are problematic for the community and for which the researchers believe they have relevant knowledge. In the second phase, the researchers enter into joint activity with the community to create an alternative set of circumstances that constitute an hypothesis about the changes in social practices needed to overcome the problem. The third phase is an evaluation of two aspects of the second one: whether the hypothesized new conditions were in fact created and, if so, whether the anticipated changes in the problem situation came about. If the team of researchers and community members failed to constitute the needed new forms of practice the research now recycles, seeking revisions of the theory of activity creation. If the new forms of activity were created but did not have the desired effect, the research recycles in order to determine what was wrong with the hypothesized theory.

But if the new activity was successfully created and had the desired effects, the research enters its fourth phase—diffusing the innovation more broadly throughout the community and seeking to sustain it. This is the "utopian goal": to diffuse the new problem-dissolving practice through the community in a sustainable way. Such a goal is rarely achieved, but even when it not accomplished the ways in which diffusion fails offer a critique of the theory at all levels, enabling a reevaluation and initiating a new cycle.

Brown and Cole illustrate these ideas with a description of a project to create new forms of educational activity for children during after-school hours: the "Fifth Dimension." The concern to which this research was addressed was the desire of a community to provide high-quality educational experiences for their children, and especially to provide the children with access to, and expertise in, the use of new communication and information technologies. The utopian goal was the creation and sustainable maintenance of after-school activities in existing community institutions brought about through collaboration between universities and communities. Brown and Cole provide an overview of the success and failure of a number of such efforts, efforts that have yielded valuable evidence about the quality of the theory guiding their work and about the kinds of condition that must be taken into account to make progress toward the utopian goal, conditions not ordinarily considered in educational innovations.

In chapter 3, "The return of the 'white man's burden': The encounter between the moral discourse of anthropology and the domestic life of Oriya women," Menon and Shweder engage in an anthropology informed by a cultural psychology. Their aim is to understand and interpret the lives of Hindu women living in a temple town in India. They seek to accomplish this through a conjunction of sensitive ethnography and interpretive analysis. One result is an account of the women's conceptions of the phases of their life, conceptions that draw upon well-articulated two-, four-, or five-phase models of the life course (and these models neatly nest hierarchically). Menon and Shweder first explore how these models are defined in terms of changes in responsibility to others, in management of the family, and in moral duty. They then step back to consider how other anthropologists have represented and evaluated Hindu women's lives. They argue that those studies that have adopted a critical feminist stance, typically portraying these women as either "passive victims" or "clandestine rebels," have adopted implicit presuppositions about the moral superiority of the West, the unitary category of "women," the ubiquity of male dominance, and consequently the moral obligation of Western intellectuals to "rescue" members of the cultures they visit and study.

It might be said that Menon and Shweder are engaged in the critique of critique, raising the question of whose values should be drawn on when (Western) anthropologists visit (Eastern) indigenous people. They seek to defend a local, "emic," moral framework against those who would critique it as embodying an abstract patriarchal ideology. Turning the tables, Menon and Shweder seek to expose the ideology, the "hidden and unexamined presuppositions," at work in anthropologists' accounts.

Such presuppositions amount to a "thin" theory of moral goods such as "autonomy" and "individuality." This theory, Menon and Shweder argue, is projected by critical ethnography onto a very different moral order, a different "cultural reality," one in which women are seen—by both genders—as playing a crucial role in the social reproduction of the family and of the larger social order, and in which men and women relate through "difference and solidarity" rather than through "equality and competition." If anything curbs the power these women have, power they view as both cultural and natural, it is self-discipline rather than subordination. Voluntary service to one's responsibilities as a devoted servant of the divine has been interpreted as humiliating subservience and abusive exploitation, but in actuality the Oriya Hindu women are not cultural dopes but reflective agents, aware of both the costs and the rewards of their choices.

Since for Menon and Shweder a culture is defined by its morality, obtuse moral critique is tantamount to a denial of the reality of a way of life. They don't wish to rule out all criticism of a culture—their stance is not a cultural or ethical relativism—but it must start with a genuine respect for the inner logic, both ethical and intellectual, of that culture. They insist that the anthropologist's journey must be a dialectical one, and reflexively so—or it can become "a late 20th century version of cognitive and moral imperialism."

In chapter 4, "Changing classes: Shifting the trajectory of development in school," Packer also engages with critical pedagogy, while using Haberma's distinction between lifeworld and system to explore differences between local educational reforms that acknowledged the cultural and relational character of teaching and learning, and state and national reforms that sought to rationalize public schooling as a "system." Packer argues that too often students' resistance in the school classroom is portrayed as their only active form of involvement. But developmentalists insist that the child is never merely a passive recipient of information, so Packer sets out to understand the active cultural work that occurs in every school classroom, whether students resist or not. He describes a participatory research project within a small school district in a midwestern rust-belt state. The community grew up during the Second World War around a massive plant constructed by the Ford Motor Company for mass production of B-24 bombers, and subsequently remodeled by General Motors (GM) for automobile assembly. GM closed the plant in 1992, providing an occasion to study the roles schools play in a community's response to economic dislocation and job loss. Packer describes how the schools had already begun to prepare by redefining the end point of learning and development—by seeking forms of pedagogy that would suit the needs and attitude of working-class children, raised within Fordism's division of labor. The local reformers, Packer argues, were aware of the fact that teaching and learning is a relational and cultural phenomenon, and he contrasts this with the efforts at rationalization that state and federal school reform initiatives brought to bear on the district, with dire consequences. These efforts misinterpreted teaching as either delivery of a public good, or production of a product.

Here the culture of the classroom is one focus, but that culture is located within larger political and economic systems. Indeed, Packer views the state and federal reform initiatives precisely as efforts to change the linkages between the individual classroom and these larger systems. He defends the "practitioners' expertise" that informed local reform initiatives, taking this as his grounding from which to critique the large-scale reforms.

Culture as the operation of power

In chapter 5, "Critical inquiry and children in day care," Leavitt reviews issues and questions that emerge from her critical inquiry into young children's lived experiences within day care programs. Her work is influenced by "multiple, diverse texts" that include phenomenology, postmodernism, interactionism, feminism, and poststructuralism, and Leavitt has crafted an interpretive ethnographic approach that allows her to question the character of her own role as researcher, and to grant that even the youngest children are active agents in the construction of their personal lives and social worlds. Yet her approach also allows her to consider how one can balance this position with a developmental perspective on children's emerging competencies and developmental limitations. How can caregivers, charged with the mission of socialization, enter into the lives of children and give them voice?

Leavitt reminds us that a critical investigation of children's lived experiences is an investigation of their political position in the social world—what they are allowed to do and how they are understood, defined, and treated by adults. Her particular focus is on forms of social control within these settings—how time and space monitor the body, and how social identities are produced by forms of institutionalized power. Leavitt, following Foucault's lead, views power as exercised rather than possessed, embedded in the microrelations of everyday life, present in the daily routines and interactions between children and their caregivers. Thus, power is studied at the level of everyday practices, "where it installs itself and produces real effects" (Foucault, 1980).

A critical perspective applied to children in day care must, it follows, explore the hegemony produced in the everyday routines and rituals of the day care center, "the terrain of conflict and struggle" (Giroux, 1991), and look for places of resistance. What is the relationship between children's empowerment and disempowerment and their caregivers' experience of power and its lack within these institutionalized settings?

Leavitt describes with subtlety the power relations that operate in the everyday, commonplace interactions among young children and their day care providers, showing that these relations flow both ways. She illuminates how children's dependency can be, given the economic and political conditions of childcare in the United States oppressive of caregivers. She reaches the conclusion that the caregivers' command over children's bodies in space and time is a fundamental, pervasive source of social power in and over children's everyday lives. But she also insists that the children must be considered competent dialogic participants, able to participate in an unmasking of the hegemony they are subjected to. By means of writing interpretive narratives, "tales from the field," Leavitt illuminates the dynamics and asymmetries of power within day care settings, and children's developmental, situated otherness.

Chapter 6, Debold's "Engendering subjects: A Foucauldian analysis of developmental gender differences," draws, like Leavitt, upon Foucault's notion of culture as a web of connections, even identities, among power, knowledge, and desire. This perspective on culture provides Debold with a critical framework for examining our fascination, both as a society and individuals, with gender identity and gender differences. Gender, Debold proposes, is a way of knowing and categorizing self, a way of disciplining self, and a basis for identity. But it is also a traumatic splitting against which resistance can be observed at specific points of discontinuity in both historical and psychological transformation.

Foucault (1980) argued that knowledge creates power and vice versa; that the use of power is evident in what we know as ourselves and our expectations of the "normal," as well as in how we experience our bodies. Knowledge of social norms creates the desire to embody those norms, and this is one of the effects of power. Foucault explored discontinuities in history—times of rebellion and resistance—as moments when power is especially at play. Thus Debold is led to explore two discontinuities in the individual psychological development of gendered subjectivity, searching for evidence of the developing child's incorporation of engendered power relations. Specifically, she examines early childhood in boys and early adolescence in girls.

Early childhood, ages 3–5, has long been understood as a time of psychological crisis for boys, evidenced by the greater prevalence of symptoms of psychological distress. Recent research indicates that early adolescence poses a similar psychological crisis for girls. These two times correspond with the development of greater cognitive capacities by which, Debold argues, children incorporate gendered power relations. Her analysis interprets the embodiment of masculinity and femininity as, in part, strategic responses to psychological distress, and so begins to explain gender differences not simply in behavior and attitude but also in mental disorder and even physical disease. Debold shows how children's expanding ability to understand the world around them, to "imagine, extrapolate and anticipate increasingly abstract forms of pleasure and pain," brings them into relations of power that are frightening, even traumatic. She emphasizes the fact that division and distinction—especially that between "male" and "female"—are not only cultural, or only cognitive. Division is a psychological process that divides each of us internally. The social practices that divide people from one another also involve a psychic splitting that each of us is subject to and which, paradoxically, renders us "normal."

Culture as the circulation of semiotic forms

Chapter 7, by Rogers, titled, "Exploring the felt pathways of the self: From experience to meaning-making in children, K–5," examines elementary school-age children's understanding of their home, school, and peer interactions. Rogers draws on Eco's (1979) semiotics to read children's narratives and interview responses in order to understand how they reacted in their understanding of the signs and symbols of their environment. She argues that it is context that shapes moral and intellectual understanding, rather than gender or developmental stage. The children she studied learned not only how their world functioned, and who was important in their interactions, but also began constructing concepts of personal identity, including concepts of gender behavior. These children used the experiences available in their immediate environment to create patterns of meaning that Rogers observes in complex narrative self-structures (Danesi & Santeramo, 1992) that deal with issues such as friendship. These ways of understanding, these "meaning making systems," were forged from the sensed life of the child, knowledge gained from making sense of doing and living, everyday experience. Rogers draws from Vico (1968) to explore how, in a world in which adults play the dominant role, children find even silence and nonresponsiveness important signs that require interpretation.

Brown is also concerned with gender identity. In chapter 8, titled "Adolescent girls, class, and the cultures of femininity," Brown, like Debold (and Tappan, as we shall see), considers the messages and pressures that culture can deliver. Her approach to culture derives not from Vygotsky and the notion of cultural tools, but from Gilligan's work on women's development and their "different voice." The notion of voice emerged casually in Gilligan's 1982 book—in phrases like "discovery of an inner voice," "voice of self and others," and "the inner dialogue of voices to which she attends"—but the concept was developed in her research group. Brown characterizes voice in complex terms, as "a relational, discursive phenomenon—linguistically constituted, socially constructed, physically embodied and, thus, by definition, polyphonic, layered, infinitely varied, often contradictory, fragmented, and rich with intentions." Brown locates her work between, on the one hand, a feminist poststructuralism that sees each of us as subject to language and, on the other hand, an appreciation of an authentic self. She thus acknowledges a tension between agent and social order, a gap between subjectivity and language, within which resistance can take place.

It is in resistance that Brown is able to ground her critique of white, middle-class messages about "femininity." A good deal of recent research in psychology and education has documented the psychological struggles and losses adolescent girls sustain as they confront cultural pressures and messages to be traditionally feminine—that is, to be nice and kind, silent, passive, and accommodating. Unfortunately, because so little attention has been given to girls who stand outside white and middle-class culture, researchers rarely interrogate the very notions of culture and femininity on which their work rests.

In an effort to counter this bias, Brown explores the ways in which sixth-, seventh-, and eighth-grade girls from working-class and poor families in rural Maine understand, express, and react to cultural definitions of femininity. She draws from videotaped focus groups and individual interviews, asking us to attend to the "class accent" in these girls' voices. Brown suggests that we think of social class as an "accent": literally and metaphorically a manner, a style, of speaking. "Voice" now has a dimension of social class as well as gender. And gender, she suggests, is a performance, a fiction, which invokes an ideal and so never quite contains the person. Consequently performance can become parody. Brown underscores the contradictory nature of what constitutes appropriately feminine behavior for these working-class girls. It is behavior radically different from the dominant white middle-class cultural ideal; behavior that offers these girls a wide range of physical and verbal expression not usually considered under the rubric of femininity. They were "raucous, active, funny, loud, and loving . . . not, as it were, a 'pretty' sight," writes Brown. She suggests, however, that while such behavior may signal a direct rejection of middle-class propriety and, in this sense, a resistance to the dominant ideologies of femaleness as passive, accommodating, and helpless, it may also work to cement the girls' lower-caste status. That is to say, the very behavior that frees them from stereotypical gender conventions may also label them, according to the dominant notions of femininity, as socially inferior.

In chapter 9, "The cultural reproduction of masculinity: A critical perspective on boys' development," Tappan draws on Vygotsky's notion of cultural tools, the "mediational means" whose appropriation shapes development. In a study of young boys' social and personality development, drawing on interviews with boys in first-, second-, and third-grades living in rural Maine, Tappan seeks to understand how identity is forged in and by culture.

Tappan locates his work in contradistinction to the psychodynamic perspective that, of course, goes back to Freud, though it is Chodorow's account of parental identification in early childhood and its connection to gender identity that Tappan wishes to question. Chorodow leaves unanswered, Tappan suggests, questions about the role of culture in gender identity formation, and to correct this omission he draws on work by Penuel and Wertsch (1995) that sees identity shaped by "cultural tools in the form of ideologies." He attends to the ideology of the messages that culture offers and circulates to young boys. With this extension of the notion of cultural tool to include messages, "cultural forms," Tappan introduces a critical dimension to his analysis.

Tappan pays particular attention to the phenomenon of "male bonding," described by Stoltenberg (1992) as a process by which groups of boys or men affirm their masculinity by verbally and/or physically harassing, abusing, and otherwise oppressing those—typically females, gay men, weaker males, or animals—who are perceived to be less powerful. Taking as his starting point an incident of sexual harassment perpetrated by some of the first-grade boys against a group of girls in their class, Tappan argues that male bonding is a ritual and discursive process by which, in the context of their interactions with peers, boys internalize and thus reproduce cultural messages about the necessary links between masculinity, power, and violence. This analysis suggests, Tappan concludes, that peer interaction deserves the attention of a critical developmental psychology, as a locus of socialization and developmental processes that perpetuate or reproduce oppressive social relations and practices. Critical pedagogy has generally approached the processes of social and cultural reproduction by attending instead to the institution of school, and the ways in which it perpetuates or reproduces social relationships, attitudes, and dynamics necessary to sustain dominant gender, class, and cultural relations of the larger society.

Tappan ends with some suggestions about how teachers and parents might encourage young boys to resist the pressure to engage in male bonding, and could, instead, develop relations with both boys and girls characterized by genuine mutuality, respect, and responsiveness.

Critical theory has taken the approach of locating communities and the lifeworld of their cultures within larger societal structures, institutions, and dynamics, thereby drawing attention to conflict and contradiction, inequality and exploitation, and to the problems of legitimation that attend the maintenance of any community. Critical pedagogy (e.g., Apple, 1982; Willis, 1977/1981; Giroux, 1983; Giroux & McLaren, 1994; McLaren, 1989) has developed the implications of critical theory for the institutions of schooling in Western society. Schools are seen as important sites for the reproduction of a society whose economic organization is capitalist, through the preparation of young people for the particular forms of their participation in its inequities and exploitations. The development of the child is seen as typically subordinated to, and directed by, the imperatives of the economy and, though less attention tends to be paid to this, to the demands of the state.

But critical pedagogy has recently taken a new direction, into the analysis of cultural forms. Giroux and McLaren (1994) have recently emphasized the fact that cultural studies should take seriously debates in education and the issue of pedagogy *(The Review of Education / Pedagogy / Cultural Studies,* a new journal of essays edited by Shannon and Giroux, undertakes this). Chapter 10, by McLaren and Leonardo, "'Dead Poets Society': Deconstructing surveillance pedagogy," illustrates this well. McLaren and Leonardo leave school for a trip to the movies. They consider one recent example of a popular genre: the "school movie." Weir's film *Dead Poets Society* is one of a kind with films like *Stand and Deliver, Dangerous Minds, The Prime of Miss Jean Brodie,* even in some respects Anderson's *If. . . .* In the main, these films portray the arrival, unexpected triumph, and ultimate downfall of a heroic figure who is able, through charismatic example and energetic exhortation, to connect with truculent students in ways others have not. In *Dead Poet's Society*, the choice of comedian-turned-character actor Robin Williams to play the teacher John Keating already suggests that this mold will not be broken.

McLaren and Leonardo explain how popular culture can be "valuable terrain for a critical study of race, class, gender, and sexual relations," and in *Dead Poets Society* in particular they find seductive themes of liberation and learning, but also a lack of attention to social contradictions that ultimately undermines the film's progressive potential. McLaren and Leonardo show this film in their graduate school classroom, and Keating is seen at first by students who view the film as an embodiment of critical pedagogy, but they are soon able to point out the limitations of his pedagogical philosophy and praxis. Keating calls into question his students' conformism with their New England boy's prep school's practices of discipline and authority, inviting them to "Seize the day!" But he provides them with no vocabulary with which to formulate a truly political project. The movie represents resistance merely as personal revelation rather than rebellion. This is, Leonardo and McLaren conclude, the "romantic pedagogy of individual expression," seductively appealing to a mainstream audience, but also instructive for a critical pedagogy.

Intersections and Projections

It becomes evident on surveying these chapters that despite their common aim and the common forum for which most of them were initially prepared, there are appreciable differences in the way in which culture is introduced as a factor to be considered, and what the "cultural perspective" brings into view in each case. There are equally important differences in the form, character, and purpose to which critique is put, and in the consequences of adopting a "critical perspective." It is helpful to consider the scope of these variations; they derive, to be sure, from the diverse sources drawn upon by the authors as the study of culture has seen "an unprecedented international boom" and emerged as "an alchemy," with "no distinct methodology" but "bricolage," and with influences as diverse as ethnography, media studies, and text criticism (Nelson, Treichler, & Grossberg, 1992, pp. 1, 2; cf. Agger, 1992).

We've distinguished three distinct approaches to culture, and three to critique. Culture can be the "medium" in which a form of life blossoms, the product of the play of power, or the flow of messages and semiotic forms. Critique can be an unveiling of the conditions of possibility, an unmasking of violence and exploitation, or the decoding of a text. These approaches are not mutually exclusive, and although we've matched them into pairs in this introduction, the chapters are not so constrained. Nonetheless a certain consistency can be perceived among them.

For example, attention to culture as the ground for a form of life is coupled here with efforts to nurture, cultivate and protect that life-form. Brown and Cole put into practice the notion that culture provides mediational means, building a system of artifacts that has diagnostic power. Their critique has a deconstructive edge to it, too, as they seek to question and overthrow a set of binary divisions that define the system their "after-school" activity stands outside of. Menon and Shweder similarly approach culture as the ground for a definition of the life course, and they then turn to protect it from feminist critique, unmasking a perpetuated colonialism, deconstructing the narratives of their own discipline of anthropology. Packer similarly seeks to protect the local culture of a working-class school district from the dictates of representatives of a "system" of public schooling, defending the ethos of the local community and contrasting it with imposed system imperatives. In each of these chapters we find an effort to disclose and defend the inner rationality and morality of a way of life (Brown & Cole in addition seek to create a lifeworld without division; to foster a culture) conjoined with sensitivity to the threats to which this way of life is vulnerable.

Attention to culture as a heterogeneity of practices where power and knowledge intersect—and to action on another's action—draws attention to the marks left by the application of power on the growing child. Leavitt moves us with her depictions of children constrained in day care settings, Debold with her portrayals of the traumatic quality of developmental transformation. In both cases the aim is to show us something hitherto obscured or unnoticed, to have us consider the costs of what has gone by the name of "education" or "progress."

And we find attention to cultural forms, to messages that circulate, and to the voices, both literal and metaphoric, with which they are produced, coupled with a critical appraisal of these performances. Brown hears the class accents of a voice that mocks the ideology of femininity; McLaren, and Leonardo view the antics of Robin Williams as a muted, well-intentioned but ineffectual critique of schooling; Rogers reads children's narratives as resistance to adult dominance; Tappan finds the bonds of male identity forged in the flames of male violence.

Viewing the chapters in this volume as a whole, we can see several respects in which the work they report and represent offers significant contributions to the study of human development. First, by bringing an increasing awareness of the position and stance of the researcher. Second, by providing an increased understanding of the linkages between development, society, and history. Third, by encouraging an appreciation that development involves the creation of a subject, a human being. We close by briefly considering each of these contributions in turn.

Youniss has declared that "developmentalists have to start from a different definition of science and perhaps create that science anew," in a manner that "places the discipline in a historical and sociological context and, by necessity, does the same for the subjects of our studies" (1983, pp. 49–50). The chapters in this volume aim to do just this. Several of the chapters draw the reader's attention to conceptions of development that stem not just from the children who are studied, but also from the assumptions, the values, and the cultural background, of the investigator, researcher, and theorist. For example, Menon and Shweder articulate the newly dialectical character of their own inquiry and of cultural psychology more broadly: it is "a means to understanding one's self and one's own culture by journeying through other selves in other cultures." Brown and Cole write as researchers who have become designers of alternative activities; here the divide between research and practice is overthrown. Leavitt considers the dilemmas of the "critical researcher." Debold interrogates the notion that we all need a sense of "identity." All draw our attention to the ways in which accounts of development are legitimized, not least of which is a declaration by a "scientific" psychology concerning what is normal. Furthermore, inquiry feeds back to influence the very practices it seeks to describe. Writing about one's research can change the phenomena one studies. Recent debate over child-centered and behaviorist approaches to such seemingly straightforward matters as toilet training and parent-child sleeping arrangements illustrates the role of values in inquiry, and the effect of such professional judgments on social practices. With all of this, developmental psychologists have surely relinquished forever the right to appeal to a criterion of natural and universal progress.

Marcus has proposed that we make a final break from the Western historical metanarratives employed unthinkingly by classic developmental theory, and with its historical determination. The relation between the process of human change and its description must, he says, be recognized as complex and two-way: an ethnography, for example, is "a story that is synonymous with addressing the construction of personal and collective identity itself" (1986, p. 317). Development and its investigation fuse together. In this volume crafts new kinds of narrative, as developmentalists find new places to stand. And it presents new types of inquiry that break the mold of "method."

The second contribution the authors in this volume have begun to make is a more powerful grasp of the connections between individual development and the historical reproduction and transformation of society. As Debold puts it, "We develop . . . along two axes of history—cultural history and the individual lifespan."

Throughout the history of developmental psychology, most descriptions of children's development have portrayed it as universal, natural, and so asocial and ahistorical. Early descriptions tended to base their proposals for improved parenting and schooling on claims about children's "nature"—whether that nature be described as an inherent plasticity that society might shape to its ends, or whether it be portrayed as passions and impulses that amounted to a recapitulation of earlier social forms. Empiricist theories of development, from Locke to Skinner, typically insisted that the child is inherently plastic and malleable, and has a final form that is shaped by society. Romantic theories emphasized the educability of human nature, and even linked this to a recapitulation of history; Hall, for instance, saw in the stages of psychological growth "a repetition of racial history" (1904, p. viii). Even genetic epistemology, despite its emphasis on the active child, still sometimes turned into a recapitulation theory: although the child is presented as an active explorer of, and theorizer about, the world, what is discovered through this exploration is, somewhat inexplicably, the same for all (cf. Popkewitz, 1998).

Of course disciplines other than psychology, notably anthropology and sociology, as well as interdisciplinary fields such as cultural studies, have grappled with varying success with the relationship between individual, society, and history. Nonetheless, these disciplines have often neglected to consider how the social agent develops, and have taken adults as the objects of their examination. Miller and Goodnow have noted a growing recognition that development occurs in context, but "models that integrate the cultural with the developmental . . . are still not readily to hand" (1995, p. 7). Psychology is pretty much alone among the social sciences in paying serious attention to the processes whereby infants become effective—or ineffective—members of society. The other social sciences either reduce these processes to the supposedly unproblematic "socialization" of the individual, or ignore them altogether, starting with the adult, when such processes are supposedly completed.

Clearly the trajectory of change that we call "development" is not natural and pregiven, nor uncontested and agreed-upon by all. Communities in which a single pathway to adulthood is accepted unquestioningly are found rarely, if at all. In postindustrial societies any apparent consensus over the value of ubiquitous movement toward ends such as "freedom" and "autonomy" disguises "profound rifts" and disparate appeals to moral ends thin enough to permit multiple interpretations and implementations (Taylor, 1989, p. 495). We need to understand how a child becomes a skilled participant in the traditional historical practices of a community, and at the same time how, in doing this, the child makes an active contribution to reproducing and transforming these practices.

Critical pedagogy, for example, has adopted an interpretive framework for thinking about human development in which development is seen first of all as intimately linked to the reproduction of society. At its best, critical pedagogy articulates the historical dynamic that runs through human development: the way changing economic and political circumstances lead to changed demands on children, and the active way they engage with adults.

The contributors to this book see the connections between children's development and societal organization and change as intimate and complex. What counts as development, and the pathways whereby that end point is sought, are defined by societal practices and institutions. Viewed at the level of cohort rather than individual, children's development is the reproduction of a society. "Any theory of child socialization," wrote O'Neill, "is implicitly a theory of the construction of social reality, if not of a particular historical social order" (1973, p. 65).

And so, to give just the simplest summary, we find the contributors engaged in subtle efforts to trace how children and adults move along the social trajectories that define class (Brown, Packer, McLaren, & Leonardo), gender (Tappan, Debold, Menon, Shweder, Brown, & Rogers), and ethnicity (Menon & Shweder).

There is, of course, much work to be done. The task, as we understand it, is to characterize and study the reciprocal relationship between child and society with particular attention to temporality and transformation over time, at two scales, those of psychological development and historical change. The complexity of this task is illustrated by a preparatory framework drawn up by Habermas (1971), who has distinguished the same three modes of human relationship as Foucault: instrumental, communicative, and emancipatory knowledge-constitutive interests. Habermas has sketched a model of ontogenesis, of human development, in which social reproduction processes are associated with each of these domains (1981/1989). In this way he is able to speculatively explore the links between social evolution (i.e., history) and children's development. These reproduction processes operate at the same time on the structures of culture, society, and individual. In terms of individual development, *cultural reproduction* is a matter of the reproduction of knowledge pertinent to such tasks as childrearing and education, *social integration* is a matter of the reproduction of patterns of social membership, and *socialization* leads to the formation of identity. Standards of rationality, of solidarity, and of responsibility can be applied to these three developmental trajectories respectively.

This is an ambitious formulation, and a speculative one, as Habermas grants. It also rests on questionable rationalist presumptions: Habermas accepts the basic strategies of Kohlberg's rational reconstruction of moral cognition, Piaget's cognitive developmentalism, and Selman's stages of perspective-taking (but cf. Habermas, 1983/1990, pp. 116ff.). We mention it here because, despite its limitations, it provides a rare model for the design of a project to formulate an account of development in a social context where the latter is not static but dynamically both a precondition and a product of human development.

But a quite different kind of framework is suggested when one reads these chapters as a group. It is a framework that distinguishes among—and explores the linkages among—the basis of a way of life (in its larger societal contexts); the relations of power and emotion in caretaking, parenting, teaching, and so on; and the circulation of utterances, texts, and other symbolic forms. To be sure these three interrelate: the exchange of cultural forms reproduces or transforms relationships, and sustains or fractures the language games within which relationships are possible. And in all this "culture" the child is transformed.

While Habermas considers ontogenesis a matter of growing cognitive competence, the third contribution this book makes to a refurbished developmental psychology is to highlight the significance of a notion that development is not simply a matter of the child coming to construct or acquire more effective knowledge, knowledge that is more adequate to the world. The child herself becomes a subject; becomes— in modern industrial and postindustrial societies like the United States—an "individual." Leavitt quotes Polakow. "The child as a conscious *becoming* being pursues a 'project' of freedom in order to become some-one else and not a being-for-others" (1992).

We begin to glimpse how we can answer the question that "Vygotsky recognized but did not answer . . . how the child comes to be a person like the adult" (Litowitz, 1993, p. 184) in a process that is "gradual, complex, and conflictual" (p. 194). Development is to be understood not just as a transfer, or even a construction, of cultural knowledge, but as the construction of a person, a process "in which "selves are continually created and re-created" (Miller & Goodnow, 1995, p. 13). Whatever changes are deemed developmental, they are not simply a matter of knowledge, of epistemology, but of changing motivational and personality structure—ontological changes, transformations in the child's being.

We start to get a feel for what we call "development" and the transformation that comes about in relationships formed in a shared lifeworld, albeit relationships that can be traumatic as well as nurturing, misleading even when well-intentioned, relationships nonetheless that provide a sense of purpose and a moral framework. Development entails profound transformations in who the child is, the emergence of the subjectivity of a subject who may be just as neglected in the postmodern declaration that the subject is dead as it was in the cognitivist declaration that the subject is irrelevant. Piaget insisted that "structuralism calls for a differentiation between the *individual subject,* who does not enter at all, and the *epistemic subject,* that cognitive nucleus which is common to all subjects at the same level" (1970/1988, p. 139). In a similar vein Levi-Strauss dismissed the phenomenological subject as an "intolerable spoiled child who for too long has held the philosophical scene and prevented any serious work, drawing exclusive attention to itself" (cited in Pettit, 1975, p. 77). The child may sometimes be a spoiled brat (there's a developmental outcome worthy of greater attention!), but let's not dismiss her so quickly. A hasty rejection of the feeling, caring subject in favor of structure, and reduction of the psychological subject to the role of intangible "generator" of structures which are always "under construction" (Piaget, 1970/1988, p. 140), was no less misleading than a "deconstructed" subject whose existence is said to be illusory. The position adumbrated in this book is humane without being overly humanistic.

It is a position in which culture provides the basis for relationships in which human nature is nurtured and mind created; where development is the never-ending effort to understand oneself in a complex world; where evidence of self-understanding is found in cultural forms, prosaic as well as elite; in a constant struggle against scattering and splitting. Marcus (1986) points out how identity is dispersed as children move from one setting to another, and hence multiply. The state and the economy integrate and rationalize these settings and, consequently, our sense of sameness and unity. Marcus has suggested that we think of development not in terms of the biological metaphor of accommodation and assimilation but in terms of a political metaphor of accommodation and resistance. The changes that have been portrayed cozily as "knowledge-construction" are also a subjugation to, and struggle against, power that divides people from each other and also from each one of us internally.

The time is ripe, therefore, for publication of the dialogue that takes place in this volume, among scholars whose work is at the intersection of the critical, the cultural, and the developmental. This book presents an array of exciting studies of developmental phenomena; the authors consider the implications of their work for those who are exploring new pedagogical practices, and also for those who seek new insights about the lived experience of children, adolescents, and adults living in the contemporary world.

References

Agger, B. (1992). *Cultural studies as critical theory.* Falmer Press.

Apple, M. W. (1982). *Education and power.* New York: Routledge.

Brown, L. M., & Gilligan, C. (1992). *Meeting at the crossroads: Women's psychology and girls development.* Cambridge: Harvard University Press.

Bourdieu, P. (1979/1984). *Distinction: A social critique of the judgement of taste.* (Richard Nice, Trans.). Cambridge, MA: Harvard University Press.

Bruner, J. (1996). *The culture of education.* Cambridge: Harvard University Press.

Cole, M. (1995). Culture and cognitive development: From cross-cultural research to creating systems of cultural mediation. *Culture and Psychology, 1*(1), 25–54.

Cole, M. (1996). *Cultural psychology: A once and future discipline.* Cambridge: Harvard University Press.

Danesi, M., & Santeramo, D. (1992). *Introducing semiotics: An anthology of readings.* Toronto: Canadian Scholars Press.

Donmoyer, R. (1996). This issue: A focus on learning. *Educational Researcher, 25* (4), 4.

During, S. (Ed.). (1993). *The cultural studies reader.* London: Routledge.

Eagleton, T. (1991). *Ideology: An introduction.* London: Verso.

Eco, U. (1979). *A theory of semiotics.* Bloomington: Indiana University Press.

Engestrom, Y., Miettinen, R., & Punamaki, R.-L. (Eds.). (1999). *Perspectives on activity theory.* New York: Cambridge University Press.

Foucault, M. (1980). *Power / knowledge: Selected interviews and other writings 1972–1977.* New York: Pantheon.

Foucault, M. (1982). Afterword: The subject and power. In H. L. Dreyfus & P. Rabinow (Eds.), *Michel Foucault: Beyond structuralism and hermeneutics* (pp. 208–226). Chicago: University of Chicago Press.

Gilligan, C. (1977). In a different voice: Women's conception of the self and of morality. *Harvard Educational Review, 47,* 481–517.

Gilligan, C. (1982). *In a different voice: Psychological theory and women's development:* Cambridge: Harvard University Press.

Giroux, H. A. (1983). Theories of reproduction and resistance in the new sociology of education: A critical analysis. *Harvard Educational Review, 53,* 257–293.

Giroux, H. A. (1991). Moderism, postmodernism, and feminism: Rethinking the boundaries of educational discourse. In H. Giroux (Ed.), *Postmodernism, feminism, and cultural politics* (pp. 1-59). Albany: State University of New York Press.

Giroux, H. A., & McLaren, P. (Eds.). (1994). *Between borders: Pedagogy and the politics of cultural studies.* New York: Routledge.

Gunn, G. (1987). *The culture of criticism and the criticism of culture.* New York: Oxford University Press.

Habermas, J. (1971). *Knowledge and human interests.* (J. Shapiro, Trans.). Boston: Beacon.

Habermas, J. (1981/1984). *The theory of communicative action. Vol. 1. Reason and the rationalization of society.* (T. McCarthy, Trans.). Boston: Beacon.

Habermas, J. (1981/1989). *The theory of communicative action. Vol. 2. Lifeworld and system: A critique of functionalist reason.* (T. McCarthy, Trans.). Boston: Beacon.

Habermas, J. (1983/1990). *Moral consciousness and communicative action.* (C. Lenhardt & S. W. Nicholson, Trans.). Cambridge: Massachusetts Institute of Technology Press.

Hall, G. S. (1904). *Adolescence: Its psychology and its relations to physiology, anthropology, sociology, sex, crime, religion and education.* (Vol. 1). New York: D. Appleton and Company.

Hall, J. R. (1992). The capital(s) of cultures: A nonholistic approach to status situations, class, gender, and ethnicity. In M. Lamont & M. Fournier (Eds.), *Cultivating differences: Symbolic boundaries and the making of inequality* (pp. 257–285). Chicago: University of Chicago Press.

Kant, I. (1787/1965). *Critique of pure reason.* New York: St. Martin's.

Kessel, F. (1981). On cultural construction and reconstruction in psychology: Voices in conversation. In F. S. Kessel & A. W. Siegel (Eds.), *The child and other cultural inventions.* (Vol. 4.) *Houston Symposium* (pp. 224–259). New York: Praeger.

Kessen, W. (1990). *The rise and fall of development*. Worcester, MA: Clark University Press.

Lamont, M., & Fournier, M. (Eds.). (1992). *Cultivating differences: Symbolic boundaries and the making of inequality*. Chicago: University of Chicago Press.

Lave, J. (1988). *Cognition in practice: Mind, mathematics and culture in everyday life*. New York: Cambridge University Press.

Litowitz, B. E. (1993). Deconstruction in the zone of proximal development. In E. A. Forman, N. Minick, & C. A. Stone (Eds.), *Contexts for learning: Sociocultural dynamics in children's development* (pp. 184-196). New York: Oxford University Press.

Lukács, G. (1923/1988). *History and class consciousness: Studies in Marxist dialectics*. Cambridge: Massachusetts Institute of Technology Press.

Marcus, G. E. (1986). Contemporary problems of ethnography in the modern world system. In J. Clifford & G. E. Marcus (Eds.), *Writing culture: The poetics and politics of ethnography* (pp. 165–193). Berkeley: University of California Press.

McLaren, P. (1989). *Life in schools: An introduction to critical pedagogy in the foundations of education*. New York: Longman (2nd. edition, 1994).

McLaren, P. (1995). *Critical pedagogy and predatory culture*. London: Routledge.

Miller, P. J., & Goodnow, J. J. (1995). Cultural practices: Toward an integration of culture and development. *New Directions for Child Development, 67,* 5–17.

Nelson, C., Treichler, P. A., & Grossberg, L. (1992). Cultural studies: An introduction. In L. Grossberg, C. Nelson, & P. A. Treichler (Eds.), *Cultural Studies* (pp. 1–22). New York: Routledge.

Newman, D., Griffin, P., & Cole, M. (1989). *The construction zone: Working for cognitive change in school*. Cambridge, MA: Cambridge University Press.

O'Neill, J. (1973). Embodiment and child development: A phenomenological approach. In H. P. Dreitzel (Ed.), *Childhood and socialization. Recent sociology No. 5* (pp. 65-81). New York: Macmillan.

Packer, M. (1993). Away from internalization. In E. A. Forman, N. Minick, & C. A. Stone (Eds.), *Contexts for learning: Sociocultural dynamics in children's development,* (pp. 254-265). New York: Oxford University Press.

Packer, M. J. (1985). Hermeneutic inquiry in the study of human conduct. *American Psychologist, 40,* 1081-1093.

Packer, M. J. (1999). Critical interpretive research: An introduction. Available at <http://www.mathcs.duq.edu/~packer/>.

Packer, M. J., & Addison, R. B. (Eds.). (1989). *Entering the circle: Hermeneutic investigation in psychology.* Albany: State University of New York Press.

Packer, M. J., & Goicoechea, J. (2000). Sociocultural and constructivist theories of learning: Ontology, not just epistemology. *Educational Psychologist, 35 (4),* 227-241.

Penuel, W. & Wertsch, J. (1995). Vygotsky and identity formation: A sociocultural approach. *Educational Psychologist, 30,* 83-92.

Pettit, P. (1975). *The concept of structuralism: A critical analysis:* Berkeley: University of California Press.

Piaget, J. (1970/1988). *Structuralism.* (C. Maschler, Trans.). New York: Harper.

Polakow, V. (1992). *The erosion of childhood.* Chicago: University of Chicago Press.

Popkewitz, T. S. (1998). Dewey, Vygotsky, and the social administration of the individual: Constructivist pedagogy as systems of ideas in historical spaces. *American Educational Research Journal, 35*(4), 535-570.

Ricoeur, P. (1973/1990). Hermeneutics and the critique of ideology. In G. L. Ormiston & A. D. Schrift (Eds.), The hermeneutic tradition: From Ast to Ricoeur. (pp. 298–334). Albany: State University of New York Press.

Rogoff, B. (1990). Apprenticeship in thinking: Cognitive development in social context. New York: Oxford University Press.

Rogoff, B. (1995). Observing sociocultural activity on three planes: Participatory appropriation, guided participation, and apprenticeship. In J. V. Wertsch, P. D. Río, & A. Alvarez (Eds.), *Sociocultural studies of mind,* (pp. 139-164). New York:Cambridge University Press.

Salomon, G. (1995). Reflections on the field of educational psychology by the outgoing journal editor. *Educational Psychologist, 30*(3), 105-108.

Schutz, A., & Luckmann, T. (1974). *The structures of the life world.* (R. M. Zaner & H. T. Engelhardt, Trans.). (Vol. 1). London: Heinemann.

Shotter, J. (1993). *Cultural politics of everyday life: Social construction-ism, rhetoric and knowing of the third kind*. Toronto: University of Toronto Press.

Shweder, R. A. (1989). Cultural psychology: What is it? In J. W. Stigler, R. A. Shweder, & G. Herdt (Eds.), *Cultural psychology: The Chicago symposia on culture and human development*. New York: Cambridge University Press.

Shweder, R. A. (1991). *Thinking through cultures: Expeditions in cultural psychology*. Cambridge: Harvard University Press.

Stoltenberg, J. (1992). *The end of manhood*. New York: Dutton.

Taylor, C. (1989). *Sources of the self: The makings of the modern identity*. Cambridge: Harvard University Press.

Thompson, J. B. (1990). *Ideology and modern culture: Critical social theory in the era of mass communication*. Stanford, CA: Stanford University Press.

Valsiner, J. (1987). *Culture and the development of children's action: A cultural-historical theory of developmental psychology*. Chichester, England: Wiley.

Valsiner, J. (1989a). How can developmental psychology become 'culture inclusive'? In J. Valsiner (Ed.), *Child development in cultural context* (pp. 1-8). Toronto: Hogrefe and Huber.

Valsiner, J. (1989b). Organization of children's social development in polygamic families. In J. Valsiner (Ed.), *Child development in cultural context* (pp. 67-85). Toronto: Hogrefe and Huber.

Valsiner, J. (1995). Editorial: Culture and Psychology. *Culture and Psychology*, 1(1), 5-10.

Vico, G. (1968) *The new science of Giambattista Vico* (T. G. Bergin & M. H. Fisch, Trans. Ithaca, NY: Cornell University Press.

Vygotsky, L. S. (1978). *Mind in society: The developmental of higher psychological processes*. Cambridge: Harvard University Press.

Vygotsky, L. S. (1986). *Thought and language* (A. Kozulin, Trans.). Cambridge: Massachusetts Institute of Technology Press.

Walkerdine, V. (1988). *The mastery of reason: Cognitive development and the production of rationality*. London: Routledge.

Walkerdine, V. (1997). Redefining the subject in situated cognition theory. In D. Kirshner & J. A. Whitson (Eds.), *Situated cognition: Social, semiotic, and psychological perspectives* (pp. 57-70). Mahwah, NJ: Lawrence Erlbaum Associates.

Willis, P. (1977/1981). *Learning to labor: How working class kids get working class jobs*. New York: Columbia University Press.

Youniss, J. (1983). Beyond ideology to the universals of development. In D. Kuhn & J. A. Meacham (Eds.), *Contributions to human development. Vol. 8. On the development of developmental psychology* (pp. 31–52). Basel: Karger.

I. Culture as the Ground for a Form of Life

CHAPTER 2

A Utopian Methodology as a Tool for Cultural and Critical Psychologies: Toward a Positive Critical Theory

Katherine Brown
Michael Cole

Introduction

This chapter offers an introduction to a program of research, teaching, and community development that can serve as a model for what we refer to as a *positive critical theory*. *Critical theorizing* has roots in several corners of the humanities and the term means different things across discourse communities. Our use of the term marks our attempt to supersede those forms of criticism that offer no possibility for remedy or redress within the reach of people who don't benefit from reading academic texts.

We reject, for example, the position of the "negative dialectician" Theodore Adorno, who denounced "concrete and positive" suggestions for social change. Adorno's criticism of reform efforts, which he viewed as sad attempts at "administrating the unadministratable," was in a word, paralyzing. Adorno thought such reforms would inevitably "call down the monstrous totality of repression upon themselves," and reinscribe the status quo (Bronner & Kellner, 1989, p. 275). Adorno's equally bitter rejection of the notion that theory and practice might productively converge is conveyed in his announcement that "no practice can ever be radical enough" (1984, p. 24); practice will never escape its dulling effect on theory.

Our project violates both of these provisos. The term *positive critical theory* is intended to reflect our emphasis on constructing and sustaining alternative arrangements to those decried in critical pedagogy, communication, technology studies, and the communities within which we work. While such efforts may be expected to fail, as Adorno asserts, they provide a crucial means through which we can deepen our understanding of the world, and an empirical basis for critiques of our own theorizing—essential goals in constructing theory as well as in reorganizing practice.

Our discussion is located at the juncture of several critical theory discourses. We begin by reviewing the work of key theorists of communication and technology studies to frame what might be called a "standard critical theory" approach to our research area. In that review, we take up recent work on access to technology, literacy, and social justice.

Bryson and De Castell (1996) study women's access to new information technologies. The authors seek exceptions to the rule that women and girls are marginalized in educational contexts where new information technologies are prominent. Their project is to document practices, policies, and contexts that are supportive of women's access to, and development of, competence in using new information technologies.

Stuckey attempts to unmask and redirect "the Violence of Literacy" (1991). She argues that in both the theories and practices of research and intervention, literacy programs and mainstream research on illiteracy fail to take seriously social class as a controlling factor in framing literacy and illiteracy.

Giroux's *Border crossings: Cultural Workers and the Politics of Education* (1992) offers strategies for practicing critical pedagogy to round out our brief survey of a landscape upon which to construct a positive critical theory. With these theorists and "calls from the field" in view, we describe and critically analyze our own project, which derives from a model activity system called the "Fifth Dimension."

The Fifth Dimension model, explored at length elsewhere (LCHC 1982; Cole 1996; Nicolopolou & Cole, 1993), is our way to bring adults, adolescents, and children together to learn and play within educational activities during the after-school hours. We describe an example of how community institutions and institutions of higher education can collaborate to provide the resources to create and develop new Fifth Dimension adaptations.

Such partnerships can only be sustained if they effectively identify, share, circulate, and enhance the resources of all participants. We conclude with a critical assessment of our own success and failure to theorize, implement, and sustain Fifth Dimensions as alternatives to dominant practices in terms of the notion of a positive critical theory.

Review of Key Theorists

Communication research

One of the seminal texts in the history of the field of communication is Lazarsfeld's classic overview of the purpose and direction of critical theory in the then-emerging field of communication. Looking ahead (and at the recent past), deeply troubled over the use of media channels (radio, advertising, and cinema) for political propaganda and mass persuasion, Lazarsfeld outlined his strategy for critical communication studies with four points of entry: (a) it should be informed by a theory about prevailing trends toward a promotional (advertising-based, privatized) culture; (b) it should involve special study of any phenomenon expressing and contributing to the trend; (c) it should track the valorizing of homogeneity that resulted; and (d) it should offer remedial possibilities (1941, p. 13).

Interdisciplinary critical communication studies

Subsequent critical communication research had a broad mandate to investigate the relationships between communication media, trends in culture, politics, and economics, and individual and institutional behavior. Critical communication scholars have generated many cross-disciplinary theories and methods of inquiry with ethical and institutional commitments different from those of the mainstream programs that Lazarsfeld referred to as "administrative." Administrative communication research often takes interdisciplinary forms, but remains interested in promoting technologies, methods, and content sought by practitioners and governmental and corporate clients of radio, electronic, and print forms of entertainment and persuasion.

An example of the persistence of this critical/administrative division within the field of communication is present in the clash between those who celebrate and those who condemn new communication technologies. Pool's *Technologies of Freedom* (1983) is representative of research that finds democratized access to a free flow of information, expanded educational opportunities, new jobs, hobbies, fantasy realms, and easier living associated with these new technologies. Critical voices question this bounty, wondering if we are finding only new ways of "amusing ourselves to death" (Postman, 1995) by embracing more effective delivery mechanisms for the entertainment values that anesthetize citizens against their proper concerns. Critics following this line of argument focus on the erosion of privacy (Schiller, 1989, 1996); the neutralization of real political debate (Herman & Chomsky, 1988), the loss of jobs and whole occupational categories to automation (Shaiken, 1985); and the rise of an amorphous "service economy."

Technology and education

Noble (1977) connected the proliferation of research and development in science and technology sectors in the United States, including communication technology, with the rise of corporate capitalism. His book established an important model for tracking and evaluating the forces, arrangements, decisions, and compromises that inform present-day relationships between technological innovation and higher education. Noble suggested that we interpret technology as social production rather than as a "thing." This move was crucial to understanding the foundation upon which (and machinery through which) research-and-development came to shape the character of American universities during the latter half of the twentieth century.

According to Noble, partnerships between educational institutions and private concerns evolved in a way that provided a humanitarian facade for capitalists who invested in new knowledge, the future, and learning for their own sake. These partnerships were also a source of income for basic researchers to build up their facilities independent of the uneven, shrinking operating budgets of their own institutions.

The resulting norm, Noble suggests, is that corporations save or write off millions of dollars while setting the agendas of public universities, prioritizing research that promises lucrative returns on the investments in the marketplace. After Heidegger (1977), scholars of new technologies cannot escape the research question, technology for what—to support what ways of being in the world? Noble's analysis supports the conclusion that science and technology have developed mainly as instruments for capitalist expansion, with education funded in a hierarchy determined by the serviceability of its subject matter to those interests.

In the end, Noble warns, social scientists, the public, non-hard-science users, affluent consumers, and others come to believe that the power of technology lies at our fingertips, and exult in our increasing reach through the Internet. Yet we have accepted arrangements that can only deepen our reliance on private, corporate control, and therefore implicate us in *their* "designs."

Twenty years later, what has been learned about how these public-private alliances are playing out, and the status of alternatives? Conley and the Miami Theory Collective of Oxford Ohio ask, "What is the position of technology in the humanities, especially with regard to a rapid transformation of the experience of space and time?" Their book contains familiar allegories of simulated worlds being "about forms of death," and ends with a noncommittal postmodern paean to the multiple seductions of cyberspace. The Internet is celebrated as the locus of opportunity for "rechannelling productive modes of singular and collective becoming" (1993, pp. xi-xiv).

Some of the articles in that volume have a definite critical tone, such as those on computer technology as it bears on warfare, sovereignty, and law in global conflicts. These articles critique the effects of hi-tech numbness and information overload as well as the feeling of "narcotic modernity" that characterizes technophile populations, and the dangers inherent in ignoring effects on the environment that are linked to computerization.

That volume does not give us the comprehensive assessment of the interplay between an agenda and the forms of knowledge and technology that Noble's work launched, but it is representative of the genre of the middle ground that is increasingly adopted across fields that have technology studies as their major concern. That is to say, the jury is still undecided about what is enabled and what is denied to individuals and groups in the Internet age.

Gender: Learning to make a difference

In their article "Gender, new technologies and inequity," Bryson and De Castell tell us that their research began with a critique of a familiar discourse of optimism about computer technologies. They expected resistance to implementing gender-equitable pedagogies and curricula, but still underestimated the pervasiveness of support for existing gender arrangements at all levels.

Bryson and De Castell faced censure and noncooperation from project sponsors and gatekeepers on basic issues of project design and implementation. The authors trace this resistance to the fact that they asked difficult questions and dealt with the hard and embarrassing facts of gender inequity with respect to access to new information technologies, despite their interest in finding exceptions to the rules.

The researchers call for identification of contexts and practices that focus on the inclusion of girls and women using new information technologies. Their methodology explicitly emphasizes maximizing the likelihood of optimal outcomes, as well as the use of principles, practices, and relations contributing to competence rather than focusing on explaining failure (1996, p. 125).

Bryson and De Castell report the conflict between themselves and research subjects and other project participants stemming from resistance to gender-equitable practices on several different fronts. They encountered little collaborative research on community and equity. They experienced their students' resistance to feminist ideals and discussions of gender equity (pp. 132-133). They also had to deal with the scrutiny of their sexuality. In an e-mail exchange about their recent progress, the authors say, "We positioned ourselves as researchers and yet once identified as lesbians we could no longer occupy that identity position."

Echoing Adorno, earlier they had written,

Learning to make a difference is a project doomed to fail. Let's consider why: school contexts are a) highly resistant to change b) locales where scripts for the enactment of appropriate gender identities are always already entrenched in an exquisitely fine tuned dance of heterogenesis." (p. 120)

Two years into the project, Bryson and De Castell reflect on the work.

> Whereas we began . . . with the goal of creating produc-
> tive links between school based and non-school based organ-
> izations, what we have learned is that by narrowing our sights
> to a single school community, and accepting the narrowness
> of having created a microclimate, we have been able to accom-
> plish many of the goals with which we started our work. It
> just leaves us with a much less exciting set of stories to tell,
> and without any of the outputs that scientists expect, like
> models, bullets etc.

Literacy, illiteracy, and community

Stuckey, an implementer and critic of adult literacy programs and author of *The Violence of Literacy* argues that literacy programs and those who implement or study programs targeting illiterates fail those they purport to serve. She emphasizes that barriers to social mobility persist for literacy program participants following acquisition of reading and writing skills. The numerous programs Stuckey reviewed were "designed as if to fail" (1991). She concludes the literacy programs often do more violence than good in their premises and promises.

One of Stuckey's criticisms of research and reform targeting illiteracy is that scholars and policymakers assume illiteracy to be the cause and not the consequence of institutionalized poverty and social injustice. Stuckey dares to interrogate literacy as a universal good, a skill attainable by all given the right opportunity, an index of democracy, and of progress in a society. Such formulations are, for her, aspects of the myth of a classless society "doing the bidding of class."

Politicians point to literacy as an avenue to social mobility that any individual can walk down, while routinely discriminating against groups who speak nonstandard English. By cutting funding and by rolling out programs that cannot cope with heterogeneity in the goals or needs of their clientele, policymakers and implementers can appear to be "addressing the problem" without opening the field of inquiry to the intractable problem of class conflict.

Stuckey argues that a definition and standard of "literacy" couched in the rhetoric of "upward mobility" is decidedly a white middle-class standard, a red herring that draws attention away from the real sources and consequences of poverty. This tactic makes it possible to ignore the possibility of multiple literacies, or to question the way skills are valued and devalued in ways that covary with the race and gender of the people who exhibit them.

Stuckey's experience as a literacy worker and her research on the impact of adult literacy programs leads her to conclude that (1) literacy programs usually fail to accommodate the basic realities of the lives of the illiterate, (2) most programs are located outside of target communities, and (3) programs are typically staffed by volunteers (preprofessionals on their way to something better—elderly women, retired teachers, and charity groups). When paid, literacy work is done by a low-waged/ high-turnover corps of literacy "scut workers" who burn out or move on when funding dries up as a matter of course. Stuckey's advice to "literacy workers" is to make connections between the marginality of their own work and the experiences of the brown and black people from the underclass who remain subject to the historical machinery of discrimination that adult literacy programs do not dismantle.

Critical pedagogy

For Giroux, a critical pedagogy is potentially radical when it aspires to rewrite the relationship between theory and practice as a form of cultural politics, whether this practice is teaching, scholarship, introducing new educational technologies, or research. There is an affinity between Giroux's relational approach; Noble's view of technology as social production; and Stuckey, Bryson, and De Castell's examples of gender inequity reproduced in the norms of research.

Giroux's goal is "a pedagogy that proceeds from a respect for the complexity of the relationship between pedagogical theories and the sites in which they might be developed" (1992, pp. 3–4). Critical pedagogy must also work in the "spaces between binaries" (p. 24), inherited from universalizing-prescriptive approaches to theory. Borrowing from critical work in modernist, postmodernist, and feminist traditions (p. 73) Giroux calls for attention to pedagogy as connected to the practices of scholarship, ethics, relations between the self and the other in research, and implementation of new approaches.

Giroux is also concerned with understanding "difference" in an ethically challenging and politically transformative way rather than suppressing difference. What practices does Giroux propose? Starting points are breaking down disciplinary boundaries, and engaging in critiques of the notion of reason to discover some of the ways in which people take up subject positions out of habit, intuition, desire, or affect.

In Giroux's discourse of possibility, the role of "imagination" and the "not yet" are key ideas for teachers confronting their own social and political locations, as transformative intellectuals. It is quite a challenge to verbalize what we want to happen, how we want things to be. Doing so generates reflection on the gaps between one's ideals and the practices that we are invested in even as we critique them.

One example could be taken from the ideal of "imagination" and the possibility of "occupying border locations." Bryson and De Castell have remarked in conversations with the authors that it is difficult to "imagine oneself" out of harm's way to avoid being a target for routine violence. Furthermore, they ask, who really believes it is desirable to embrace "occupying border locations"? The reality for those who are not "tourists" at the borders, those who have to live in the schism, is an exhausting series of confrontations with chaos and double standards.

Summary of classic critical theory

This selective review of a landscape of danger and possibility in the high-tech 1990s is not very different from Lazarsfeld's initial take on the field in the 1940s. The privatizing forces, commercial interests, and "enframing" tendencies of communication technologies (now with microcomputers and the Internet) are ever poised to overshadow democratization of access, and educational or noncommercial content.

Persistent inequity in access to new communication technology for the poor, women, and other minorities points to a lack of focus on user competencies, goals, and community ownership in the development of literacy oriented programs (Greenwood-Gowen, 1992). Stuckey, Bryson and De Castell, and Noble each offer some insights into why this is so, and what happens to alternatives.

Our own approach, which has been realized over many years, shares the key concerns of all the theorists we have cited. Like Adorno, we expect to fail. But that does not mean the effort was theoretically or practically insignificant. One does not ineluctably reinscribe the status quo. Here, we side strongly with Giroux's emphasis on the need to reorganize the relations of theory and practice. Like Stuckey, we view the benefits of, and paths to, literacy as represented in educational discourse as highly problematic.

Like Bryson and De Castell, we have taken as our focus a knot of interlinked issues that confront the people in our region, centering on transformations in technologies that mediate work, education and community life. These issues can be cataloged as a set of binary relations. But we see them as Engeström (1987) does: as potentially generative contradictions. They include intellectual work vs. play, university vs. community, inschool vs. after-school, researcher vs. subject, theoretical vs. practical, teaching vs. research, male vs. female, white vs. nonwhite, and monolingualism vs. bilingualism.

Our way of addressing these binaries while seeking to create and sustain conditions that supersede them has been to grow a special hybrid form of activity we call the "Fifth Dimension."

What is Fifth Dimension?

It is a little difficult to characterize a Fifth Dimension briefly because it is designed as a strategy for occupying border locations between the binaries just listed. In brief, it is a specially designed activity system that mixes play, affiliation, learning, and peer interaction (Cole, 1996). The activities occur in community settings during the after-school hours and are linked to university practicum courses. The local activity system includes computer games and programming environments, non-computer-based games, and other activities. Telecommunications access affords local and regional interaction between participants at project sites. There are currently more than a dozen adaptations of the Fifth Dimension model in the United States, and several in Europe and Mexico.

Interestingly, the term Fifth Dimension is usually used by participants to describe the most visible aspect of these community-university collaborations—the places and times when the "site" is running, when children are using its special artifacts, moving through the maze, writing to the Wizard, and so forth. The Fifth Dimension in this context denotes the physical location and the special form of activity within community institutions where children interact with researchers, undergraduate and graduate students, other children, and community institution personnel in ways that differ from those when and where the Fifth Dimension is not in effect. Being on school grounds in the computer room after school in the Fifth Dimension becomes different from being there at other times; and being at the Boys and Girls Club or the YMCA "for the Fifth Dimension" invites different forms of participation than being anywhere else in the facility.

A basic characteristic of Fifth Dimensions conceived at the community site level is that they differ greatly from one another in ways that are entwined with local conditions. The Fifth Dimension at our local school feels different from the Fifth Dimension at the Boys and Girls Club across the street. Each creates its own idioculture (Fine, 1987).

Our own interest includes the developmental transformations that occur within the activity "at site" in the community setting, but extends to intermediating levels of activity produced by institutional routines that constrain and enable the joint formation of Fifth Dimensions. We are especially concerned with documenting phases in internal dynamics that undermine or realign the ability of universities, colleges, community institutions, and clubs to form synergistic relationships.

A prototype (caveat emptor)

Recognizing that these activity systems exist only with respect to local constraints, we are frequently asked for a normative description of the model. What follows should be taken as a sketch of some key conventions that have developed across numerous adaptations of the prototype.

In a prototype Fifth Dimension system[1] (local names for them vary), a dozen or more six–to fourteen–year-old children encounter a large variety of off-the-shelf computer games and gamelike educational and entertaining activities. A Fifth Dimension room usually contains both Mac and DOS machines, low-end and high-end, at a ratio of one computer for every two to three children.

The computer games and other offerings are part of a make-believe activity system, a play world, whose conventions mediate the way in which activities and games are experienced by the children. We try to avoid single-player, "arcade" style games, often called "twitch games," because the Fifth Dimension play world emphasizes skills that such games don't often cultivate. Some of the non-computer-based activities include origami, chess, boggle, mancala, and producing materials for the World Wide Web. The activities are arranged so that there are several types assigned to each room in a tabletop or paper-drawn maze.

Games are not played bare-handed, however. "Task cards" or "adventure guides" accompany each game or activity, to help participants get started, to specify expected achievements, and to provide evidence necessary for obtaining credentials as an expert. Task cards are developed by adults who look for ways to highlight and combine the educational and playful moments embedded in an activity or game proposed for inclusion in the maze. Researchers, students, or site coordinators play the game and identify opportunities that invite children to reflect, think strategically, cooperate with someone more or less skilled, and document their experiences in writing.

The task cards provide a variety of obligations to write to someone in the Fifth Dimension (the Wizard, or another child), to look up information in an encyclopedia, or to teach someone else what has been learned. Task cards are developed at "beginner," "good," and "expert" levels. Each level of play requires a combination of choice, chance, and consequences.

A Wizard

There is a "real make-believe" bigendered Fifth Dimension Wizard who is alleged to have created the Fifth Dimension. S/he lives in the Internet, writes to the children, chats with them via modem, and acts as their patron. The Wizard, (names for these totemic electronic entities vary) has a home page, and helps the children gain access to the World Wide Web, where they too have a home page that displays their creative work. Each Fifth Dimension has special ceremonies (e.g. birthdays for the Wizard) that promote interaction with other Fifth Dimension sites in other locales around the country and the world.

The Wizard is an important mediating force in the Fifth Dimension, giving both children and adults someone to appeal to when help is needed.

The children

Children typically visit a Fifth Dimension on a drop-in basis. Some children spend four to six hours per week of their after-school time participating in the Fifth Dimension, while others may only come once a week for a few hours. Opportunities and constraints vary across locations, seasons, populations and sites. Girls outnumber boys in some Fifth Dimensions even where larger setting activities are dominated by boys. In other places, boys are in the majority. While ages six to twelve are dominant in most Fifth Dimensions, the systems tend to include preschoolers and high schoolers as they grow.

At some locations, adults expect the children to participate regularly in the Fifth Dimension and arrange for them to do so, while at other sites children are free to choose if and for how long to participate, with homework, basketball, and reading as some of their alternatives. Many children enter the Fifth Dimension directly after school or homework sessions, and remain there until their parents or school transportation services take them home.

A site coordinator

In our model system, there is a "site coordinator" who greets the children and supervises the flow of activity in the room. This person is trained to recognize and support the pedagogical ideals and curricular materials that mark the Fifth Dimension as "different"—as a different way for kids to use computers, as a different way for adults and children to interact with each other. The site coordinator monitors the balance of education and play in interactions between children and undergraduates.

A site coordinator may be employed by the community institution, and may have taken university courses that support the Fifth Dimension, but this not the case everywhere. Arrangements for funding the site coordinator position vary—sometimes the partner university or college provides research or outreach funds that cover the salary to help grow a Fifth Dimension in a setting with modest resources. In other cases, site coordinator salaries can be absorbed into the operating budget of a club or school.

The undergraduates

In addition to the presence of computer games and a mysterious Wizard who writes to them and pays attention to their progress through the maze, the chief draw for the children is the presence of university and college students in the Fifth Dimension who are there to learn and play with them. In our model, an important feature of the Fifth Dimension is that the participating college students are enrolled in an intensive research methods course focused on fieldwork in the community and on the confrontation of theory with practice.

At the University of California, San Diego, the university course associated with student participation is an intensive, six-unit class that emphasizes deep understanding of basic developmental principles, familiarity with the use of new information technologies for organizing learning, and methods for collecting and analyzing the processes that undergraduates help to put into play. Students are treated as, and act as, junior researchers. They write detailed clinical field notes after each session with the children. These notes are read and critiqued by the professors and by their teaching assistants.

The class meets twice weekly to discuss assigned readings and to evaluate the scholarly articles they read at the university for their fit with their own field experiences with the children. Students also discuss their work with students in other Fifth Dimension-linked courses in the UC system through the UC system's Distance Learning network. Finally, the undergraduates write papers tracing the development of individual children, the relative effectiveness of different games, differences in the ways in which boys and girls participate in the activities, or other developmental topics.

Superseding binaries

In this "play world" we try to organize opportunities for practical experience in transcending "business as usual" on as many levels as possible. Giroux's notion of exploring alternative subject positions through imagination is a mainstay of the Fifth Dimension. Success in the Fifth Dimension requires children and adults to cooperate and to use multiple dimensions of their life experience and talents in their journey through the maze.

It is difficult for everyday and arbitrary forms of hierarchy, exclusion, and segregation to be effective in such a setting. We see this feature as an embodiment of Giroux's pointer toward ethics in research and pedagogy. An explicit exploration of "difference" is made possible through our blending of learning and play, the real and the imaginary.

Having characterized the Fifth Dimension prototype, we can return to the discussion of the major binaries that we deal with in our work and how we attempt to supersede them: intellectual work vs. play, university vs. community, in-school vs. after-school, researcher vs. subject, theory vs. practice, teaching vs. research, male vs. female, white vs. nonwhite, and monolingualism vs. bilingualism.

University vs. community. A boundary routinely exists between the priorities and motives of academic researchers and those of community members who participate in activities of interest to researchers and to other university people. The Fifth Dimension as a joint activity is constructed on the border of in-school (research and educational activity) and after-school (recreation and community well-being), requiring members of both "worlds" to invest in its survival and regular repair.

Consider, for example, the implications of a concept of university "outreach" that implies that one side exerts effort—traffic flows from the entity that possesses "resources" (the university) to a distant other entity (the underserved), which has a "need." Our understanding of outreach is that it is a process of bridge construction, requiring the alignment of university and community resources and interests. Traffic must flow both ways across the bridge for it to be a relevant structure in the long term.

In-school vs. after-school. A related example of how the Fifth Dimension model promotes dissolution of binaries concerns its origins and its present status. The model was originally designed to offer not merely after-school, but nonschool activity. The idea was to provide children (especially those who weren't succeeding in school) with resources and forms of guidance that evolved from a critique of school practices like tracking students, teaching by drill, and testing for memorization. Evidence of this critique is the Fifth Dimension's emphasis on nonauthoritarian older peers; culturally relevant modes of instruction; multiple modes and goals for problem solving, and the mix of friendship, play, and intellectual work. By 1994, Fifth Dimension adaptations had taken hold on school grounds after-school, and in some cases in classrooms during the school day, blurring the school/nonschool boundary.

Researcher vs. subject. The binary "researcher vs. subject" is destabilized as Fifth Dimension researchers position themselves as members of the subject population—actors in the systems we grow and study. Theoretical and practical academic instruction are blended as we simultaneously deal with implementing the activity (staffing, organizing, and getting technical equipment in place) and developing theoretical tools to analyze data gathered from the sites, courses, meetings, and e-mail exchanges. In many cases, Fifth Dimension implementers have gone on to conduct evaluations of the project, and in some cases, people who entered the project as outside evaluators have gone on to start Fifth Dimension adaptations in their own communities.

Stereotypes: gender, ethnicity, and language use. Another set of constraining dualisms that reinforce and coconstruct each other are those associated with gender and ethnic stereotypes. We undermine the logic of stereotypes by modeling anti-essentialism through the behavior of the electronic entity that each site develops as its patron, mascot, and correspondent. The entity assigned to each Fifth Dimension is male and female, ageless, and often multilingual. Dubbed El Maga, the Wizard, the Wizardess, Proteo, Golem, Volshebnik, Zarfen, and so forth, the "entity" sends provocations, observations, and challenges to support participants' reflections on their own role conflicts and assumptions about sex, gender, race, and ethnicity in working with, and observing, diverse groups of children and adults in community settings.

For the citizenry of the Fifth Dimension, appropriate behavior for children and adults is not cast in terms of sex roles, sex-appropriate knowledge, or a single preferred language for expression. The use of ethnicity labels as markers of "otherness" is challenged by intersite activities, the omnipresence of bilingual artifacts, and cocelebration of special holidays across sites.

Undergraduates in the practicum courses study peer group and cross-age power relations and the politics of representation in their coursework. They compare their experiences in the Fifth Dimension with the literature on sex-roles and gender, Attention Deficit and Hyperactivity Disorder, minority achievement, bilingual education, and other issues in human development. This process often prompts students to confront their own investments in gender and language biases, providing occasions to reflect on their own experiences of empowerment and disempowerment in technology, language use, and gender relations.

At the University of California, San Diego, women outnumber men among the students taking the practicum courses. Our students frequently report that participating in the Fifth Dimension occasioned their first experiences of using computers or their first opportunities to use computers for something other than data entry or word processing. Playing games with children, moving between platforms, authoring fieldnotes, sending and reading e-mail, using the World Wide Web, and trouble-shooting involve a range of easy and difficult tasks and frequent role shifts from teaching to learning. This flexibility in combination with the ethos of exploration and play in the Fifth Dimension helps to hold the interest of both self-professed "computerphobes" and experienced users.

Undergraduate fieldnotes reveal moments of fruitful discoveries and anxieties around language issues arising from participating in bilingual and bicultural sites, such as La Clase Magica.[2] Monolingual and bilingual participants are encouraged to explore a realm where playing, speaking the language spoken at home, speaking the language spoken at school, and intellectual achievements co-occur. It is useful for the undergraduates and the children to experience an environment where first and second languages are drawn upon to solve different kinds of problems.

Ageism and the equation of "older" with "more expert" are also undermined, because adults are enjoined to have fun while being educators and more expert children are all around. Expertise is situated, distributed, and jointly mediated. This is possible because authority and discipline is distributed in the Fifth Dimension (through the Wizard, the site coordinator, the constitution, the maze, etc.). The rules of engagement and roles (learner, teacher, and helper) are less rigid than those encountered in settings that position adults as *de facto* authorities and children as receptacles for instruction.

By participating in a Fifth Dimension play world, children and adults discover that seniority and authority in this realm are a function of familiarity with its artifacts and processes. Young people learn to teach older newcomers. Visiting researchers accustomed to observing adult interactions with children in traditional classrooms frequently remark on the contrasting ease with which adults interact with children in the Fifth Dimension.

Cycles of Reflective Practice: Implementing the Methodology

The strategy we refer to as "positive critical theory" requires the embodiment of theory in the normal institutional/social life of a community. Not just any community will do.

The ideal solution has been to ground our activities in a "hometown" where we are both citizens and actors. As actors, we work at the university where we create and try to sustain forms of activity which, according to our academic theories are "good for children." As citizens, we walk our dogs in the morning, support the library, participate in community activities in our respective neighborhoods, participate in election time discussions with neighbors, and complain about the way the city is run. Consequently, we occupy multiple subject positions with respect to the key people and institutions (community clubs and universities) we are seeking to connect.

The researchers' self-consciousness of their multiple positions allows for amplification of feedback on all the ways in which, having positively "prescribed" reality, our theory of the processes involved underrepresented reality to an embarrassing degree. That is, we test theory in practices located in the criss-cross of values and culture of the researchers' own communities. Those communities will decide the value of our efforts.

How does such an intervention get underway?

Phase one: Identify problematic areas

First, researchers identify problematic areas in their own community. The issue should be one for which the researcher believes she has relevant knowledge. The researcher is a participant in fashioning existence proofs that the requisite activity to address the issue can be assembled.

In our analyses of institutional forces that constrain individual and social development, and in an effort to build sustainable alternatives, we often locate the rationale for our work at the crossroads of three local concerns.

Pressure on children and parents. There is a shortage of places for a majority of children to go after school that provide for their immediate safety and for their ability to cultivate opportunities to engage in learning for a variety of purposes. There are even fewer places where they might interact with other children and adults around information technologies in ways that are intellectually and affectively beneficial. There is a contradiction between a household need for two incomes and provision of childcare at home.

Concern about ethnic conflict and academic achievement. There is a growing split between resources and needs that communities have and what the public sector, the private sector, and tax base provide for and demand of their inhabitants. While watching public resources dwindle, members of ethnic minorities and low-income groups increasingly view the institutional norms and missions of colleges and universities as out of touch with their day-to-day lives.

For example, parents from communities where achieving a college education is the exception and not the rule continue to sacrifice and plan for "college," hoping that higher education will make a difference for someone in their family. The idea that colleges and universities might form relationships and presences within community institutions is rarely expressed. Institutions of higher education are typically seen as places for their children to escape to, not as local partners.

Pressure on colleges and universities. Universities and colleges are increasingly seen by their local communities as inaccessible, indifferent, and out of touch with the general public. At the same time, universities are being pressured to address themselves to a constituency far more diverse than they have historically been willing or able to accommodate. There is also increased demand from undergraduate students and from their prospective employers for forms of higher education that include opportunities to combine, not merely to decide between, learning associated with theory and learning through practice.

For example, on the one hand, programs in education and human development are criticized for promoting idealistic theories that don't address the daily goals and problems of exhausted parents, teachers, and social workers. The general public believes that degree inflation is limiting their access to good-paying jobs, while colleges become wealthy and self-serving "degree mills" that matriculate students with no experience of putting theory into practice in the "real world." These institutions are also blamed for producing radicalized students with few skills valued by conservative employers.

On the other hand, faculty members and researchers in programs and departments that offer "fieldwork" or require practical tests of theory are at often at odds with colleagues and administrators who devalue "applied" work in communities, questioning the research value and publication rates of studies coming from these labor intensive activities.

These and other local problems require the first phase of research to involve extensive participant observation, interviews, document collection, and use of ethnographic research to map such barriers. The goal is to uncover, understand, and historicize these types of conflicts as they play out in local settings.

Phase two: Joint activity

In the second phase, the researcher enters into joint activity with community members to create an alternative set of practices that constitute an hypothesis about changes needed to overcome the problem that has brought them together. In our case, it is a nexus of problems focused on children's experiences in the after-school hours.

The Fifth Dimension serves as the occasion for collaboration between universities, colleges, community centers, and schools in several U.S. cities and towns. Our research design picks up where Stuckey concludes—that successful literacy programs ought to focus on communities as a locus of sustainability.

Stuckey indicts the "literacy profession" for its failure to see community members as having resources to offer, defining the poor as always in need of ideas and management by the middle class. By entering into relationships of genuine exchange and cooperation between community and university members, we have been able to organize and sustain opportunities for learning that flow bidirectionally across generational, linguistic, gender, and ethnic and institutional lines.

As designers and implementers of educational interventions, we struggle to recognize and redirect counterproductive patterns in the process of coordinating community and university agendas. It is difficult but worthwhile to try to normalize circumstances and opportunities for children and adults to make common cause with people they ordinarily avoid.

A central premise of our network of community and university partnerships is that by joining together to create a Fifth Dimension, the parties can do together something that they cannot easily do on their own. Stuckey's work resonates with our interest in learning from how community members define their own diverse resources and needs. In Bryson and De Castell's work, we recognize familiar experiences of going against the grain of business as usual. Their work also bespeaks the wisdom of distributing the work of documenting and interpreting sources of resistance to, and acceptance of, challenges to the status quo.

The process of creating new practices is invariably arduous, and requires careful attention to the establishment of trust, reciprocity, a commitment to mutual understanding, and a willingness to repair misunderstanding. People agree at the outset that they are in it for the long term.

Phase three: Evaluation

The third phase involves evaluation of two aspects of the second phase: Were the hypothesized alternative practices in fact created and if so, did the hypothesized changes in the problem situation come about? If the researcher/community team fails to create the needed new forms of practice, the research recycles at this point, requiring revisions of the theory of activity creation. If the new forms of activity are created, but do not have the desired effect, the research recycles to determine what was wrong with the hypothesized theory in the first place.

Assuming a new Fifth Dimension adaptation is underway, we have several ways of evaluating the effectiveness of its constituent parts that are respectful of diversity across adaptations.

Person-computer interaction. It is ideal if children and adults are using software and hardware in ways that allow them to reflect critically on their activities, to work cooperatively, and to communicate their problem-solving strategies to others. The key mediating structures in Fifth Dimension adaptations are provided by task cards and interaction with undergraduates.

Fifth Dimension site. We expect a Fifth Dimension to be a place where rules and roles of learning and play are organized differently than in the surrounding context, and where this difference is valued by children and adults. Despite differences across Fifth Dimensions around the country and in diverse institutions, universal among them is the creation of a culture of collaborative learning which, mixed as it is with play, is a pleasure for all of its participants, young and old. It is this mixture that attracts children to the Fifth Dimension and provides it with the extra enrichment needed to convert "playing computer games" into something with a good deal more social and psychological potential.

Undergraduate instruction. Fifth Dimension-linked undergraduate courses are labor and time intensive, yet across the system, undergraduate and graduate student evaluations of the courses are consistently positive. Undergraduates frequently comment in their fieldnote reflections on the significance and relevance of course issues and requirements to their other educational and life experiences.

School effects. We have consistent evidence from sites where we can obtain data from treatment and control groups that participation in the Fifth Dimension positively influences children's development of academic skills (mathematics, reading, writing, and computer use) and social competence (Blanton, Moorman Hayes, & Warner, 1997; Schustack 1997). There is also evidence that schools themselves change as a consequence of hosting Fifth Dimensions (Underwood & Taub, 1998).

Funds/publicity. We pay special attention to how community leaders and participants represent and demonstrate their interest in our university-community institution partnership. For example, there are three sites close to each other in neighborhoods north of our university. Area community leaders (parents, Head Start staff, and club program directors) have declared themselves a "Coalition for Community Education" devoted to raising funds and community awareness to support the continuation of Fifth Dimension after-school initiatives.

This coalition has been successful in attracting significant financial support. Meanwhile, local philanthropists, university administrators, and politicians have funded, endorsed, and commended the academic and community directors of Fifth Dimension adaptations throughout the state.

Dissemination. Several dozen scholarly articles have been published about the efficacy of the Fifth Dimension approach to sustainable after-school programs from data gathered by the Fifth Dimension network. Print and television media outlets have featured the Fifth Dimension as a model after-school program. Also, a half hour documentary has been made about the local history and origins of the Fifth Dimension model and an hour-long program about the statewide spread of Fifth Dimensions aired in the fall of 1998.

Phase four: Dealing with failure

Phase four represents the "hereafter" of ordinary interventionist research. Insofar as they are successful, Fifth Dimensions don't go away; they continue to exist in dynamic relations with their institutional and community environments. However, the birth and growth of a Fifth Dimension does not confer immortality.

The research cycle of utopian methodology ends with social criticism: we address the conditions that make an ostensible social good impossible to maintain. It is a crucial part of our work to study the process of failure of Fifth Dimension adaptations to sustain themselves, and to document the ways in which institutions extrude them over time through "business as usual."

As Adorno said, the best intentions of individuals are usually no match for the existing institutional barriers to cooperation and access.

For over a decade, we have documented some of the same intractable, cynical, and divisive processes at work that Stuckey associates with the failure of mainstream literacy programs.

Diversity is somewhere else. In one such case, failure came within two years of start-up because the mission of a Teacher's College was delimited to the classroom. Even as the leaders of this institution viewed themselves as having a strong record in community service and outreach, preservice teachers and their mentors were doubtful that something pedagogically complementary or significant (much less transformative) could come from rearranging their system to put college personnel and students in the local community in the after-school hours. A practicum course for this Fifth Dimension was approved for only one semester per year. Ultimately, this college preserved its customary approach to "diversity" and cross-cultural education. Its leaders seemed less interested in the ethnic and linguistic diversity of neighborhoods surrounding the campus than they were with encouraging an appreciation of diversity through missionary work oversees in Asian countries.

Rank and risk. Sometimes a would-be implementer is too junior in academic status to bend rules or to reinterpret their institution's mission statement.

Conflict between innovation and business as usual can be seen, for example, in the waves caused when a junior person pushes for a courseload reduction or for a change in a course description to make a "practicum" course intensive enough for significant community involvement and not for short-term "tourism." The frustration and career hazards for the junior academic who takes on this kind of work in an indifferent or hostile academic setting are significant.

As daunting as this prospect is at the start of a career, it is no less damaging to the senior scholar who must grapple with the fear that years of time and effort can be erased in a matter of months when bureaucracies are left to run their course.

This issue is similar to that faced by Stuckey's literacy scut workers who take on exhausting challenges at one or the other end of the labor market, moving up, moving on, or burning out more often than they stay with the work. In some academic circles, resources and legitimacy can be marshaled when an implementer points to the larger network of Fifth Dimension colleagues participating in research and implementation throughout the country, but at other times this larger context has no resonance.

Finally, the leading cause of death for Fifth Dimension programs is that an ostensibly enthusiastic institution cannot provide material commitments to support the desired form of activity when the initial funding is gone. This major step in sustainability is the hope and the failure of many university and community partnerships.

Each case of failure is frustrating, but is extremely valuable for our research program.

Informing Critical Theory

There are elements of our work that we think suggest possibilities for critical theorists interested in reforming educational practice and policy. These elements include insights gleaned from participating in a distributed consortium of implementers and evaluators of the Fifth Dimension projects as well as findings from evaluators about social and intellectual benefits of participation in the Fifth Dimension and the importance of local variability in Fifth Dimension cultures.

The Consortium

In some cases, Fifth Dimension implementers are evaluators of data from their own site and from other sites. Having many roles in the project helps cultivate appreciation for the diverse perspectives and backgrounds of colleagues. This kind of arrangement starts from the opinion that collaboration and interdisciplinarity are good, to risky practices such as confronting traditional professional biases (toward individual scholarship and disciplinary chauvinism) by taking risks through academic collaboration.

As a national and international consortium, we create and exchange resources and data as a matter of necessity. Learning to participate in this network of opportunity and responsibility requires cooperation from members of different statuses and interests over time. Conversations on the "x-mellon" listserve[3], joint production of annual reports, and face-to-face meetings expose consortium members to a variety of possible questions about units and levels of analysis for looking at data. With a data inventory that ranges from Cloze test scores to painstakingly coded videotapes of undergraduate/child computer interaction, the choices of what to look at are daunting. Members of the consortium often stay close to their initial issues and methods, but are ever aware of alternative interpretations of their work and different uses for their data. This experience of nonhierarchical research interest, mutual visibility, and self-conscious choices in research practices are features we think contribute to critical theory.

The organization of learning in Fifth Dimension Sites

Our colleagues from the Institute for Research on Learning (IRL), Ito, McDermott, and Greeno (1998), have evaluated Fifth Dimension activities from the standpoint of how opportunities for learning are organized differently than they are in schools. The critical theory reviewed in this article offers examples of dysfunctional and damaging processes and dichotomies in education systems, calling for alternative arrangements. Our colleagues from the IRL were charged with looking at the Fifth Dimension to see if and how it embodied an effective alternative to formal learning environments.

They found that the Fifth Dimension mediates the social and cultural space between entertainment and education, helping kids to engage in recreational and voluntary activity while engaging in practices that foster intellectual mastery. They also found that the Fifth Dimension allows people of varying ages, seniorities, and backgrounds to take turns being expert and beginner with respect to different tasks. Finally, they observed that social relations are negotiated between players in the system, with kids and adults both displaying knowledge and jockeying for position. In each case, the Fifth Dimension strategy offers something other than the either/or setup that creates haves and have-nots.

Language and culture in Fifth Dimensions

Another way in which our work contributes to critical theorizing aimed at educational policy and reform comes from the findings of another evaluation team, interested in the use of language and culture in Fifth Dimensions. In an era when English-only legislation and assaults on affirmative action are sweeping the nation, it is valuable to be informed about the promising work of our colleagues Gallego, Rueda and Moll (1997, 1998). They used Language Assessment Scales and the Ace Reporter computer game to document children's maintenance of Spanish language skills and children's increased ability in the use of English language skills through participation in the Fifth Dimension.

These researchers also discovered through comparative analysis of the participation structures of several sites that a common set of Fifth Dimension characteristics is shared among all sites, but that local adaptations characterize each site's cultural "personality." Definitions of success and failure are quite different in the Fifth Dimension play world. There are many ways to succeed and fail in the Fifth Dimension, as it offers many different incentives to participate, "absorbs" failure, and makes opportunities for "success" widely available.

Site enculturation is an initiating ritual as well as a continual and renewable process requiring knowledge of constant local adaptations. The children's community or native language (English, or Spanish) does not determine the language used during their participation in the Fifth Dimension. The language of the home and the language of intellectual achievement are not set apart from one another.

These are only a few of the insights we have gleaned so far. Our utopian methodology of putting theory into practice, and developing practice into fine-tuned symbiosis with local rhythms of institutional life *and death,* gives us insight into principles of learning in addition to helping us guide efforts toward strategic propagation of the model. The more these systems take root and grow in different settings, the more opportunity we have to see what difference they can make, for whom under what conditions and for how long. In such varied climates, we can only sustain these model systems if we regularly reflect on the signs of trouble and likely paths to success as steering points for the larger system.

Notes

1. Variations on this "normative description" appear in Cole (1996) and in Brown and Cole's chapter in Underwood and Taub (1998).

2. La Clase Magica (the Magic Class) is the name that parents and children gave the bilingual/bicultural adaptation of the Fifth Dimension model that was started by Olga Vasquez (Professor of Communication, University of California at San Diego) in the Catholic mission St. Leo's in a neighborhood called Eden Gardens near Solana Beach, CA.

3. The "x-mellon" listserve is an active bulletin board and archive of over eight thousand messages (and counting) exchanged among researchers and implementers of the model systems in the Distributed Literacy Consortium. X-mellon stands for "from Mellon," meaning A.W. Mellon Foundation, one of the two major funders of the initial work in the 1990s (the other being Russell Sage Foundation). The Laboratory of Comparative Human Cognition (LCHC) has many listserves and discussion groups currently in operation, with titles that begin with "x", such as xlchc, and xmca, for the list that is associated with issues of interest to the readers of the journal *Mind Culture and Activity.*

References

Adorno, T. W. (1984). *Aesthetic theory.* (C. Lenhardt, Trans.) (G. Adorno & R. Tiedemann, Eds.). Series title: The international library of phenomenology and moral sciences. Boston: Kegan Paul.

Blanton, W., Moorman, G., Hayes, B., & Warner, M. (1997). Effects of participation in the Fifth Dimension on far transfer. *Journal of Educational Computing Research,* 16(4), 371–396.

Bronner, S., & Kellner, D. (1989). *Critical theory and society: A reader.* New York: Routledge.

Bryson, M., & De Castell, S. (1996). Gender, new technologies, and inequity. *Mind, Culture and Activity, 2* (3), 119–135.

Cole, M. (1996). *Cultural psychology: A once and future discipline.* Cambridge: Harvard University Press.

64   Katherine Brown and Michael Cole

Conley, V. A., & the Miami Theory Collective of Oxford Ohio. (1993). *Rethinking technologies*. Minneapolis: University of Minnesota Press.

Engeström, Y. (1987). *Learning by expanding*. Helsinki: Orienta consultit oy.

Fine, G. (1987). *With the boys: Little League baseball and preadolescent culture*. Chicago: University of Chicago Press.

Gallego, M., Rueda, R., & Moll, L. (1997/1998). *Language and Culture Evaluation Team Reports. Annual Reports to the Andrew W. Mellon Foundation*. (M. Cole & K. Brown, Series Eds.). La Jolla, CA: Laboratory of Comparative Human Cognition.

Giroux, H. (1992). *Border crossings: Cultural workers and the politics of education*. New York: Routledge.

Greenwood-Gowan, S. (1992). *Workplace literacy*. New York: Teachers College Press.

Heidegger, M. (1977). *The question concerning technology and other essays* . (W. Lovitt, Trans.). New York: Garland Press.

Herman, E., & Chomsky, N. (1988). *Manufacturing consent: The political economy of the mass media*. New York: Pantheon.

Ito, M., McDermott, R., & Greeno, J. (1998). *Process Evaluation Report. Annual Reports to the Andrew W. Mellon Foundation*. (M. Cole & K. Brown, Series Eds.). La Jolla, CA: Laboratory of Comparative Human Cognition.

Lazarsfeld, P. (1941). Remarks on administrative and critical communications research. *Studies in Philosophy and Social Science, 9* (1), 12-16.

LCHC (1982). A model system for the study of learning difficulties. *Quarterly Newsletter of the Laboratory of Comparative Human Cognition, 4* (1), pp. 4-10.

Mosco, V. (1989). *The pay-per society. Computers and communication in the information age: Essays in critical theory and public policy*. Norwood, NJ: Ablex.

Nicolopolou, A., & Cole, M. (1993). The Fifth Dimension, its playworld and its institutional context: The generation and transmission of shared knowledge in the culture of collaborative learning. In *Contexts for learning: Sociocultural dynamics in children's development*. (E. A. Forman, N. Minnick, & C.A. Stone, Eds.). New York: Oxford University Press.

Noble, D. (1977). *Technology by design*. New York: Knopf.

Pool, I. (1983). *Technologies of freedom*. Cambridge, MA: Belknap Press.

Postman, N. (1985). *Amusing ourselves to death: Public discourse in the age of show business.* New York: Viking.

Reich, R. (1991). *The work of nations: Preparing ourselves for 21st-century capitalism.* New York: Knopf.

Schiller, H. (1989). *Culture, Inc.: The corporate takeover of public expression.* New York: Oxford University Press.

Schiller, H. (1996). *Information inequality: The deepening social crisis in America.* New York: Routledge.

Shaiken, H. (1985). *Work transformed: Automation and labor in the computer age.* New York: Holt.

Schustack, M. (1997) *Cognitive Evaluation Report. Annual Reports to the Andrew W. Mellon Foundation.* (M. Cole & K. Brown, Series Eds.). La Jolla, CA: Laboratory of Comparative Human Cognition.

Stuckey, J. E. (1991). *The violence of literacy.* Portsmouth, NH: Boynton/Cook Publishers,

Underwood, C., & Taub, L. (1998). *UCLINKS Annual Report.* Oakland: University of California, Office of the President.

CHAPTER 3

The Return of the "White Man's Burden": The Encounter between the Moral Discourse of Anthropology and the Domestic Life of Oriya Women

Usha Menon
Richard A. Shweder

Introduction

The central aim of this chapter is to characterize the life course images and domestic life of Oriya Hindu women living in extended households in the temple town of Bhubaneswar in Orissa, India. The chapter is divided into three parts.

In the first part we examine Oriya women's conceptions of the ideal phases in a woman's life. Oriya women do not conceive of a middle phase of life defined by either chronological age (e.g., 40–65) or by markers of biological aging (e.g., poorer eyesight, menopause, and loss of muscle strength) corresponding to the phrase "middle age." Yet, Oriya women do have a well-differentiated conception of the normal and desirable phases in a woman's life. Their ideal life course scheme includes a phase called *prauda* or "mature adulthood," which begins when a married woman takes over the management of the extended household and ends when she relinquishes control and social responsibilities to others. Although *prauda* is a condition that a married Oriya woman is likely to achieve by her early 30s and likely to hand over to others by her late 50s, age and biology per se are not the defining characteristics of Oriya life phase transitions. The real underlying logic of the five-phase scheme is a logic of social responsibility, family management, and moral duty. In the first part of the chapter we describe this scheme.

In the second part, we review some recent anthropological representations and moral evaluations of the lives of rural Hindu women more generally. Since the 1970s, a growing number of anthropological studies have examined the lives of Hindu women (to name but a few, Fruzetti, 1982; Dhruvarajan, 1988; Papanek & Minault, 1982; Sharma,

1980; Roy, 1975; Jacobson, 1982; Jain & Bannerjee, 1985; Liddle & Joshi, 1986; Wadley, 1980; Wadley & Jacobson, 1986; Bennett, 1983; Kondos, 1989; Minturn, 1993; Jeffrey, Jeffrey, & Lyons, 1988; Raheja & Gold, 1994). Many of these studies are implicitly, if not self-consciously, "feminist" in orientation, relying on moral concepts such as social inequality, patriarchal oppression, subjugation, exploitation, and resistance to depict Hindu women, their lives, and their situations. We identify two kinds of ethnographic portraits—the passive victim and the clandestine rebel—that have emerged from such studies.

In the third part, we raise some doubts about these recent representations and moral evaluations of the situation of rural Hindu women. Our aim is to recover a set of local meanings that have tended to be lost in the writing or invention (the "making up") of a feminist ethnography of Hindu family life. We do this by relying on Oriya women's own descriptions of their workaday lives and their own ratings of psychological well-being and physical health. Apart from women's descriptions of their daily routines, we also make use of observations of daily life in the family, of cooking and worship, of events like births and marriages, as well as everyday conversations that one of the authors (Menon) had with these women outside the interview situation. We relate women's daily routines to the different phases in an Oriya woman's life, and we contextualize the lives of Oriya "housewives" and trace some connections that exist between family statuses over the life course and the achievement of a sense of personal well-being *(hito)*.

Our strategy in this part is to rely on indigenous and locally salient Oriya moral concepts to reveal the hidden and unexamined presuppositions implicit in many portrayals of Hindu women. That unexamined presupposition is the tenet of "the moral superiority of the West," the presumption of a white man's (or in this case a white woman's) burden to liberate others from the darkness of their own cultural traditions. We describe the ways in which Oriya Hindu women derive meaning, purpose, and a sense of power from their family life practices, and we point out some of the important differences between the moral sensibilities of "Westernized" feminist writers and the moral sensibilities of the "non-Westernized" Hindu women whose lives they have sought to depict.

As we shall see, the overriding moral significance of the domestic life of Hindu women perceived by many "Westernized" ethnographers (and projected into their writings about exploitation, victimization, and resistance) are not the moral significances constructed by local Oriya women, whose voices and subaltern notions of the moral good (including their ideas about service, duty, civility, and self-improvement) articulate a vision of life in society that Westernized feminists appear ideologically unprepared to sympathetically represent.

The Oriya "Sample"

Our investigation was done in the neighborhood surrounding the Lingaraj temple in Bhubaneswar, Orissa, the "Old Town" as it is known locally. This medieval temple (it dates to the tenth or eleventh century) is one of the contemporary residences of the Hindu God Siva and his divine family. The temple is an active pilgrimage site and a necessary stop in the itinerary of pilgrims on their way to the famous Jagannatha ("juggernaut") temple forty miles away in the coastal town of Puri.[1]

Data for this chapter comes from two spells of fieldwork conducted by Menon: the first done in 1991 and the second in 1992–1993. In 1991, 92 Oriya Hindu men and women[2] were interviewed about their conceptions of the life course and about the kinds of events and experiences that they considered typical and/or significant in a person's life. They were also asked to assess their past and present life satisfaction and their expectations for the future.

The results of this initial spell of research highlighted three important issues. Firstly, Oriya Hindus tend to describe life in terms of changes in roles, duties, and responsibilities. They rarely speak of life in terms of the growth and development of a child's capacity to speak or walk; they never mention first menstruation or menopause, although the former is marked by explicit rituals and marks the beginning of restrictions on girls, on their movements; on the kinds of clothes they may wear; and on the people with whom they may associate.

Secondly, Oriya Hindus have well-articulated conceptions of the phases of the life course: the two-, four- and five-phase models. These models are described in part 1 of this chapter.

Thirdly, Oriya Hindu women of all ages tend to see middle age as, relatively speaking, the most satisfying period in a woman's life. This finding appears to be distinctive of the Oriya Hindu cultural world; for instance, it differs quite remarkably from research done with American women[3] (see figure 3.1). According to Cleary's unpublished results, American women exhibit a steady, linear decline in anticipated future life satisfaction as they move from young adulthood to advanced middle age. According to our results, however, Oriya Hindu women do not. In fact, unlike American women who view young adulthood—the period of life when individual capacities for autonomous, independent action are at their peak—as the more satisfying period in life, "mature adulthood" is the period that elicits from Oriya Hindu women the greatest anticipation of positive life satisfaction. As we shall see, there are indigenous meanings and understandings that can help us understand their evaluations.

Those findings from the fieldwork in 1991 provided the background for a second spell of fieldwork conducted by Menon a year later. Since Oriyas tend to describe their lives in terms of changing roles and responsibilities, the later research focused on women at different phases in the

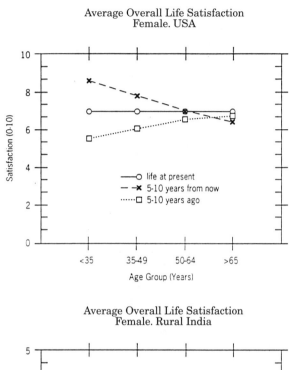

Average Overall Life Satisfaction
Female. USA

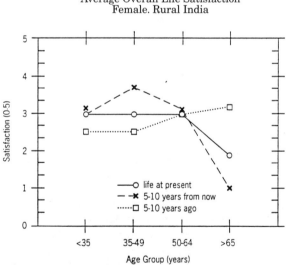

Average Overall Life Satisfaction
Female. Rural India

Figure 3.1. The American data were collected and analyzed by Paul Cleary and his associates at Harvard University. We are grateful for the opportunity to use this unpublished material as a point of comparison with the data from India.

life course, women occupying different family roles, performing different duties, and having different responsibilities. And since "mature adulthood" is perceived by many women to be the most satisfying period in a woman's life, the second set of interviews and observations tried to explicate the values and meanings that these women attach to this particular time of life, the way they define "satisfying life experiences." Keeping in mind that shifts in these women's roles, responsibilities, and personal well-being can be most clearly witnessed within the context of joint living arrangements, informants for the second spell of fieldwork were selected from extended households.

Joint living arrangements (a three-generational family consisting of adult brothers, their parents, wives and children, and unmarried sisters) are a phase of the developmental cycle of all families in the temple town of Bhubaneswar. One significant difference between joint and nuclear living arrangements in India lies in the fact that joint families are most certainly the cultural ideal. There is always a tendency to prefer such living arrangements whenever possible. In the Old Town, joint families usually break up when either the old father/grandfather (the head of the household) dies or when the old widowed mother/grandmother dies. At this point in time, the adult sons set up their own nuclear families consisting of just themselves, their wives and their children. Yet with the marriage of their sons and the birth of their grandchildren, their families extend and become complex and the cycle of joint living arrangements begins again.

Our sample of Oriya informants for this phase of the research consisted of 37 Hindu women belonging to 10 extended households, ranging in age from 19 to 78. These women follow traditional age-related family roles, those of "new" daughter-in-law, wife, mother, "old" (or senior) daughter-in-law, mother-in-law, grandmother, and widow. A couple of unmarried adult daughters also form part of the sample; they were interviewed so as to provide a same age control group and counterpoint to the experiences of "new" daughters-in-law.

Of the 10 families selected, 7 are Brahman; of the rest, 1 is a Chassa (a cultivating caste), another a Teli (a merchant caste), and the last a Maharana (a caste of carpenters). Except for one family of Brahmans, the rest are fairly well-off: they own agicultural land and other property—houses and shops—that earn rent. Signs of this relative wealth can be seen in the fact that all families have at least one scooter, perhaps two, as well as televisions, refrigerators, and other household appliances.

The number of members in these families vary from 6 to 20, with the average being 13. Of the 37 women, there are 22 daughters-in-law, 13 mothers-in-law, and 2 daughters; 2 of these daughters-in-law belong to 4-generational households and so are mothers-in-law to the newest generation of daughters-in-law. In terms of education, a generational effect is clearly noticeable: mothers-in-law rarely have more than 3 or 4 years of education while almost all the daughters-in-law have completed 10 years of formal schooling. There are, moreover, 5 mothers-in-law who state that they are unable to read or write; of these, 3 are non-Brahmans while the other 2 belong to a caste (Badus) whose status as Brahmans is contested by other Brahmans in the community.

Using open-ended, loosely structured interview schedules, women were asked to describe their daily routines, the degree of control they exercise over their own actions and bodies as well as those of others, their sense of belonging to their families, of being part of a meaningful communal life, and the extent to which they felt they had achieved well-being. In order to measure the extent to which these women experience well-being, Menon relied on the following mode of estimation. Ordinary folk in the Old Town often speak of having "not even one *anna*[4] of control over what happens in life" or of having "fully 16 *anna*s of happiness in childhood," and so when it came to asking women how healthy they were or how much well-being they thought they had, we framed the question in these commonplace terms. Therefore, the answers we typically heard were, "Six *anna*s of good health *(svasthya)*" or "Four *anna*s of well-being *(hito)*."

Almost without exception, the women were candid, articulate, and eager to participate and consequently, the interviews are long and detailed. None lasted for less than an hour. Some went on for more than two hours. The reasons for this candor and eagerness are not hard to understand. We believe most women saw the interview situation as an opportunity to engage in a kind of therapy and/or criticism of family members. They permitted themselves to speak their minds with relative freedom to an interested stranger (Menon) who spoke their language but who did not share the constraints of their lives. While most interviews were one-on-one conversations in secluded rooms, the feeling that the rest of the family was close at hand, within earshot, was not easy to shake off. Often, when the women felt that they were saying something particularly critical of other family members, their voices would drop, but at other times they would deliberately raise their voices so that their complaints could be heard by other members of the family. Thus, most "new" daughters-in-law spoke in low undertones while mothers-in-law and sometimes "old" daughters-in-law speak loudly and self-confidently, often even aggressively.

Part 1. Between Birth and Death in Orissa, India: Some Local Women's Views

Figure 3.2 is a schematic representation of the phases of life *(avastha)* as described by sixty-six Oriya Hindu women (predominantly

Brahman) living in extended households in the temple town of Bhubaneswar. All the women were interviewed by Menon in the summer of 1991. During the interview, they were presented with a sheet of paper on which there were two dots, designated "birth" and "death." The women were asked to fill in the space between the two dots by narrating the most significant events and experiences in a typical person's life, and in their own lives as well.

Some women initially resisted the request, indicating that it is really boring to talk in broad generalities about things that are obvious about life. As one elderly woman put it (a woman who was in the fifth and last phase of life, the *briddha avastha* or "stage of completion"), "What can I tell you about those kinds of things? You know about them.

	Birth	Knows right from wrong (7 - 9)	Marriage (18 - 20)	Takes over family management (30 - 33)	Relinquishes family management (55 - 60)	Death
Two stage model		*bapa gharo* life in father's house		*sasu gharo* life in mother-in-law's house		
Four stage model		*pila* child	*jouvana* sexually active	*prauda* mature adult	*briddha* completed	
Five state model	*pila* undiciplined child	*kishoro* morally formative youth	*jouvana* sexually active	*prauda* mature adult	*briddha* completed	
Quality of role	pet	guest	servant	manager	dependent	
Rank in family	High	High	Low	High (Peak)	Low	
Control over others	High	Low	Low	High (Peak)	Low	
Served by others?	Yes	Yes	No	Yes	Uncertainty	
Restrictive life?	No	Yes	Yes (Peak)	Yes	No	
Burden of responsibilities	Low	Low	High	High	Low	
Worry about welfare of others?	No	No	Yes	Yes (Peak)	Disappears	
Perceived stress	Low	Low	High (Peak)	High	High	
Karmic consequences of one's actions	Low	High	High	High (Peak)	High	
Capacity of reason	Absent	Present	Present	Present (Peak)	Declines	
Time of suffering?	No	No	Yes	No	Yes	
Perception of life-satisfaction trajectory		I will be worse off in next phase	I was better off in last phase and will be much better off in next phase	I was worse off in last phase and will be worse off in next phase	I was much better off in last phase and will be much worse off in next phase	

Figure 3.2. Oriya Woman's Conception of the Life Course

Everyone does. You are born, you grow up, 'you grow old', you die. Do you want to hear that?" Other women were initially skeptical about the task on the grounds that "each person's life is different from everyone else's" and that "it depends on what kind of family you are born into, what your caste is, whether you're a boy or girl, whether you are the old-est child or the second or whatever, what your capabilities are, what *karma* you have brought with you." Nevertheless, Oriya women are quite adept at storytelling, and with just a bit of coaxing, they in fact had much to say about how a woman's life proceeds between life and death in rural India.

The tales told by these 66 Oriya women reveal an alternative cul-tural conceptualization of the phases of the life course, one based on the logic of social responsibility, family management, and moral duty. In their narrations, Oriya women tend to divide the life course into either two, four, or five phases. These three types of conceptualizations form a nested hierarchy of differentiated cultural models of the life course. All three cultural models are schematically represented in figure 3.2.

In the context of our general concern with documenting the breadth versus narrowness of the cross-cultural and historical distri-bution of the idea of "middle age," it is the four- or five-phase model that interest us the most, because within these models there is a life phase known as *prauda* or "mature adulthood." We shall have more to say about the Oriya conception of "mature adulthood" in a moment. First, however, we briefly comment on the most basic or rudimentary Oriya model of a woman's life: the one in which the life course is partitioned into only two phases, life spent in my father's house *(bapa gharo)* and that spent in my husband's mother's house *(sasu gharo)*. If an Oriya woman divides her life into only two phases, these are most likely to be the two.

In extended households in Orissa, India, married sons continue to stay at home base with their parents but daughters, after an arranged marriage, move out. From the point of view of the daughter who is mar-rying out, the marriage ceremony is the most significant phase bound-ary in her life. It is at this point that an Oriya woman's socially recog-nized status shifts from being a child who is some man's daughter (a *jhio pila*) to being a sexually active female who is some other woman's daughter-in-law (a *bou*). As a daughter-child (*jhio pila*), an Oriya female is assumed to be sexually dormant (even after she is biologically mature) and to live under her father's protection. As a young daughter-in-law *(bou)*, she is expected to be reproductively and sexually active and live under her mother-in-law's command.

Ideally, this fundamental phase shift from her father's house to her mother-in-law's house takes place between 18 and 20 years of age. However, age per se does not mark the boundary between these two basic phases in life. Rather, it is marked by the numerous changes in social responsibilities attendant upon marriage, including among other things, the responsibility to serve and be sensitive to the in-laws' needs and to become sexually active for the sake of reproducing the family line. Unlike young American females who want to be referred to as "women" (rather than "girls") as soon as they move out of their parents' homes and into the "liberating" atmosphere of a college dormitory, a sexually inactive Oriya thirty-year-old who is still unmarried and lives under the protection of her father is socially categorized as a "child," and she becomes a "woman" by getting married and by willingly and dutifully placing herself under an older woman's authority.

For the women in our study, the story of the life course, then, is the story of domestic life in someone else's house (first father's, then mother-in-law's). The fact that Oriya women are house bound, however, is not viewed by them as a mark of their oppression. Quite the contrary. The domestic realm is highly valued in Oriya culture, and domestic space *(ghare)* is understood as a kind of sacred, uncontaminating space, and contrasted with public or outside, contaminating space *(bahare)*. Men spend time outside the home and, therefore, are always at risk of becoming coarse *(asabhya)* and uncivilized *(abhadra)*. It is by virtue of being able to remain indoors that Oriyas, both men and women, believe that women are more refined than men, more capable of experiencing civilizing dispositions such as "humility," "restraint" and shame *(lajya)*, less likely to display crude emotions such as anger *(raga)* or mocking laughter *(hasa)*.

The four-and five-phase models elaborate on life in the two houses, presenting us with a more differentiated view of a woman's life course. In the five-phase model, life in the father's house is divided into two phases: first, the undisciplined early childhood phase *(pilaliya)*, when the daughter is indulged as a kind of adorable yet uncivilized family pet, and the second, the morally formative yet tender youthful phase *(kishor avastha)*, when the daughter-child becomes a kind of resident-guest in training and is given anticipatory instruction in the social responsibilities and duties of married life. The first phase ends at approximately seven to nine years, when the daughter-child is now thought to be capable of praying on her own, able to distinguish between right and wrong, and sufficiently mature to have a conscience about the social responsibilities associated with domestic life while the second ends at marriage.

Life in the mother-in-law's house is divided into three phases: the first (phase 3) is *jouvana*, "young adulthood" when the sexually active young daughter-in-law is expected to have children and serve the needs of her husband's family members; the second (phase 4) is *prauda* or "mature adulthood," when a woman takes over all the responsibilities for family management, including planning and control; and the third (phase 5) is *briddha*, the "age of completion," when a woman gives up on the management of the family, becomes dependent on her kin, and begins to anticipate life in yet another house, the house of *Yama,* the house of the god of death.

In figure 3.2 we have listed some of the characteristics of each life phase as revealed in these women's narratives. We have focused on those that are potentially relevant to perceived life- satisfaction or well-being, for example, being assimilated into the family, having dominance within the family, being served by others, and having control over the actions of others. The 66 Oriya women in our sample represent four of the five life phases. As a measure of perceived life-satisfaction, they were asked to estimate the ratio of good and bad events in their lives now, 5–10 years ago in the past, and 5–10 years into the future. The perceived life-satisfaction of the 14 oldest women, for example, those over 60 who are in the "last phase," that of *briddha,* can be summarized as follows: My life was much better off in the past and it will be much worse off in the future. The perceived life-satisfaction of the 19 young daughters-in-law, those women under 30 who are in phase 3, *jouvana,* can be summarized this way: My life was better off in the past and it will be much better off in the future. Neither *jouvana* (the early married phase) nor *briddha* (the phase of completion, the last phase of life) are valued times for women in this community. By way of contrast, it is the phase of "mature adulthood," *prauda,* which is highly prized. Married women in their twenties look forward to it with anticipation. The elder women look back on it as that phase of life that preceded their decline.

Prauda, "mature adulthood," may seem to be vaguely reminiscent of "midlife" or "middle age." Yet that impression is surely misleading, for "mature adulthood" is not defined by biological age and does not normally extend beyond the age of 55–60. *Prauda* begins when a married woman takes over the management of the extended household and ends when she relinquishes control and social responsibilities to others. According to these Oriya women, *prauda* is the phase in life when dominance, control, planfulness, and responsibility for others is at a peak. The perceived life-satisfaction of the 28 women who are in the prauda phase can be summarized this way: Compared to where I am now I was worse off in the past and I will be worse off in the future. In absolute terms it is when Oriya women are "mature adults" that they report the greatest life-satisfaction.

When pressed, Oriya women can estimate rough descriptively normative age boundaries for each of these phases of life. *Prauda,* for example, is likely to begin when a woman is in her early 30s and end when she is in her late 50s. Nevertheless, as we have mentioned before, age per se is not the defining characteristic of Oriya life phases, and other biological markers such as menarche or menopause are rarely mentioned when these women talk about the phases of life. The real underlying logic of Oriya life phases is a logic of social responsibility, family management, and moral duty and it is in such terms that a woman's "mature adulthood" in rural India is culturally defined.

We now turn to a discussion of the way Hindu family life and the domestic careers of Hindu women have been represented in recent scholarly literature, where for the most part the "native point of view" has either been subordinated to, or appropriated by, the moral framework of the currently popular "feminist" point of view. First we discuss the two types of constructions of the lives of Hindu women that are most prevalent in feminist ethnography. Then we offer an alternative construction derived from an alternative point of view.

Part 2. Writing about Domesticity: The Moral Foundations of Ethnographic Representation

Feminist discourse about "Hindu women": A brief overview

Feminist scholarship is, of course, neither uniform nor homogenous in its goals or beliefs. Nevertheless, in the context of South Asian studies, there are certain assumptions that seem to be widely held among anthropologists who approach their subject matter from a feminist point of view: that is, that patriarchy is bad and is responsible for the subordination of women; that "women" can be grouped into a unitary, coherent, already constituted category, made up of gendered persons who have the same objective interests and similar subjective desires; that male dominance and female subordination are not only morally outrageous but also seem to exist in almost every context; that Hindu cultural meanings systematically and regularly devalue women.

Armed with these tenets, scholars who study India from a feminist point of view seem to divide into two categories: those who view Hindu women as passive victims of patriarchy, and those who view them as active rebels against it.

The scholars who portray Hindu women as passive victims (e.g., Kondos, 1989; Dhruvarajan, 1988; Jeffrey, Jeffrey, & Lyons, 1988) focus on the "differences" that they, as "Westernized" observers see in the life circumstances of the female Hindu "other," and they are sensitive to (and feel great empathy for) the situations of the most unfortunate of Hindu women.

There is much that these scholars dislike or even disdain in Hindu society. For example, they blame Hindu religion (which they interpret as mere ideology, in the Marxist sense of "ideology") for the "subordination and subjection" of women (Kondos, 1989, p. 162), for clouding the consciousness of its victims and for withholding from Hindu women a political discourse of protest, insurgency, and victimhood. Such feminist writers tend to project an image of "the Hindu woman" as tame, domesticated, tradition-bound, intellectually unsophisticated, and sexually constrained, as a woman who has little control over her actions or her body, as a woman whose life is completely contingent on others.

Thus, Dhruvarajan, while describing her book's objective, writes,

> By elaborating on the philosophical underpinnings and the beliefs regarding the nature of men and women it is based on, it shows how women's dependent position on men is legitimized, how the ideology manipulates the motivational structure of women to accept their position as underlings of men, and how it strips them of the willpower necessary for self-reliance and personal growth. (1988, p. 108)

And Kondos, in her study of upper-caste Nepali Hindu women, concludes,

> Feminine success is predefined and not open to variation, for a woman cannot be successful in any other way or in any other terms except those specified by the structures (the domicile, the laws, the cultural imperatives to produce sons and to die before her husband). (1989, p. 190)

And Jeffrey, Jeffrey, and Lyons reveal their intellectual predispositions when they write that

> Swaleha (one of our research assistants) responded to Patricia's exasperation over women's self-abnegation with the comment: "But you see, the men here have subdued their women so completely that the idea has perched in women's minds that they are indeed inferior." (1988, p. 157)

The foregoing image of the Hindu woman as passive victim is set in sharp contrast to another representation that is implicit in the writings of these feminist scholars, the image of the Western or Westernized academic woman as educated and cosmopolitan, as having control over her body and her sexuality, as autonomous, and as having the freedom to make informed decisions on her own. The message conveyed by these authors is that the discrepancy between the two images (the tradition-bound housewife vs. the cosmopolitan liberated scholar) is a measure of the failure of Hindu society to recognize and live up to a set of obvious and universally binding moral ideals (autonomy, equality, privacy, individual rights, and social and economic justice), which have been recognized and are being institutionalized in the "West." In ethnographic constructions of this sort the "native point of view" remains unvoiced or tends to be subordinated to a feminist point of view.

Yet not all scholars who study India portray Hindu women as passive victims. Recently, there has become available in the literature an alternative construction or invention—the Hindu woman as an active rebel. Those who represent Hindu women this way, as proto-Jacobins or cryptorevolutionaries, perceive in Hindu women a set of "liberated" attitudes and reactions against patriarchy that are very much like their own. These ethnographers detect "subversion" and "resistance" in Hindu women's songs and poetry and ordinary conversations. They portray Hindu women as having a bawdy sense of humor, taking pleasure in their sexuality, and relishing their female nature. They represent these symbolic actions as ways for women to express their disenchantment with patriarchy and as indications of an incipient or clandestine movement within Hindu India aimed at undermining received gender roles (see Raheja & Gold, 1994). According to this representation of South Asian moral attitudes and beliefs, Hindu women speak in multiple voices and elaborate both dominant male and subversive female perspectives. At some fundamental level, however, Hindu women, it is claimed, share with Western feminists insights that enable them to identify the ultimate cause as well as the proximate instruments of their oppression—patriarchy and men. In ethnographic constructions of this sort, the "native point of view" is equated with, and thereby appropriated by, the feminist point of view. Is there a distinctive (nonfeminist) "native point of view"?

Local Oriya discourse about Hindu women

There can be little doubt that the cultural practices of rural India in general and the family life practices of rural Hindu women in particular are a challenge to the cognitive, moral and aesthetic sensibilities of Euramerican observers. For example, most married Oriya Hindu women living in the temple town of Bhubaneswar are sequestered in family compounds, where they assume a major responsibility for the humdrum routines, tasks and duties of domestic life. Chandrama, a twenty-three-year-old Oriya woman who has been married for the last five years and is the eldest daughter-in-law in an extended household of twelve, tells us about a typical day in her life. What she has to narrate about her daily routine is not untypical of a day in the life of an Oriya woman in the third or *jouvana* phase of life.

> Chandrama: As soon as I get up, I sweep out the house and then I go to the bathroom. I clean my teeth, have a bath, and then I start the breakfast. Once the breakfast is done, people come in one by one to eat. I serve each of them breakfast. Once that is done, we have our breakfast together. *Bou* (husband's mother) and I eat together. And then, I start preparing lunch—what we'll be eating at 2:00 in the afternoon. Once that is done, again people come in one by one to eat. By 3:00,

we would also have eaten and I would have washed up after lunch. Then, I come and sleep in the afternoon. I sleep for an hour. I get up at 4:00. I again sweep out the house and then I go down to start making something to eat with tea. I knead the *atta* (wheat flour) and make *parathas* or *rotis* (different kinds of bread). Again, people come one by one to eat. I serve them and then it would be sundown by now and I offer *sandhya* (evening worship) before I start cooking the night meal. I am usually cooking till 9:00 in the night. Then I go and watch the serial on T.V. After that, at about 9:30, everyone will come to eat and I serve them. And then we eat. After finishing eating, we go to bed. The dishes are left as they are till morning. I just keep them till the morning when I wash them. In the morning, the first thing I do is take out and wash the *ointha* (polluted by leftovers) dishes, then I leave them out in the sun to dry, while I sweep out the kitchen, wash it out, and then take the vessels back in again.

Usha: Would you like to add anything more to what you've just said?

Chandrama: No, nothing else.

Usha: What about *puja* (worship)? In the morning do you do *puja* after your bath? Give water to the *tulasi* or offer water to the *surjya* (sun-god)?

Chandrama: No, I do nothing. *Bou* does all that. All I do is wash our *burhi ma's'* (husband's father's mother) feet and drink the water after my bath and before I go to make breakfast. I used to do it for *bou* and *nona* (husband's mother and father) in the beginning but they stopped me from doing it. They said that it was enough to do it for *burhi ma* and get her blessings. But apart from that I don't do any *puja*. I offer *sandhya* but that is only in the kitchen—*bou* offers it in the *puja* room and over the rest of the house.

Now as every interpretive anthropologist knows, a storyteller's intent is not always equivalent to a listener's response. One theme of our chapter is that, from the point of view of "authorial intent," Chandrama's chronicle of her daily routine is really a narrative saturated with locally salient yet universally recognizable moral meanings about her self-conscious engagement in a project of doing *sewa* or "service" for her husband's family. Her narrative is about the positive moral implications of voluntarily enduring the specific life phase (and hence temporary) responsibilities of a family *sevaka* (a devoted servant of the divine).

One of the things this storyteller, Chandrama, does not know, however, is that some of her listeners will be cosmopolitan liberated Westernized scholars who will reflexively perceive her *sewa* as humiliating subservience, oppressive subjugation, and/or abusive exploitation. Minimally we can expect that the daily routine of an Oriya "housewife" as described in this narrative will appear at first blush to give new meaning (both literal and figurative) to the idea of the "daily grind." At least that is the first impression it is likely to create in the minds of many cosmopolitan and liberated academic observers.

A second theme of our chapter is that first impressions can be misleading. This is especially true when those impressions have been formed or take shape under the influence of a relatively thin theory of moral goods, such as the honorable yet incomplete (and hence "partial" or "biased") "morality of autonomy" privileged by "Western" liberal thought. In this case the (objectively) partial yet (subjectively) totalizing moral significance projected (and then perceived) by "Western" and "Westernized" feminist ethnographers as they gaze upon the lives of "unliberated" Hindu women are almost neocolonial in character, for those significances carry with them the implications of a moral imperialism or a "white (wo)man's burden" to emancipate and uplift Hindu family life and to disenthrall "uneducated" and "superstitious" Hindus of their "unjust" and "oppressive" gender roles.

In this chapter we wish to suggest, however tentatively, that the Oriya Hindu women of the temple town of Bhubaneswar are neither passive victims nor subversive rebels, but rather active upholders of a moral order that Western feminists have largely failed to comprehend. High on the list of virtues and values in the moral order upheld by Oriya women are chastity, modesty, duty, self-discipline, the deferment of gratification, self-improvement, and the ideal of domestic service *(sewa)*. Low on the list are liberty and social equality. [5]

This chapter is about the cultural agency displayed by the Oriya Hindu women of the temple town as they go about their daily lives, agency that supports and affirms rather than denies or undermines the cultural order. These women are not cultural robots who go through life mechanically and unthinkingly. Rather, they are self-reflecting people who acknowledge the constraints they live with, recognize the choices available to them, and are well aware of the costs and rewards of conforming to cultural norms.

Hito, the Oriya term for well-being, is an analytic category familiar to the women who participated in this study. Defined very broadly, it refers to the state of being satisfied with the way in which one's world has turned out. A more nuanced definition, one that includes the indigenous meanings that this term conveys to Oriya women, will emerge during the course of this chapter. It is that nuanced definition that enables us to critique the rather dismal feminist representations of the lives of

Hindu women and to relocate Oriya domestic life within an alternative moral order. (On the idea of plural moral "goods" such as autonomy, community or divinity and alternative moral orders see Shweder, 1990, 1994; Shweder, Mahapatra, & Miller, 1990; Shweder, Much, Mahapatra, & Park, 1997; Haidt, Koller, & Diaz, 1993. On the idea of plural moral "goods" such as fairness, sympathy, duty and self-improvement, and alternative moral orders see Wilson, 1993.)

Our representation of women's lives in Oriya households highlights the way a woman's access to, and achievement of, wellbeing *(hito)* systematically varies across the life cycle. There are periods when an Oriya "housewife" is so valued within the family, when her activities are so significant for the material and spiritual prosperity of the entire household, that her own sense of well-being peaks; and there are periods when she is less essential to the household's well-being, and her own sense of well-being declines. No Oriya Hindu woman's life is uniformly successful nor uniformly a failure, just as there is no woman in this community who always makes her own decisions nor one who never does. These are facts well recognized by the women themselves. Oriya women will tell you that success or failure, control and lack of control, and well-being and distress characterize different phases in a person's life and ultimately mesh together to form the fabric of a self-disciplined life. This chapter is thus an attempt to describe the moral texture of that self-disciplined way of being in the world as understood by Oriya woman.

Part 3. Understanding the Cultural Construction of Gender in a Hindu Temple Town

For the sake of our analysis we shall define a "culture" as a reality lit up by a morally enforceable conceptual scheme or sub-set of meanings instantiated in practice (Shweder, 1996). In this section we examine the alternative cultural reality of gender relations in the temple town of Bhubaneswar and some of the concepts, beliefs, and practices so that Oriya gender relations are understood as a justifiable or defensible moral reality.

To an outside observer unfamiliar with the concepts, meanings, and practices of the temple town the women who live there may at first glance seem to be docile, submissive, withdrawn, and relegated to the background, women without voices. But appearances can deceive, revealing more about the observer than the observed. A closer acquaintance suggests a radically different picture, for these Oriya women do not see themselves as powerless, and they confidently believe that it is they who hold families and society together. Oriya men share this view. In this section, we attempt to show the ways in which such self-understandings grow and develop among these women.

Kakar's comment that, in Hindu India, "the preferred medium of instruction and transmission of psychological, metaphysical and social thought continues to be the story" (1982, p. 1) accurately describes much of indigenous cultural discourse in the temple town of Bhubaneswar. Oriya men and women frequently use stories from the various Puranas (texts about the old times and the often-times), as well as regional Oriya folktales to give logic and meaning to everyday or mundane experience. For most of the Oriya women who spoke at length and in intimate detail about their lives with Usha Menon, the stories from the Puranas are far more "real" and relevant to everyday life (and thus more worthy of repetition) than events reported in the daily newspapers.

The female protagonists (divine and human) of these stories— Durga, Kali, Kunti, Draupadi, Sita, Radha, Savitri, and Anusuya— exemplify womanly virtues. Their experiences elucidate a woman's *dharma,* define a woman's *prakriti* (*svabhava,* "her nature"). Their qualities *(guna)* tell them what it means to be a Hindu woman. Women see these figures as paradigmatic, partly because they represent ideals worthy of emulation, and partly because it is believed that by virtue of being female, these heroines and ordinary Oriya Hindu women share the same configurations of female substance.

In addition to the Puranic orientation in the temple town, the *Sakta*[6] tradition is also strong. Oriya Hindus of the temple town, both men and women, are liable to say that women embody, as the goddess does, *sakti* (vital energy, power, and strength), that they have more of the *gunas* in terms of absolute quantities than do men, which is why women can turn the *asadhya* (undoable) into the *sadhya* (doable), the *asambhav* (impossible) into the *sambhav* (possible). Women are commonly described as *saktidayinis* (givers of vital energy and strength) and as being *sampoorna sakti* (full of vital energy and strength). Women are depicted as *samsarore*[7] *chalak* (controllers and directors of the familylife in this world), as those whose duties include satisfying everyone *(samasthonku santhusta koriba),* maintaining the family *(samsaroku sambhaliba),* and ensuring peace and order *(shanti shrunkhala rakhiba).*

Most Oriya Hindus in the temple town believe that social reproduction is the primary task of any group. And they believe that the family represents the most appropriate site for social reproduction. For most Oriyas the idea of a voluntarily childless marriage is a contradiction in terms (why would anyone marry, Oriyas ask, if they had no intention of having children and contributing to the reproduction of the group?). Both men and women will say, "We are born into this world to play our roles in *samsara,* to participate in the ebb and flow of life, to build families, to raise children." They emphasize the impermanence of all things in this world, the fact that continual change is the only stable feature of life. They believe that only through procreating and raising children to responsible adulthood does a group achieve immortality.

It is thus not surprising that Oriya Hindu women, and their menfolk too, regard the home and the family—the domestic domain—as a more important sphere of human action than action in the public domain. Since women control and manage all household activities, whether what men earn is utilized effectively and productively depends on the sagacity and capability of the women of the household, particularly the seniormost woman. Men readily acknowledge that women shoulder many more responsibilities than they do (striro daitya purusa opekhya jyateshtha adhika) and that the work women do is six times as much as men have to do (stri jatinkoro karma chho guna adhika). As a sixty-year-old husband, father, and one of the most articulate of informants says,

> Look, as a 20-year-old man, a 20-year-old child, he knows nothing; he just roams here and there, but a 20-year-old girl, she has become the mother of two children; she runs her household and family; she cares for the cows and calves under her care, the children, and the house; she cooks and serves her husband; she cleans the children, dresses them, and sends them to school, makes sure that they are well; she manages the parents of her husband; she cleans the house. Compared to a man's, a woman's responsibilities are far more. When you compare men and women of the same age, that is what you find.

In contrast to the premises of modern liberal thought, the view of the world espoused by Oriya women and men is built on a logic of difference and solidarity rather than on equality and competition. To understand the Oriya moral universe as it applies to gender, one must understand that the popular Oriya recognition of the worth of women's work and widespread acknowledgment of greater female effectiveness is not a local idiomatic Oriya expression of a feminist viewpoint, for quite emphatically, neither women nor men in Orissa believe that women and men are equal.

Indeed, most Oriya women and men find the notion that one should be indifferent to gender or treat the genders as though they were the same as either incomprehensible, amusing, or immature. For these Oriyas, the most common metaphor for society is the human body: no organ is exactly substitutable for any other and yet all work together so that the body functions efficiently so that it survives and lives. Most Oriya women and men believe that of all the jatis (castes) in the world, male and female are the only really real jatis because male and female are the only two jatis whose fundamental differences cannot be transcended.

For Oriya Hindus then, "difference" and "interdependency" are givens. Yet, this "difference" and the character of the "interdependence" are not fixed or global. The prerogatives and privileges enjoyed and the power exercised by women and men are fluid, varying, as Ramanujan (1990) has said, with particular contexts. Men, in terms of the constitution of their bodily substances, have disproportionately more of the *sattva guna* (qualities of transparency, lucidity, and coherence), and so, are regarded as "purer" and because of this relative purity enjoy certain privileges in some situations (e.g., they can approach divinity with fewer restrictions); while women because they possess more of all the *gunas* in absolute terms, exercise considerable power and control in other situations (for example, they manage household finances and activities with little interference). We will now document and elaborate these points.

Some Oriya women's discourse about well-being

In this section, we rely on the voices of thirty-seven Oriya women from our broader sample to construct a representation of the way in which personal well-being is understood and defined by women who belong to this orthodox Hindu community whose practices and institutions are premised on moral goods and ethical virtues other than those privileged in feminist writings and Western liberal thought.

Family role (rank and status) appears to be the significant variable in determining an Oriya woman's well-being. As noted earlier, considering the fabric of adult life across the life course, access to personal well-being is at its maximum when an Oriya woman enters the managerial stage of *prauda* (typically as either an "old" daughter-in-law or as a married mother-in-law). And while most Oriya women achieve this rank or status some time between thirty and forty years of age, biological age per se is not a crucial variable.

Similarly, the sense of well-being reported by daughters and "new" daughters-in-law vary according to their particular family roles. In Hindu extended households, unmarried adult daughters and "new" daughters-in-law live in the same family compound and are often of approximately the same age (both may be in their early twenties). Yet, their well-being assessments vary widely, with unmarried daughters reporting strikingly higher levels of *hito*.

Because an Oriya woman's duties, responsibilities, social status, and ways of being enmeshed in interpersonal relationships seem to be the major factors giving her meaning, purpose, and fulfillment in life, it is one of our aims as ethnographers of Hindu family life to characterize their moral meanings, to describe changes in those duties and responsibilities over the life course, and to understand the way in which access to those moral meanings is related to personal well-being.

The "daily grind": The moral meanings of domestic service (sewa)

It has been reported that in most societies as a woman ages there is a relaxation in the restrictions under which she lives (cf. Brown & Kerns, 1985). While this may be true on a worldwide scale, it would be a mistake to infer that increased "autonomy" is the central moral "good" that explains the association between personal well-being and "mature adult-hood" (prauda) in our sample. We believe that in the temple town a woman's sense of well-being hinges on the particular kinds of family rela-tionships she has succeeded at developing or failed to develop as she ages.

An important part of the story about *hito* concerns the values and meanings that Oriya Hindus attach to the roles of "old" daughter-in-law and married mother-in-law. By incorporating such indigenous values and meanings, we will try to construct an ideal typical model of the development of well-being among Oriya women. We believe this model is culturally salient, although because this model is an idealization, summarizing and typifying thirty-seven Oriya voices, it will not neces-sarily coincide with the lived experiences of each and every woman.

The most striking feature of the daily routines of these Oriya women lies, we think, in the ways in which such routines highlight social relational patterns within families. These daily routines bring to the fore the ways in which duties, responsibilities, and opportuni-ties get distributed among women according to the needs of the fam-ily. In this section, we discuss and contrast five particular family roles: daughter, "new" daughter-in-law, "old" daughter-in-law, mother-in-law, and widow. We discuss the social relational patterns that are revealed by their daily routines.

We begin with the "daughter" of the family. As an unmarried adult an Oriya Hindu girl enjoys a carefree and relatively irresponsible life. She is far more carefree, in fact, than even her brothers, for whom, given the unemployment statistics in India, the pressure to obtain an ade-quate source of livelihood makes these years of early adulthood very dif-ficult. An unmarried adult girl is indulged. She has no prescribed duties. Whatever she does, she does voluntarily. The daily routines of the two daughters in the sample makes this abundantly clear. (Although there were only two unmarried adult women in our sample, over the years, the authors have observed this pattern of behavior in scores of families.) As Sudhangani, one of the unmarried adult daughters, says,

> After eating rice, I may stitch something or I may knit or if I wanted to, I may watch some T.V. or I may go to sleep. I do things like that.

And as the other daughter Ameeta says explicitly, daughters have no responsibility toward anyone in their fathers' households:

> My responsibility? What responsibility? I have no responsibil-ity. As long as my father and mother are alive, I have no respon-sibility toward anyone.

At the same time, however, they are aware of their positions as temporary residents in the *kishoro* stage of life, whose permanent homes are elsewhere. Although these unmarried girls have few illusions that life in the homes of their mothers-in-law is going to be anything less than strenuous, the interviews communicate quite plainly the sense of positive anticipation they feel as they look ahead to life as daughters-in-law.

Now let us consider the situation of a "new" daughter-in-law. The differences in well-being between daughters and daughters-in-law are quite striking. Daughters report almost double the level of personal well-being reported by daughters-in-law. This reflects, perhaps, the comfort, the sense of belonging that daughters feel in their fathers' homes, and a feeling of comfort that "new" daughters-in-law lack during their initial years in their husbands' homes. Since these two groups are of roughly the same age, the relationship is clearly not between age and access to wellbeing but between the family role occupied and well-being.

Unlike an unmarried daughter of the house, who is in the *kishoro* phase of life, a "new" daughter-in-law is in the *jouvana* phase and has explicitly understood duties. She is put through something like the domestic Oriya version of military "boot camp." The most important of these duties lies in doing *sewa*—service to members of her husband's family. Such *sewa* has, in the Oriya Hindu context, very concrete dimensions. She has to do all the cooking and some of the serving of the food, much of the cleaning and washing, as well as perform explicit rituals of deference to her husband's mother and father. These rituals include massaging their feet daily, drinking the water used to ceremonially wash their feet before eating, and eating out of the *thali* (metal plate) previously used by either her mother-in-law or her father-in-law.

It is crucial to recognize that the meaning of these rituals are easily misunderstood if they are comprehended only within the moral framework of "Western" individualist liberationist ideals. From the "native point of view," these rituals of family life are culturally defined ways available to a daughter-in-law for "reconstructing" (see Lamb, 1993) her physical substance, and for expressing her solidarity with the patrilineage into which she has merged at married. This is not to say that every Oriya newlywed is temperamentally inclined to life in a "boot camp" or tolerates harsh treatment without suffering and physical distress. It is to say, however, that within the framework of indigenous South Asian understandings such rituals of deference continue the process of "reconstruction" of the bride's bodily substance begun explicitly during the marriage ceremonies and symbolized by the new name given the bride at marriage (see Inden & Nicholas, 1977). In keeping with Hindu notions of the body that emphasize the relative openness to external influences (Marriott, 1976), the new given name, the marriage ceremonies, and the rituals of deference mark the continual "reconstructions" that a woman's body undergoes as her bodily substance slowly becomes that of the patrilineage into which she has married.

Such rituals contribute directly to an increase or decrease in a daughter-in-law's sense of well-being. Thus when an angry mother-in-law withholds permission to perform such rituals, all daughters-in-law interpret such refusal as a rejection by the family to her assimilation and experience that rejection with considerable sorrow and distress. The cognitive and emotional reactions of "Westernized" feminist scholars to such practices do not further, indeed they obscure, our understanding of the local moral world supporting extended family life in India.

Most "new" daughters-in-law echo Chandrama with only minor variations. In the early years of marriage, daughters-in-law do not worship any gods. For them, it is enough to worship their mothers-in-law and fathers-in-law, earthly gods having the power to withhold or bestow blessings. As Sabitiri, a "new" daughter-in-law, married for just four months, told Menon,

> At my time in life, it is appropriate that I worship *bou*. What need is there for me to worship any other god? She is my god.

These "new" daughters-in-law are working up a spiritual ladder to the gods. At this point in their moral careers, they regard the opportunity to worship their husbands' mothers and fathers rather than the gods as opportunities for promotion, not a deprivation. At this stage, given their position in the family hierarchy, "new" daughters-in-law appear to have few other responsibilities. As Chandrama says further along in her interview,

> For the moment, I have no responsibility. There are so many people older than I am—they take all the responsibility of this household.

Nevertheless, as she herself is aware, *daitva* or "responsibility" is never completely absent. A competent daughter-in-law has to learn to be adept in maintaining harmony among the younger members of the family. She must take on the role of friend and advisor. She may even intervene as an intermediary between them and her mother-in-law, when the latter's consent and approval is required but unlikely. And it is this aptitude, this capacity to, as she says, "understand what lies in the minds of the *nanad* [husband's younger sisters] and *diyoro* [husband's younger brothers]" that is the distinctive mark of a successful daughter-in-law, trusted by her affinal family.

Further in the interview, Chandrama describes the restrictions under which she lives. They are fairly severe. She rarely goes out, she hardly meets anyone but family members. Her trips to her father's house are infrequent and depend on the wishes of her husband's mother and father. Even within the house, she is unable to move freely, because given the pattern of avoidance relationships within the family, she has to hide from (avoid) those male affines who are senior to her husband. As Sandhyarani, another "new" daughter-in-law says, "All that one does in a *sasu's* (husband's mother) house is hide."

Given the stressful circumstances in which "new" daughters-in-law in the *jouvana* phase live their lives, it is hardly surprising that only a couple of them claim to have achieved substantial well-being, 15 to 16 *annas* of it. The ones who do experience high levels of *hito* live in relatively small families having only 7 or 8 members and their mothers-in-law are both noninterfering and not very demanding. At the other extreme, there are two daughters-in-law who appear to suffer considerable distress, one claiming to have no well-being at all and the other only 2 *annas* of well-being. For the most part, daughters-in-law have rather low feelings of well-being: if 16 *annas* indicates that one has achieved complete well-being, a "new" daughter-in-law, on the average, has less than 8 *annas* of well-being.

A notable and distinctive feature of these interviews with junior, "new" daughters-in-law in the *jouvana* phase is fairly clear evidence for the somatization of emotional distress. "New" daughters-in-law who give themselves low scores on well-being complain of night fevers, chest pains, and fainting. Such somatization is explicitly recognized in local discourse. There are "new" daughters-in-law who say that they are so sad that they cannot digest their food and this leads to chest pains that cannot be explained by the doctors they consult. Their husbands' mothers and sisters say that these women make no effort to integrate with the rest of the family, that they are angry and resentful of everyone else and this anger and resentment hinders digestion of food leading to chest pains.

There are also daughters-in-law who feel so unappreciated in their husbands' homes, so diminished in respect, so anxious to receive regard, that they experience (by their own accounts) a fall in their blood pressure and often faint. Of course, all this has to be seen against the background of a strong cultural aversion to excessive self-concern and reflection about oneself. Generally speaking, people in the Old Town believe that too much thinking (meaning, worrying about oneself) is deleterious. They believe that attention to oneself leads in and of itself to illness and physical distress—one makes oneself vulnerable to disease by thinking about oneself too much.

Thus there are multiple explanations for the somatic symptoms of emotional distress and they vary depending on who is speaking— whether it is the "new" daughter-in-law or the mother-in-law or the husband's sister. Nevertheless these multiple explanations have one thing in common. They all ascribe the lack of well-being not to the severity of the restrictions under which "new" daughters-in-law live nor to their having to perform deference, but to their incomplete assimilation into their husbands' families. Oriya women say quite categorically that the greater the assimilation, the greater the well-being that is experienced.

Before a "new" daughter-in-law gives birth to children, she receives more from the family than she gives to it and she does not control any of this exchanging. Oriya women state quite explicitly that a "new" daughter-in-law has to learn to open herself, during this phase, to influences from the family, to learn to become as permeable as she can so that her "reconstructing" and the process of assimilation can occur rapidly and effectively. Those women who are unable to open themselves—and Oriya women recognize such a possibility, saying that often *lajja* (modesty and a heightened awareness of oneself) makes such opening painful and difficult—cannot make use of the opportunities available, even during *jouvana,* for achieving well-being and so feel less well-off.

Let us now consider the situation of an "old" daughter-in-law. With age, the birth of children, and the entry of younger daughters-in-law, a woman progressively attains a status that is referred to locally as "old" daughter-in-law—*purna bou. Purna* is an interesting word because it also connotes "completeness," and in a sense it is when a woman matures, becomes a mother, and becomes senior to others like herself that she finally becomes the "complete" daughter-in-law. While maturing and seniority happen on their own, women actively complete themselves as daughters-in-law by giving birth to children. By providing new members to the families they have married into, they are entrenching themselves within the household, embedding themselves in the families, and laying claim to being heard in family debates and discussions.

In reading the daily routines of these women, it is possible to detect a gradual relaxation in some of the restrictions women experience as "new" daughters-in-law. The insistence by their seniors that they do a substantial part of the cooking declines. The restrictions on movement, on meeting people who do not belong to the family grow fewer. Even the emphasis on the performance of explicit rituals of deference grows steadily weaker.

Thus, Dukhi, a forty-year old *purna bou,* makes very clear her promotion out of the kitchen. When asked if she helps her husband's younger brother's wife *(sana ja)* in the cooking, she says, referring to herself as a sasu (husband's mother);

> No, no. I don't have anything to do with the cooking. The *sana ja,* she does all that. We *sasus* don't even enter the kitchen. She will do all the work; won't she? She does the cooking; doesn't she? Why should I do all that? I don't cut the vegetables. I don't grind the *masala.* I don't touch the cooking utensils.

And Pranati, a thirty-three-year-old *purna bou,* says,

> If people drop in, then it is my responsibility to serve tea to them, snacks, talk pleasantly to them, till whoever they have come to see is ready to meet them.

Most "old" daughters-in-law do not strictly observe the rituals of deference toward the mother-in-law. Most *purna bous* explain it as merely a result of increased familiarity with one's mother-in-law, a consequence of the passage of time, a function of the number of years they have lived within their husbands' families. An alternative, perhaps more plausible, interpretation would appear to be that such rituals are no longer needed: *purna bous* have completed their "reconstructions" into fully acknowledged members of their husbands' patrilineages. Indeed, nonperformance of such rituals figures as a factor playing into their sense of well-being by underscoring their sense of finally belonging to their husbands' families. As *purna bous,* it is not a question of being prevented from performing such rituals (as "new" daughters-in-law sometimes are) but rather that such rituals are no longer needed, having served their purpose of "completing" the "reconstruction" of the newlywed into a "real" daughter-in-law.

With the passage of time and the birth of children, "old" daughters-in-law have merged with their husbands' lineages. Although they are still some time away from being the seniormost woman of the household, they see themselves as well on the way to it. They have begun to take advantage of the privileges that that position is likely to bring with it, privileges that include commanding those subordinate and junior to themselves. A concomitant of this improved position within the family is greater well-being: on the average, a *purna bou* states that she has thirteen *annas* of well-being.

Let us now consider the situation of a mother-in-law. For the average Oriya Hindu woman, her position reaches its apogee when her sons marry and a new generation of daughters-in-law enter the family.[8] A reading of the following daily routine brings home in sharp detail the shifts that occur in duties and privileges when a woman becomes a mother-in-law. Priyambada, a sixty-two-year-old mother-in-law who lives with her own mother-in-law, husband, four sons, two daughters, daughter-in-law and two grandsons, describes her day in the following manner:

Priyambada: Getting up in the morning. We get up at 3:30 or 4:00 in the morning. As soon as we get up we wash our faces and then we bow our heads to god. We then clean our teeth, go and defecate. After defecating, we may do some polluting work. And then we go for our baths. While we are returning from our baths, we pluck a few flowers for the god. After we return, we pray to god, we light a lamp, *agarbatti* [incense sticks], offer flowers, repeat a few *slokas* [verses] and after that we have some tea to drink. After tea, I arrange the *thali* [tray] that I will be taking to the temple later on. Once I have finished arranging, I turn my attention to cutting vegetables or grinding *masala*—I have to do all that. It varies from day to day. Once that is done, I have to go to the temple. Once I have gone around the temple and returned, I have to see who has come, who has eaten, who has gone out, who is in the house, and then again, I have the job of arranging the flowers and other things for the god. And then, I may sit down, go from this room to that, look out of the front of the house, whatever needs to be done in the house—that has to be settled, that has to be cleaned and washed. And then comes the business of serving food and seeing people eat. All the business of running a house.

And then the children return home from tuition and it's time to see to their eating, their studies—this would be about 3:00 in the afternoon. Sometimes it may be a little later but my work of arranging things for the temple goes on. I make the wicks for the temple lamps. I make garlands with flowers for the deity. I gather together whatever will be necessary for tomorrow, and then. I move around the house, from here to there and then we have tea. I join in the cutting of vegetables for the evening meal. After tea, I offer *sandhya*. Once I've given *sandhya,* I go and lie down. I cover myself and lie down right here. I only get up at about 9:30 or 10:00 at night. I eat food then and go to bed soon after. Nowadays, because it's cold, I cover myself and lie down, but even in summer, I lie down and close my eyes. After all, the food won't be ready till 10 o'clock—so what is there to do but lie down and close one's eyes?

Usha: As you were saying, before you go to the temple in the morning, you bow your head to the god?

Priyambada: As soon as we get up, early in the morning, as soon as we have washed our faces with water, we turn to the one or two photos we have of the god and we bow our heads three times. Then we clean our teeth; after that we defecate. After defecating, before going for our baths we may clean out the house, throw out the garbage, do all that kind of polluting work, and then we go for our baths. On the way back from Bindusagar [9], we pick a few flowers and after returning home, there is again prayers in the puja room upstairs. After doing *puja*, I water the plants that we grow and then I come down for tea.

Clearly, this daily routine's emphasis is quite different from that of the earlier ones. Priyambada is freed from the strenuous work of cooking and feeding a large family; in fact, she does more than most mothers-in-law. When she says, "I turn my attention to cutting vegetables or grinding masala. I have to do that," she is subtly directing our attention to what she sees as her daughter-in-law's incompetence, her inability to manage the kitchen independently. Furthermore, her work now is more of a supervisory nature, of ensuring that her little community runs efficiently. She has considerable geographical mobility: she goes alone for her daily bath to the temple pond, she worships everyday at the Lingaraj temple, and she admits that during the day, she looks out of the front of the house, watching the world going by—all activities that are strictly forbidden a "new" daughter-in-law and often limited even for an "old" daughter-in-law.

Most important, however, is her regular communication with god and her uninterrupted association with offerings meant for divinity. This privilege of approaching divinity without reservation is a direct consequence of her ability to maintain her physical body's purity, an ability that is relatively recent for her and the direct result of two factors.

First, among Oriya Hindus of the Old Town, when a son marries and brings his wife into the family, his parents usually cease being sexually active. The job of reproduction has been passed onto the son and his wife. Many Oriya adults are disgusted or feel desanctified by the idea of two generations copulating under the same roof. Priyambada is no exception to this custom and she believes that this cessation of sexual activity makes it easier for her to maintain bodily purity.

Secondly, she is past menopause, and so there is no time of the month when she is *mara*, "polluted" or "impure." Both of these reasons make it appropriate that as the mother-in-law she is the intermediary between the family and the god, a position that she enjoys considerably and is the source of a substantial sense of well-being, the average score for mothers-in-law being twelve *anna*s of well-being. In fact, there are three married mothers-in-law who say quite categorically that they have fully sixteen *anna*s of well-being.

Let us now consider the situation of a widow. It is as a married mother-in-law that an Oriya Hindu woman's position is least assailable. Yet time is an accuser and a degrader and with old age and widowhood, there is usually a sharp reversal in a woman's situation. As an old widow, a woman is often relegated to the background, expected to contribute nothing to the family and expecting to get little in return.

Sociologically speaking, a widow in the Old Town is a nonperson: During the funeral rites of her husband, there are several rituals that emphasize this erasure of her social existence and mark her entrance into the status of a perpetual mourner whose preoccupations ought to be both transcendant and otherworldly. This erasure of social standing is symbolized by her lack of a family name: as a widow, a woman can no longer use her husband's family name and is known only by her given name (the one given at marriage, not birth) and the title *bewa,* a local contraction of *vidhwa* or "widow."

Harsamani, seventy-eight, has been a widow for thirty-six years and her poignant story of an ordinary day's activites typifies this

particular experience of widowhood among Oriya Hindu women of
the Old Town.

> Harsamani: I get up at 3:00 in the morning. I put some water for
> heating and then I go and defecate. After that I bathe. People
> would be still sleeping—it would be dark; some people may be
> awake but others would be sleeping. After bathing, I get back into
> bed. I cover myself up and go to sleep. I get up only when the tea
> comes. With tea, there would be something to eat—whatever they
> had made, maybe some *upma* or whatever—they will call me and
> I get up. But I eat lying in bed—do you understand? Sometimes I
> sit and eat but sometimes I lie and eat. These days the weather is
> cold and so I wrap myself and go and sit in the doorway. By about
> 10:00 or 11:00, they would have finished cooking and they come
> and call me. My daughter would have come, she goes to the
> kitchen, and serves for me and herself and the two of us eat
> together. We eat here in this room. After eating, we go and wash
> our hands and then we come back to this room. If my daughter is
> not there, they serve me and bring the food here. On days when
> I'm not feeling well, I get back into bed after eating, I eat *paan*
> [betel leaf] and I lie down once more. But on days when my mind
> is active, I sit in the doorway and chew *paan*. I see you going by
> sometimes, sometimes I see an aunt going by, sometimes a mother,
> sometimes a grandmother, and they will say, "You're sitting here?"
> After sitting for sometime, when I again feel cold, I get back into
> bed, I cover myself and lie down.
>   Then again tea and snacks will come and I will eat, again my
> middle daughter will be here and we have tea and snacks together.
> And then dusk falls; once dusk falls, there is no work whatsoever.
> You understand? My daughter will put the mosquito net over my
> bed and once again I lie down all covered up. In the middle of all
> this the evening meal arrives. At night, whatever comes, if I feel
> like it, I eat it. I eat a little of it and then I lie down. *Parathas*, milk,
> curry, fried vegetables, whatever they have made that is what is
> served. After eating, then again I make myself some *paan*. I eat
> one and keep one under the pillow. I lie down. I have no work to
> do, neither night nor day. At no time during the day do I have any
> work. I have nothing to do. When I get up in the morning, again I
> put water for heating, I shit, clean my teeth, bathe. This is the
> month of *Magha* [January/February], all the women get up early,
> bathe, and go to the temple; they do what they want to after
> bathing; I go back to bed. The *nathani-bou* [grandson's wife], she
> comes and calls me, "Ma, you've fallen asleep; get up; get up; here's
> your tea and breakfast." Again the tea and something to eat—some
> days it's *suji;* some days its *parathas*.

Usha: When do you pray?

Harsamani: There's no more praying for me. Why? Do you want to know why? Our gods are kept upstairs. By the time I walk up those stairs, my strength disappears. God is taken care of nowadays by the bous [sons' wives]. Now that they do all that, what is left for me to do? On days when I have the strength I pour a little water on the tulasi at the back but otherwise all I do is put a few drops of *nirmaliya*[10] in my mouth. Everyday, everyday, I put a few drops of *nirmaliya* in my mouth and then I lie down. Then the same things happen every day—over and over again, the same things.

Usha: How often do you go to the temple?

Harsamani: I can't go to the temple. It is now two years since I went to the temple. My strength is declining; my body trembles; I may fall down somewhere and then people will say, *"Hou, hou,"* people will criticize me for that.

Harsamani appears to have been effectively marginalized by age and widowhood. She is forbidden to provide sustenance to the family, for she is not allowed to cook for and feed others. She is forbidden to provide spiritual sustenance, for she is not allowed to intercede with divinity to ensure the health and prosperity of family members.

The "auspicious heart of the family"

In the context of one of Menon's interviews about their roles and responsibilities across the life cycle, an articulate Oriya woman described a mature, married woman as the auspicious heart of the family *(parivararo mangaliko antahkarano)*. That particular description seems apt as one reads and rereads these accounts by Oriya women of their daily round of activities and their feelings of well-being. As the interviews demonstrate, a "new" daughter-in-law gradually becomes an "old" daughter-in-law and her access to, and enjoyment of, greater well-being occurs almost imperceptibly as she attains the domestic managerial responsibilities associated with mature adulthood *(prauda)*. Mature adulthood *(prauda)* (in which she has many juniors and still commands all sustenance) is a peak period in the lives of these women.

For a daughter-in-law to grow "old" (and well), she has to move out of the kitchen. This move out of the kitchen need not be complete nor even substantial, but the possibility that she could move out if she wanted to has to exist. However, her ties to the kitchen continue to be strong enough to make her the primary server of food—a responsibility steeped in prestige that emphasizes the central nature of her role within the family. Through ensuring that each member of the family gets his or her fair share of food, she sustains, very concretely, the life and health of the family. If someone should come over to the house for social or business reasons and if the men of the family are otherwise busy, she entertains them. She represents the family, underscoring once more her importance. She performs less and less frequently the rituals of deference, indicating her full assimilation into the family. Finally, she begins to represent the family in its relations with divinity: one of the first tasks of any ritual significance that an "old" daughter-in-law does is to offer *sandhya,* a ceremony performed at sunset that seeks to keep malevolent spirits at bay while inviting Lakshmi, the goddess of wealth and auspiciousness, into the home.

Of course, other factors, physiological and cultural, limit this involvement in household worship: usually, an "old" daughter-in-law is young enough to menstruate. She is sexually active and she is still involved in the care of her children, feeding and cleaning them. All of these factors make it difficult for her to maintain bodily purity and compromise her ability to approach the divine. It is as a married mother-in-law that these factors begin to lose their salience.

With daughters-in-law entering the household, the business of reproduction is passed onto the younger generation. The older couple withdraw from sexual activity, enabling the mother-in-law to maintain bodily purity more easily. This is also the time when one is no longer involved in taking care of the very old or the very young. One's own children are past needing such care. One's own mother-in-law and father-in-law are either dead or their care has been handed over to the newest daughter-in-law. At this time of life, most Oriya women go through menopause, which means there is no time of the month when a woman is impure. Finally, for these postmenopausal women, it is both culturally and physiologically appropriate for a woman to go to the temple whenever she wishes to, to pray whenever she wishes to, to perform the daily *puja* for her family without hindrance, and to function as the intermediary who seeks divine blessings for every member of the family.

Apart from this, an older married woman is also relieved of the physical labor of cooking and cleaning for a large family. While she still retains the responsibilities and privileges associated with *prauda,* she continues to administer the affairs of the household and remains aware of everything that happens to family members. The possibility of geographical mobility, of traveling, of going on pilgrimages, and of visiting relatives also contributes in some measure to her heightened sense of well-being. As a mother-in-law, explicit deference is paid to a woman by the junior women of the household. While this explicit display of social power must surely increase her sense of well-being, it also provides her with a forum in which to express her opinions. By refusing to accept a daughter-in-law's deference she conveys unmistakably her feelings of displeasure and disapproval without saying a word. A mother-in-law, therefore, has greater opportunity to express negative feelings about other family members and this perhaps does make her feel better. Unlike the other women in the family, she does not, for the sake of family harmony, have to control what she says or does.

There are of course anxieties that may work to reduce the married Oriya Hindu mother-in-law's feelings of well-being. Firstly, there is the prospect of widowhood and all the connotations that Oriya Hindus attach to that condition. Secondly, there is the process of growing old and losing the ability to care for oneself physically. While the junior wife has to shake off the constraints that are attached to being "new" to gain in well-being, the mother-in-law loses some of her wellness because she is looking to an uncertain future.

A culturally salient model of well-being

In general, women expect the middle phase of their lives, that of "mature adulthood", *prauda,* to afford them the most satisfying experiences. According to their accounts, during this phase, they will be either the most senior woman in the household, or the next to most senior. As such, a woman is dominant—she has control over her own body and her actions, but more importantly, considerable control over the activities of others within the family. She is also very productive during this phase—she is likely to feel and to be felt central to the order and material prosperity of the family. Finally, she feels coherent—her connections and communication with divinity are now regular and uninterrupted. Dominance coming from seniority, productivity emerging from centrality within the family, and coherence resulting from the capacity to approach divinity, without restriction, are thus three salient measures of well-being for an Oriya Hindu woman. All imply controlling and managing the transacting and exchanging that she is involved in with those above, around, and below her, within the household and between the household and beyond.

There is another, subsidiary aspect of women's well-being that needs to be mentioned here—the skill and competence with which a woman manages and controls these processes and transactions. In Bhubaneswar, as Lamb (1993) reports for Bengali women, the processes of "reconstruction" and "deconstruction" that women undergo as they marry, give birth, assimilate with the family, mature, age, and become widows, require them to manage these processes skilfully and competently—if they are to achieve well-being. Those women who are less competent at managing these processes experience low well-being even during the middle phase of their lives, while those who know when and how to expand and encompass others and when to curtail their transactions, withdraw into themselves, minimize their exchanges, are more likely to achieve higher levels of well-being during all phases of their lives.

Furthermore, we suggest that these three measures of well-being are not competing but complementary. Having control over one's own activities and those of others makes one central to, and productive of, the family's well-being. Both of these conditions enable one to control one's interactions with divinity, to approach the gods in a coherent, ordered way. When a woman achieves all three, usually during the middle phase of mature adulthood, her well-being is complete.

Variations around the ideal model

What we have described is, of course, an ideal model extracted from our interviews. However, even thirty-seven interviews are enough to make the point that this ideal rarely has a perfect fit to anyone's lived experience. There are women in other family roles who claim to have achieved substantial well-being as well as some married mothers-in-law and "old" daughters-in-law in the *prauda* phase of life who claim to be miserable. For instance, Priyambada, the married mother-in-law whose description of an average day was quoted earlier, says that she does not even have two *anna*s of well being. She ascribes her lack of well-being to the conflicts within the family, conflicts that result from the lack of respect that younger members display toward their elders.

> Everyone thinks he is the superior of the other, everyone thinks he is the family elder, everyone thinks he has to speak out, that he has to say what his opinion is . . . I'm not preventing others from talking, I'm only saying, "Think of everything, the person who is talking and the consequences of your talking back before you answer.

In a community in which asymmetry of privilege and responsibility has such salience, it is hardly surprising that lack of respect should lead to such a diminishment of well-being.

It is also possible that Priyambada was using the occasion of the interview to inform others in the family of her displeasure with what she perceived as discord within the family. Her daughter-in-law definitely interpreted her statements to indicate just that. This daughter-in-law believed that her own conduct was the focus of the mother-in-law's criticism. The daughter-in-law's attribution seems plausible. At the time of the interview Menon suspected that Priyambada was using her low assessment of her own well-being as a means to arouse the younger woman's guilt at being an "usatisfactory" daughter-in-law.

And the reverse, too, occurs. There are widowed mothers-in-law who continue to be valued and respected members of the family. There are "sonless" (Kondos, 1989, p. 185) mothers who become the mainstay of their husbands' families. There are "new" daughters-in-law who dominate household affairs almost as soon as they step across the threshold. Even in this small sample of thirty-seven women such examples can be found, demonstrating, we think, quite conclusively that one must be suspicious of such simplistic feminist representations (see, e.g., Kondos, 1989, p. 108). Kondos claims that Hindu women lead such contingent lives that only those who produce sons and who predecease their husbands are deemed successful. The following excerpt, from an interview with a seventy-two-year-old widow, Labanya, whose husband died almost forty years ago, holds particular relevance here. She describes her day.

> Labanya: I get up in the morning. I clean my teeth; I have tea. After having had tea, it's necessary to make sure that the children have gone to school and I go and do that. And then, maybe someone comes over, like you have come over, and I sit and talk. I have become the elder *(murabbi)* in the family; when people come over, I have to sit and talk to them; we discuss things. They may have tea; I may have some more tea. And then, I go for my bath. After my bath, the cooking would be almost finished, and so I eat. After eating, I take some rest, I lie down. I rest till afternoon. At about 4:00, I get up and again, if people come over, I sit and talk to them. I talk to them till the sun sets. After the sun sets, once more tea is made, I drink some tea. . . .I have no work. So right here, I take some rest. While I'm resting, the children will come, and the *bous* will come and they will say, "*Ma*, come, eat your rice," and so, I go and eat. And then, I go to bed—what else is there to my day? . . .
>
> Usha: Do you do *pujas* to God?
>
> Labanya: [long pause, till finally, hesitantly] . . . yes, yes. This elder *bou*, she does all that. I have become an old woman. I can't have a bath that early in the morning. They all have their baths early and then they pray to God. Eldest son, he bathes, he is the *kalasi* at the *Thakurani mandir*. He goes there. . . .
>
> Usha: Do you offer *sandhya* in the evening?
>
> Labanya: No, I don't offer any *sandhya*. I don't have that responsibility anymore. That is a responsibility that the *bous* have and that they fulfil. I no longer touch the cooking vessels; they do and so they offer *sandhya*. This *bou* offers *sandhya* or if this one can't,

then the other or the other or one of the granddaughters, they offer *sandhya*. That is a burden that has slipped from my head.

Usha: Do you tell them what to cook?

Labanya: No, no. I don't bother my head with all that. When they first came to this house then I had to teach them everything. "*Arre, ma*, do this like this; do that like that," I used to tell them. "This food won't be enough" or "That is too much," but now I have grown old and they have all raised their families; what is there for me to teach them now? Now that I am old, I eat a fistful of rice that they give me and I sit. What else is left for me in life? Why should I continue to keep all that in my head?

Usha: When did you give up giving directions?

Labanya: It is now thirty years since I left all that. Once this eldest *bou* came into the house, a few years after that, I stopped running the house. A few years after the eldest *bou* came, another *bou* came into the house, and a few years later, another *bou* came. In this way, three bous came. They gave birth to children, and they managed running the house. Why should I try to keep the nuisance and trouble of running the household on my head? All that I do nowadays is soothe my grandchildren when they cry, carry them on my hip when they're small, clean them when they're dirty, and see that they go to school regularly. Or when someone wants advice or when someone wants to give or take money, I do that—that's my business now.

He [her eldest son] keeps nothing. He comes and gives me everything. I keep all the money, when he needs money, he asks me. He needs 5,000 rupees or 6,000 rupees to pay the laborers who are repairing this house, he comes to me; I give him the money. Vegetables have to be bought; I give the grandsons the money to buy the vegetables. I keep all the money. When I go away to Unit 6 to be with my middle son, then I leave some money with the eldest bou for household expenses but the rest of the money is still with me and he'll come to Unit 6 when he needs money.

One can see that Labanya is hardly involved in the day-to-day activities of the household and has little contact with divinity. But even a casual reading of her daily activities makes it clear how she continues to be the center of her family. She holds the family purse strings. Her sons choose to give her all their earnings. No expense is incurred without her knowledge. More importantly, according to her account, her sons and her daughters-in-law make it explicit that they care for her: they are concerned that she relish what she eats, that her clothes are decent. They desire her comfort.

And then there is Pranati, an "old" daughter-in-law, mother of three daughters, who recognizes that she has disappointed her mother-in-law and father-in-law by not providing sons for the *kutumba* (lineage). This affects her sense of well-being, her score of eight *anna*s being the lowest among all the "old" daughters-in-law. While this score may reflect her sorrow at not having had sons, that inadequacy clearly does not cramp her style when it comes to running the household. She is not relegated to some corner of the house, ignored and despised because she is "sonless"; instead, as one reads her interview as well as those of her mother-in-law and her younger sister-in-law it becomes quite clear that the entire household depends on her for its efficient functioning. She decides what will be cooked. She shops for the entire family, selecting the clothes that others will wear. She entertains guests and relatives when they visit. She plays the lead role when it comes to arranging her husband's younger brother's marriage. Sonlessness, though a matter for personal sorrow, does not determine her position within the family; in fact, it does not even define her as inauspicious. For these women, success and failure are not "predefined." Being a widow or "sonless" are constraining circumstances but they do not absolutely define success or failure.

Labanya and Pranati are examples of ways in which "psyche and culture make each other up" (Shweder, 1991, p.73). Cultural meanings and possibilities are picked up these women, each according to her particular talents, and then they create their own life situations. Thus Labanya is not just a widow; she is also the loving mother who single-handedly raised her three sons to adulthood. As such she is entitled to their respect and devotion, an entitlement that she appropriates in full measure. Again, Pranati is not merely a "sonless" mother. She is also the dutiful daughter-in-law who has never stinted in her performance of *sewa*. As such, she has extended her influence through the family, making her its single most important member. According to Kondos' formulation, these women are "failures," and yet, by all accounts, they participate fully in running their households and raising their children. More importantly, they feel good about themselves.

The question of "subversion / resistance"

On the basis of our experience in the Old Town, we have come to harbor the suspicion that the representation of the Hindu housewife as a rebel or subversive is largely a projection of critical ethnography grasping at straws. Quite baldly stated, almost nothing we have encountered in our interviews and observations implies a deep political critique of family or social life or the desirability of subverting the social system.

There is an absence of subversive voices in the Old Town. While complaint could, perhaps, be regarded as a language of "subversion" and the dragging of feet while performing household chores as acts of "resistance," it is curious that only "old" daughters-in-law and mothers-in-law do so. "New" daughters-in-law who have the most to gain from subverting the system do not complain and rarely drag their feet. Some of the reasons, of course, could be that they are trained to suppress their words, to anticipate negative consequences from expressing themselves. It is true that their positions within the family are too fragile, and that they have yet to accumulate power or exercise substantial influence. Only an "old" daughter-in-law or a mother-in-law, secure of her position within the family, could engage in such verbal and nonverbal displays of discontent with impunity.

We believe, however, that a more accurate representation of the situation is that neither complaint nor dragging one's feet can be credibly viewed as "subversion" or "resistance." In the Old Town they are just the ways in which confident women express their dissatisfaction or displeasure with what is happening within the family, without indicating any desire for radical change.

Ultimately extended families do break up. Each brother lives separately with just his own wife and children. This is the nuclear beginning for a fresh cycle of joint family living. A catalyst is usually needed to set the splitting up into motion. Often this happens to be the death of the father or of both father and mother. Yet joint family living remains the ideal. Daughters-in-law, both "new" and "old," continue to live jointly because they are realistic and pragmatic about the options open to them. They make the best of whatever resources they have, realizing that they often gain thereby. Apart from the advantages that these women themselves mention when explaining why they continue to live within the joint family—those of greater security, economic and otherwise, the sharing of household chores and child rearing—an important reason lies in the fact that there *is* room for maneuvering, for achievement, and for working toward personal goals—such as increased power within the family, a greater say in the process of making decisions within the family, a sense of getting newly recruited women and their children to do what one wants them to do, and the possibility of ensuring the future success of one's children.

What is remarkable and worth noting is not the insurgency of these women but rather their attitude of active acceptance. Sudhangini, a daughter who was to be married just six weeks after the interview, in talking of her future life in her mother-in-law's home, says,

> In truth, however affectionate the new family, I will feel sad for some time remembering this home but then as one day passes and then another and then another, the sense that this is mine will begin even with respect to the other home and the people

there ... one has to accept everything as one's own. *Nona-bou* [father-mother] haven't given us our *karma;* they have given us only *janma* [birth]. They have given me birth, and they have also given me *sikhya* [learning]; they have given me *jogyata* [competence]; that is my good fortune. Now with that, if I decide to do good work in their house, then it will arouse their appreciation, but if I don't do good work, they will criticize me and that I will have to endure. But it is all in my own hands—my *karma* is in my hands. If I want to do good and gain appreciation, it is in my hands.

Most people in the Old Town hold to this future-oriented notion as a major aspect of the karmic process. This sense of having control over what happens in one's life, of being responsible for one's own destiny, this belief that "human intentions really do matter" (Babb, 1983, p.180) runs through several of the other interviews, though perhaps no other woman articulated the idea so fluently. All these women, daughters, daughters-in-law, and mothers-in-law recognize the givens in each of their situations. They recognize the factors that they cannot change. But they also realize that it is possible to work within an emerging situation for success. In fact, these women see such compromise and accommodation as admirable signs of maturity.

Furthermore, these women share with other Oriya Hindus a particular way of looking at life. They look on family life as a process, one that is continuously shifting and changing, never complete or static. And so, when they marry and enter a household, they do not see themselves as "new" daughters-in-law for the rest of their lives. They can see in front of them women at different stages in the life course. They see themselves as occupying those positions in the not too distant future. If one has to understand their motivations and actions, one has to assume their future-oriented, developmental perspective. They never see themselves as victims. They are looking ahead into the future, perhaps ten or fifteen years ahead, seeing themselves contributing to and controlling family decisions. Even the very old do not lack this future orientation. Indeed, most people in the Old Town see death as merely a punctuation mark in the process of living numerous lives and they are clearly busy at work preparing the way for their future postmortem rise.

Oppressors and victims? More on gender relations in the Old Town

Among Oriya Hindus in the temple town of Bhubaneswar, men and women recognize each other as social actors, equal in importance and effectiveness who complement each other's activities. To cast men as oppressors and women as victims is to try and establish a false dichotomy, one that does not exist within the Oriya point of view. If one wants to organize Oriya social life in terms of those in control and those controlled, then it makes much more sense to discuss the matter generationally, the older generation controlling the activities of the younger. But even here one needs to temper this statement because age is not valued in and of itself. Only those older people who care for and are responsible for the welfare of others are respected and their opinions valued.

Furthermore, as anyone familiar with life and society in Hindu India knows, men (especially younger men) as well as women live with major constraints. Neither a young man nor a young woman has the right to choose but they do have some rights to veto. Most Oriya men and women, just like most Hindu men and women in other parts of the subcontinent, do not decide for themselves what people in the West would regard as the two most crucial decisions of a person's life: their professions and their marriages. This is not to say that there is no difference between men's and women's lives, for most significantly men can move and interact with others quite freely.

Whether women regard this freedom as an unmitigated advantage is doubtful. Many women pitied Menon's predicament, one that necessitated "wandering from door to door looking for people to talk to." Menon remembers asking a widow whether she planned to send her seventeen-year-old daughter to college, and she responded good-humoredly, "Why? So that she will become like you going from door to door talking to people?"

Sakti: What it means to be a woman in the Old Town

Even today, most Oriya Hindus believe that female power *(sakti)* energizes the natural and social world. In ordinary, everyday conversations, women in the Old Town describe a "woman," as the embodiment of *adya sakti* (primordial power), *matru sakti* (mother power), and *stri sakti* (woman power). According to these women such *sakti* is harnessed for the good of society and the family. It is power reined in, power that is controlled from within, power that is exercised responsibly. A woman is said to hold the destiny of her husband's family in the palm of her hands. If she is irresponsible in her management of the family's resources, the household does not prosper. If she commits adultery, the family disintegrates.[11] These women say that a woman maintains her chastity not because she lives in a joint family and others exercise a watchful eye over what she does, but because she disciplines herself. This is a remarkable assertion quite unlike what Derne (1993) found among Hindu men in Varanasi who relied on family structure and external forces to control their behavior. For Oriya Hindu women, to be truly effective, control has to come from within, and only this ensures the spiritual and material prosperity of the family.

It is relevant to mention here some of the understandings that Old Town residents have about a popular icon of the goddess Kali in which she is shown with her foot placed squarely on the chest of a supine Siva (for a detailed description of this study, see Menon & Shweder, 1994). When men and women interpret this icon, they describe the protruding tongue of the goddess as the mark of her "shame," *lajya,* at having stepped on her husband, her personal god. Acknowledging her husband's social and ritual superiority enables her to become calm, to rein in her power to destroy. Many of those knowledgeable about this icon say that Siva does not do anything to stop her, because, in fact, he *can* do nothing to stop her (Kali is far too powerful). Rather, she *chooses* to recognize what she owes her husband in terms of respect and deference and so stops her destruction. According to the Oriya Hindus of the Old Town, her choice is an entirely "autonomous" act.

From the perspective of many Oriya Hindus, Ortner's formulation (1974) nature:culture and woman:man, seems unnatural. For Oriya Hindus, a woman derives her strength and power from her closeness to nature. She, like nature, creates and reproduces, but such power gathers its full significance only because it is subject to cultural, ultimately moral, control that originates from within her. As Ramanujan points out the Levi-Straussian opposition between nature and culture is itself culture-bound. In the Hindu alternative, "culture is enclosed in nature, nature is reworked in culture, so that we cannot tell the difference" (1989, p.50). This is yet another of the "container-contained relations" (ibid) that extend to other Hindu concepts and ideas.

So, Oriya Hindu women think of themselves as intrinsically powerful. Simply by being female, by sharing the gendered physiology of the Great Goddess of Hinduism, they believe they share her power to create and destroy. But, they also recognize the fact that unrestrained exercise of such power inevitably leads to destruction. Such power has to be curbed not by an external force but from within, through a voluntary, autonomous act of self-discipline. And it is this self-discipline that those who are ignorant of Oriya Hindu cultural meanings could misinterpret as subordination.

Culturally available means to power

Personal growth, then, for these women is not conceived by them to be some kind of egocentric process that involves detaching themselves from others. Instead, it is a power that involves an increasing denseness in one's relations with others. It depends on one becoming a strong weaver of the fabric of the family.

An Oriya Hindu woman achieves this kind of personal growth in a variety of ways. Behavior, which from a Western perspective may be misconstrued as an index of subordination and passivity, often lends itself to being seen as something quite different when understood from a Hindu perspective. The Hindu notion of the body emphasizes (Kakar, 1982;

Zimmerman, 1979) its relative openness to both improvement and con-
tamination. Thus when a "new" daughter-in-law takes orders from her
mother-in-law or eats her leftovers, or massages her feet or drinks the
water that has been used to wash the older woman's feet, these practices
are not a measure of her subordination or passivity. Instead this is how
she takes into her body, potent substances from a superior. Ultimately
these internalized substances empower her. Progressively, with time, such
behavior increases her influence and control within the family.

Again, *sewa* or "service to others" is a culturally significant way of
achieving power. When a woman cooks, serves, and takes care of members of the joint family, she is building relationships in very concrete
ways. Many women compared cooking and serving to acts of *bhakti* or
"devotion," requiring the same degree of concentration and attention to
detail as that involved in worshiping God and leading to similar feelings of serenity and contentment.

Self-abnegation or self-denial is yet another culturally salient way
of gaining moral authority. While from a Western perspective self-abnegation could be interpreted as a kind of deprivation, that is not what it
means to an Oriya Hindu woman. By fasting, eating last, and eating
leftovers, she is able to garner moral authority. And when, after years
of self-denial, a woman requests or decides or commands that something
should be so, her husband and her adult sons cannot but accede to her,
for no man in the family equals her in moral stature.

Conclusion: The Moral Discourse of Anthropology

Think of the Oriya Hindu woman's life as a movement in three dimensions: both outward and upward with time being the third dimension.
Her life moves outwards, because with time, she is no longer restricted
to the kitchen, and she can ultimately move freely within the house and
sometimes go outside the house accompanied by only a child. Her life
moves upward, because with time it becomes socially and physiologically possible for her to approach divinity.

A "new" daughter-in-law is essentially locked into the kitchen,
which is often referred to as the "heart of the household", because it is
the place where the ancestral spirits *(pitru loku)* reside and are fed. But
with time and age, when she begins to play a greater and greater role in
making decisions within the family, she moves to other spaces within
the house. She has access to the *puja* room and to "higher" gods, the
household deities *(ishta devata)*. With old age and widowhood, this outward movement is completed and old widows, who are now peripheral
to household affairs, often live in an outer room that overlooks the street.
On the other hand, the upward movement is temporarily halted, for
although old widows continue to pray, they are relatively inauspicious

members of the family who are no longer involved in family rituals. They are free to absolve themselves of their own accumulated spiritual debts for the sake of their own personal salvation but little more.

To represent women's lives is a difficult and complex task. If anthropology as a discipline views itself as a means to understanding one's self and one's own culture by journeying through other selves in other cultures, then it is important that feminist anthropologists understand the dialectic they are engaged in. At the moment the intellectual insights of feminist anthropology cannot be easily disentangled from their political agenda, for there is a transparent attempt in feminist literature to unversalize women's oppression and to indulge in myth-making for political ends. If anthropology is a discipline that studies differences then it is necessary that feminists devise the means to analyze and interpret differences that they find disturbing without disrespecting the objects of their study (cf. Boon, 1994). To ignore the alternative moral goods of family practice in India, to presume that inner control, service, and deferred gratification amounts to subordination and acceptance of oppression, to represent Hindu women in South Asia as either victims or subversives is not only to dishonor these women—it is to engage in little more than a late twentieth-century version of cognitive and moral imperialism.

Notes

1. For more on this temple and the community that serves it, see Mahapatra, (1981); Seymour, (1983); Shweder, Mahapatra, & Miller, (1990); Shweder, (1991); Shweder, Much, Mahapatra, & Park, (1997).

2. For a complete description of this sample see Menon and Shweder (1994).

3. Cleary and his associates at the Harvard Medical School have collected comparable data on American women. In a telephone survey women were asked to assess their satisfaction on a ten point scale.

4. An *anna* is a coin that is no longer in circulation. In pre-independence India, there were 6 *paisa* (or *pice*) to an *anna* and 16 *anna*s to a *rupee*.

5. We should, perhaps, clarify that our particular understanding is neither unusual nor peculiar to us. Today, in India, there is a burgeoning women's movement (see *India Today*, September 30, 1995) that disdains the label *feminism*, distances itself from Western-inspired feminist movements, and does not identify gender equality at home or in the workplace as a significant goal. Instead, it seeks to identify potential sources of female power defined in Hindu terms and works to achieve female empowerment.

6. The tradition that worships the Sakti or Devi, the Great Goddess, of Hinduism, believing that the world is energized by her and that in her lies the ultimate meaning of life in this world.

7. For the Oriya Hindus of the Old Town, *samsaro* stands for the family, for household life, and for the entire world of living beings as well as for the never-ending cycle of rebirths and redeaths, which characterizes all existence this side of release and liberation.

8. Not all Oriya Hindu women have sons, but traditionally, people in the Old Town have sought a way out by adopting a relative's son, preferably one's own daughter's second or third son. The child is adopted formally into his maternal grandfather's lineage and all ritual ties to his biological father are severed. In the present sample, Dukhi, the "old" daughter-in-law quoted earlier, and her husband have done just that.

9. The Lingaraj temple tank.

10. *Nirmaliya* is a solution made of water and dessicated *prasad* from the Lingaraj temple.

11. According to Oriya Hindus of the Old Town, the effects on the family of a man committing adultery are far less profound than if a woman does so because men are considered to be marginal to the well-being of the family.

References

Babb, L. A. (1983). Destiny and responsibility: Karma in popular Hinduism. In C. F. Keyes & E. V. Daniel (Eds.), *Karma: An anthropological inquiry*. Berkeley: University of California Press.

Bennett, L. (1983). *Dangerous wives and sacred sisters: Social and symbolic roles of high-caste women in Nepal*. New York: Columbia University Press.

Boon, J. A. (1994). Circumscribing circumcision/uncircumsion. In S. B. Schwartz (Ed.), *Implicit understandings*. Cambridge: Cambridge University Press.

Brown, J. K., & Kerns, V. (Eds.) (1985). *In her prime: A new view of middle-aged women*. South Hadley, MA.: Bergin and Harvey.

Derne, S. (1993). Equality and hierarchy between adult brothers: Culture and sibling relations in N. Indian urban joint families. In C. W. Nuckolls (Ed.), *Siblings in South Asia: Brothers and sisters in cultural context*. New York: Guilford Press.

Dhruvarajan, V. (1988). *Hindu women and the power of ideology*. South Hadley, MA.: Bergin and Garvey.

Doniger, W., & Smith, B. W. (1991). *The laws of Manu*. Middlesex, England: Penguin Books.

Fruzetti, L. M. (1982). *The gift of a virgin*. New Brunswick, NJ: Rutgers University Press.

Inden, R. B., & Nicholas, R. W. (1977). *Kinship in Bengali culture*. Chicago: University of Chicago Press.

Jacobson, D. (1982). Studying the changing roles of women in rural India. *Signs 8* (1), 132-137.

Jain, D., & Bannerjee, N. (Eds.), (1985). *Tyranny of the household: Investigative chapters on women's work*. New Delhi: Shakti Books.

Jeffrey P., R. Jeffrey, & Lyons, A. (1988). *Labour pains and labour power*. London: Zed Books.

Kakar, S. (1982). *Shamans, mystics and doctors*. New York: Knopf.

Kondos, V. (1989). Subjection and domicile: Some problematic issues relating to high caste Nepalese women. In J. N. Gray & D. J. Mearns (Eds.), *Society from the inside out*. New Delhi: Sage Publications.

Lamb, S. (1993). *Growing in the net of Maya*. Ph.D. Diss. University of Chicago.

Liddle, J., & Joshi, R. (1986). *Daughters of independence: Gender, caste and class in India*. London: Zed Books.

Mahapatra, M. (1981). *Traditional structure and change in an Orissa temple*. Calcutta: Punthi Pustak.

Marriott, M. (1976). Hindu transactions: Diversity without dualism. In Bruce Kapferer (Ed.), *Transaction and meaning: Directions in the anthropology of exchange and symbolic behavior*. Philadelphia: Institute for the Study of Human Issues.

Menon, U., & Shweder, R. A. (1994). Kali's tongue: Cultural psychology and the power of "shame" in Orissa, India. In H. Markus, & S. Kitayama (Eds.), *Culture and the emotions*. Washington DC: American Psychological Association.

Minturn, L. (1993). *Sita's daughters: Coming out of Purdah*. New York: Oxford University Press.

Ortner, S. (1974). Is Female to Male as Nature is to Culture? In M. Rosaldo, & L. Lamphere (Eds.), *Women, culture and society*. Stanford: Stanford University Press.

Papanek, H., & Minault, G. (1982). *Separate worlds: Studies of Purdah in South Asia*. New Delhi: Chanakya Publications.

Raheja, G. G., & Gold, A. G. (1994). *Listen to the heron's words.* Berkeley: University of California Press.

Ramanujan, A. K. (1983). The Indian Oedipus. In L. Edmonds & A. Dundes (Eds.), *Oedipus: A folklore casebook* (pp. 234-261). New York: Garland Publishing.

Ramanujan, A. K. (1990). Is there an Indian way of thinking? An informal chapter. In McKim Marriott (Ed.), *India through Hindu categories.* New Delhi: Sage Publications.

Roy, M. (1975). *Bengali women.* Chicago: University of Chicago Press.

Seymour, S. (1983). Household structure and status and expressions of affect in India. *Ethos 11,* 263-277.

Sharma, U. (1980). *Women, work and property in North-West India.* Honolulu: University of Hawaii Press.

Shweder, R. A. (1990). In defense of Moral realism. *Child Development, 61,* 2060-2068.

Shweder, R. A. (1991). *Thinking through cultures.* Cambridge: Harvard University Press.

Shweder, R. A. (1994). Are moral institutions self-evident truths? *Criminal Justice Ethics, 13,* 24-31.

Shweder, R. A. (1996). True ethnography: The lore, the law, and the lure. In R. Jessor, A. Colby, & R. Shweder (Eds.), *Ethnography and human development: Context and meaning in social inquiry.* Chicago: University of Chicago Press.

Shweder, R. A., Mahapatra, M., & Miller, J. G. (1990). Culture and moral development. In J. Stigler, R. A. Shweder & G. H. Herdt (Eds.), *Cultural psychology: Chapters on comparative human development.* Cambridge: Cambridge University Press.

Shweder, R. A., Much, N. C., Mahapatra, M., & Park, L. (1997). The "Big Three" of morality (autonomy, community and divinity), and the "Big Three" explanations of suffering. In A. Brandt & P. Rozin (Eds.), *Morality and health.* Stanford: Stanford University Press.

Wadley, S. S. (1980). *The powers of Tamil Women.* Asia Series no. 6. Syracuse: Syracuse University Press.

Wadley, S. S. (1986). Women and the Hindu tradition. In S. Wadley & D. Jacobson (Eds.), *Women in India.* New Delhi: Manohar Publishers.

Wadley, S. S. & Jacobson, D. (1986). *Women in India.* New Delhi: Manohar Publishers.

Zimmerman, F. (1979). Remarks on the body in Ayurvedic medicine. *South Asian Digest of Regional Writing, 18,* 10-26.

CHAPTER 4

Changing Classes:
Shifting the Trajectory of Development in School

Martin J. Packer

What has become increasingly clear in these debates is that education is not *just* about conventional school matters like curriculum or standards or testing. What we resolve to do in school only makes sense when considered in the broader context of what the society intends to accomplish through its educational investment in the young. How one conceives of education, we have finally come to recognize, is a function of how one conceives of the culture and its aims, professed and otherwise.
— Bruner, *The Culture of Education*

[M]any current trends in critical pedagogy are embedded in the endemic weakness of a theoretical project overly concerned with developing a language of critique. Critical pedagogy is steeped in a posture of moral indignation toward the injustices reproduced in American public schools. Unfortunately, this one-sided emphasis on critique is matched by the lack of ethical and pragmatic discourse upon which to ground its own vision of society and schooling and to shape the direction of a critical praxis.
— McLaren, *Critical Pedagogy and Predatory Culture*

Introduction

How does school change young people? What do teaching and learning consist of? I spent a lot of time thinking about these questions during visits over a period of three years to a small urban fringe school district in southeastern Michigan. Believing we still lack adequate answers to these questions, believing that education, as Bruner puts it in the opening quotation, "is not *just* about conventional school matters like curriculum or standards or testing," I was keen to understand the *developmental processes* of schooling. I did this in part by putting everyday classroom practices under the microscope (cf., Packer & Greco-Brooks, 1999), but also by considering the schools' relations to broader contexts. Too often, school classrooms are studied as self-contained entities, when in actuality they exist in complex, contested, and changing relations to the local community and to society's political and economic arrangements and priorities. Examining the "situatedness" of schooling—viewing the institutions of public schooling against the backdrop of community context and against the shifting political and economic landscape—highlights the ways in which schools turn children into particular kinds of adults (Packer, 2001; Packer & Goicoechea, 2000). Specifically, in this chapter I try to answer the question, What do schools do? by exploring disparate answers school reform efforts offered to the question, What *should* schools do? Every attempt to change schooling assumes some conception of how schooling works; by comparing reform efforts we can draw some inferences about the adequacy of these conceptions.

This might seem to be an unusual way to study development, since it doesn't look directly at children but at the institutional arrangements into whose custody children are placed, and at the efforts of practitioners, bureaucrats, and politicians to alter these arrangements. But the institutions of schooling define the practices and relationships in which children participate and develop. Looking at these arrangements, and at attempts to reform them, offers a way to move beyond sociocultural accounts of children's development that are purely face-to-face and explain how contexts and processes operate on schools—and on children—to make their influence felt (cf. Serpell, 1993 for a review of the complexities of this task).

In the modern Western postindustrial world, becoming an adult means participating in a society which, often regrettably, assigns people very different and unequal structural positions of class, gender, and ethnicity. Critical theorists have insisted that school is an institution that plays a crucial role preparing children for this aspect of adult life. But developmental psychology has only just begun to explore and explain how children take up such adult positions. On the one hand, socialization theories typically reduce the whole process to the simple transmission and internalization of values and norms; on the other, structuralist developmental theory has generally insisted that all children's development, follows with logical necessity, a universal pathway. Such accounts remain blind to the political and economic significance of schooling and school reform; blind too to the intimate connections between human development and societal continuity and change.

To try to do justice to these complex connections requires drawing from both cultural and critical perspectives. Cultural psychology is changing our understanding of human development, showing how social and historical circumstances provide the artifacts, the mediational means, whose appropriation is a central aspect of development, and showing us that what counts as development, as maturity, as adulthood, varies with time and place. Developmental psychology has typically viewed development as a natural process, but we now appreciate that it is a praxis both social and historical. At the same time, critical pedagogy is changing our understanding by showing how the development of the person is a crucial facet of the economic and political processes upon which society depends. No social order is self-sustaining: its continued existence depends on the continuous and appropriate actions of its members, and its continuity over time requires a continual supply of properly prepared newcomers. That the development of children to adulthood is one phase—and a crucial one—of the reproduction of society is an important insight. And the two perspectives can correct each other's omissions. Cultural psychology has generally not taken time to consider the political and economic institutions in which culture and community are located (cf. Packer, in press). Critical pedagogy, on the other hand, while cognizant of these larger influences, has adopted an unduly restricted view of "cultural production" in schools.

This chapter is organized around a case study, the description and analysis of events in a single school district in one region of the United States. A single case, but this district was caught up in debates and forces whose significance was far larger than its small and particular geographical compass might suggest (cf. Packer, 2001). My work was intended to be concrete, practical, and relevant; I aimed to leave the ivory tower and make a contribution in the real world, yet still bring something of relevance back to the academy. The latter is the focus of this chapter: implications for our understanding of children's development in school, informed by both cultural and critical perspectives. My conclusion will be that a sociocultural account of development must include both the recognition and relationships of "lifeworld" interaction, and the way in which "rationalization" of school along with other social institutions implements a distal ontology.

Willow Run Community School District

Willow Run is a small rust-belt community in the industrial Midwest. Largely working class, about 40 percent African American, 60 percent Caucasian, the district has just eight schools—an early childhood center, five elementary schools, a middle school and a high school—with a total enrollment of around four thousand. The community is poor; across the district around 46 per cent of students are on the free or reduced-price lunch program.

The community was hit hard in 1992 by the announced closing of a large auto-assembly plant. Its identity and survival had been intimately tied to this massive industrial plant, built in the 1940s for assembly-line production of B-24 bombers. Workers flooded to the plant from all over the country, and others followed after the war when it was retooled for automobile production. It provided well-paid jobs on the assembly-line to generations of young adults, most without a high school diploma.[1] But now General Motors (GM) decided to consolidate production with a plant in the south, and suddenly the economic basis of the community was threatened. This painful event offered a unique opportunity to witness the relations among classroom, district, community, and larger political and economic processes, made visible in historical change. How, I wondered, would the district schools respond?

I discovered immediately that significant efforts were already underway to change the practices of classroom instruction in the community schools. In order to both understand those changes and to try, in an appropriate way, to facilitate them, I joined the committee that was trying to encourage "systemic change" throughout the district. — the Willow Run Systemic Initiative (WRSI) Committee. As their "official observer" I attended the meetings of this committee, school board meetings, and Town Hall meetings; traveled to the state Department of Education with other committee members; visited and observed classrooms; and interviewed teachers, students, parents, the superintendent, and other administrators. I focused my attention on transitions—in and out of school, from one grade to the next, the first day of the school year, and so on—believing that here too changes make customary practices and expectations more evident.

It turned out that there was much more complexity to the economic and political context of these local reforms than I had expected. First, the Willow Run plant closing was a small, though significant, part of a major structural transformation in the U.S. economy, especially in the auto-manufacturing industry that had dominated Michigan for almost a century. Second, Michigan's governor soon initiated reforms of the state's public schools. Third, the National Science Foundation had recently organized a national program of school improvement, and Michigan and Willow Run became part of this. And, fourth, the history of the community turned out to be unusual and important.

I can only summarize these influences briefly in this chapter (cf. Packer, 2001, for more details). I begin with the economy, then describe the local reform efforts in the community schools and the two larger reform initiatives. Before turning to the history of the community I point out our current lack of an adequate conception of the "cultural production" of the classroom. Then I describe how the local reformers recognized that the children brought their class origins into the classroom, needs and attitudes that stemmed directly from the fundamental organization of working-class life under Fordism. I'll argue that the local reforms' hands-on, student-centered pedagogy was grounded in a tacit understanding that teaching and learning are relational and cultural phenomena, an understanding grounded in a practitioner's involvement in the "lifeworld" of schooling. A more adequate conception of cultural production can be found here. In contrast, the tacit conceptions of schooling that underlay the large-scale school reform initiatives arose from our society's rationalized economic and political systems, and amounted to efforts to rationalize public schooling. The developmental processes in school involve ontological change—change in the kind of person a child becomes—and increasingly this is becoming a "relationalist ontology" as rationalization has its effect.

School and the Economy: Structural Economic Transformation

The economy of the United States is being transformed, undergoing a structural upheaval in which "Fordist," standardized production is replaced by "postFordist," flexible production. Fordism, as one might guess, began at Henry Ford's Highland Park factory in Michigan, where the Model-T was built. Assembly-line production, with labor divided into a myriad repetitive tasks, provided Ford with dramatic cost-savings and productivity gains. It required and imposed a fundamental division of labor: planning, ratiocination, and control by engineers and management; and execution and obedience by assembly-line workers. And this division of mental labor from manual labor came to shape the lifestyles, and attitudes of the two social classes of capitalist society, including the different attitudes the working class and the middle class have toward work, and to education.

But a new way of organizing production is being adopted in many industries, not least (though arguably last) by the auto manufacturers. Japanese auto imports, produced using techniques of "smart production," challenged the Big Three in the 1970s. Now Chrysler, Ford and General Motors are striving to make production more efficient and profitable by rationalizing design and manufacturing, outsourcing, increasing worker productivity, downsizing, and relocating plants. All of these strategies played a part in GM's decision to close its auto-assembly plant in Willow Run.

Much is made of the fact that flexible production requires new skills and attitudes on the part of workers. The Fordist division of labor is now too simple and inflexible; workers on the line now must be computer literate, able to work collaboratively, identify inefficiencies in the production process, monitor quality continuously, and—above all—be "flexible."

In the eyes of many, these new job skills call for new kinds of preparation by the public schools. Indeed, schools have been blamed for failing to keep up with the changing workplace, for failing to provide the kinds of workers needed in the "new economy." By 1992 the United States was in a recession considered the worst since the 1930s Great Depression, and the new chairman of IBM, Louis V. Gerstner, Jr., wrote an Op Ed piece for the *New York Times*.

> Our schools are failing: do we care? . . . It is a deeply dangerous situation. We cannot transform business and the economy without a labor force that is prepared to solve problems and compete on a global level. . . . If public education does not reinvent itself to meet these goals [the national goals of the first Bush administration and the Clinton administration's Goals 2000 legislation], and fast, it is the entire country that will be out of business. (Gerstner, 1994)

Gerstner's views were shared by many, nationally and certainly in the state of Michigan, which was faring especially badly. The state's economy had faltered due to the national recession and to the deep problems facing the Big Three auto manufacturers, slow to adopt the new organization of production. A group calling itself "Michigan Future, Inc." put it this way:

> The emerging New Economy demands employees who can solve problems with fellow employees without being told what to do by a supervisor or foreman. It demands employees who can keep learning new skills and master sophisticated technologies. The new economy requires very different schools and ways of learning—schools where students learn by working together, and where teachers coach students instead of telling them what to do. (Michigan Future, Inc., 1992)

Local Reforms Efforts in the Willow Run Community School District

But the Willow Run schools were already in the midst of change. A new superintendent had succeeded in boosting the district's image—Willow Run is literally the other side of the railroad tracks from the working-class city of Ypsilanti, and both are looked down on by "liberal" Ann Arbor—and in their attempt to get voters to permit bond refinancing to purchase technology, including a media center in each school and computers in most classrooms, and to refurbish buildings. He was widely credited with boosting morale, balancing the budget, and raising test scores. And several of the district's schools were experimenting with new approaches such as integrated instruction, common planning time, teachers working in teams, consensus-driven decisions, and with new kinds of curriculum material and academic task.

For example, in the 1992–1993 school year students in Kettering Elementary School's grades 3 through 5 took part in a semester of project-driven inquiry. Students worked in groups to design and construct scale model buildings—a mall, homes, and the school itself. Team-taught, they moved between their classroom and the artroom, drew, cut, glued, decorated, then wired the buildings with batteries-and-bulbs lighting. Math, science, art, and writing came together, and parents became involved too, helping their children cut foam board in the art room. In "process writing" the children reported on their project, going through as many as seven drafts, reading each another's work and giving feedback.

These innovations were not smooth sailing. The staff grappled with problems of timing, issues of ownership, and the dilemma of striking the appropriate balance between discovery learning and direct instruction. For example, children didn't use scientific concepts as clearly in their writing as the staff had expected. But this was a trial run whose goal was to draw the children into literacy and numeracy, into cooperative work and collaborative problem solving, through "hands-on, minds-on" academic tasks. The children struggled with new social and intellectual demands. Some of the buildings were destroyed in frustration several times over. But the structures were rebuilt, and some children built more houses at home without the teachers' help. The group building the model of the school discovered the concept of π as they measured the circumference of its pillars to work out the radius for their model. Parents came to help cut the foam board, and to help with the children's work in the artroom. The art teacher had to tell one parent, "No you don't; this is your daughter's painting," when they did what the principal called "copping a paint." Another parent told a teacher, "The kids know more about measuring than I do!" "But we didn't scare her away! And she still helped the child! . . ." the teacher told me, in a tone of awe.

The GM plant closing provided both renewed impetus and increased opportunity for these efforts. The day after the closing was announced the superintendent was quoted in the local newspaper, saying, "We were getting encouraging news, so we were feeling good about it. It's very bad, very, very bad." In 1997, five years later, in an interview with the same paper, the superintendent spoke in highly optimistic tones of the community becoming "freed" from its past. The closing loosened the auto-industry's grasp on the community for a moment, and lightened the pressure of the iron hand of capitalism. The relationship with the plant had provided security but it had also been deadening.

But before the success of the these local reforms could be judged, their direction and impetus were altered by two large-scale initiatives for school reform.

School and Politics: Marketplace Reforms

It was concern with the economic problems of the state and its "business climate" that led the new Republican governor of Michigan, John Engler, to demand reform of the state's public schools. This was necessary, Engler said, to better meet the needs of industry in Michigan so as to attract new businesses and to lessen dependence on auto manufacturing. These "marketplace" school reform initiatives immediately had an impact on the pace and direction of the local reforms.

In July 1993 the Michigan legislature was debating, not for the first time, the problem of inequitable funding for public school districts. A Democratic senator, reportedly trying to call the governor's bluff, proposed complete elimination of property tax funding for the state's public schools. Startlingly, the Republicans accepted her proposal, and it passed state Senate and House in a record twenty-four hours. School began that year with funding set to vanish in December, and no alternative source of revenue identified.

Each party proposed plans for funding the schools, and Engler insisted that the debate address not only finance reform but also what he called "quality reform" initiatives. He reported the views of Michigan business executives that "the state's education system is broken and needs dramatic repairs to boost its quality."

And so in 1994 the citizens of Michigan voted to approve raising the sales tax to finance the state's public school system. But they were not offered the chance to vote on the "quality" reforms, which went into effect through legislative action. Engler went on to accomplish sweeping changes in Michigan's schools. He backed redesign of the Michigan Educational Assessment Program (MEAP) tests, so that they test student achievement in "higher-order" thinking and problem solving. He successfully proposed charter schools (Public School academies), parental choice across school district lines, a longer school year, teacher certification tests, and new school accreditation standards. He repealed many provisions of the school code—for example, bilingual education is no longer mandated, districts can determine their own definition of sex education, and professional development funds must be spent on training directly related to student achievement. In addition the governor can now declare a district "educationally bankrupt" when test scores or graduation rates are too low.

School and the Government: State-wide Systemic Initiative Reforms

A federal school reform effort was building at the same time. In 1990 the National Science Foundation launched its "statewide systemic initiative"

(SSI) program, targeting math and science education in the nation's public schools.[2] The concern behind the initiative was that new emphases on teaching children to solve complex problems and to apply knowledge to novel situations threatened to leave minority and poor children behind, because the schools serving these groups often lack the trained teachers and other resources for such "higher-order" learning (Smith & O'Day, 1990; O'Day & Smith, 1993).

The architects of systemic reform, Smith and O'Day, were convinced that an "equality of educational opportunity" is *necessary* for responsible citizenship in our diverse modern society" (1990, p. 262, original emphasis). Our modern democracy and complex world needs people who can grasp "differing perspectives and novel approaches" (p. 263). Their concern was moral and political, not economic, with a focus not on efficiency but on equality. "Simple justice dictates that skills and knowledge deemed *necessary* for basic citizenship and economic opportunity be available to *all* future citizens" (p. 263, original emphasis).

For the systemic reform initiative, the task was to "deliver" the new "higher-order" knowledge and skills fairly, without regard to race, class, gender, or language, and to do so in a way that still allowed local school districts freedom to choose curriculum, instructional strategies, topics, and language of instruction (O'Day & Smith, 1993, p. 265). The approach sought to avoid problems previous "top-down" and "bottom-up" reform efforts had encountered: local responsibility and control would be "married" to the "vision and guidance" of the federal government.

To do this would require "aligning" the elements of the public school system—course content, curriculum materials, teacher training and certification, in-service training, and student assessment. Direction would be provided through a "common content"—the "curriculum frameworks" many states have developed, defining what children should know at each grade level. State and federal policies would also be aligned to provide "coherent" support to local schools.

Michigan submitted a request for SSI funding in 1991 and was awarded funds on the second attempt, in September 1992. (Altogether NSF funded twenty-five states, plus Puerto Rico, awarding each around $10 million for five years.) The "Michigan State Systemic Initiative" then issued a Request for Proposals to local school districts willing to become "focus districts" modeling change. Willow Run submitted a proposal in May 1993 and received notice of funding that summer.

The Classroom: Site of Production, or Just Site of Exchange?

How to interpret these three very different but intersecting reform efforts? And what light do these reforms throw on the structure and processes of the school classroom? It might seem that critical pedagogy has already thoroughly explored the linkages between school and society. But ironically the analytical tools critical pedagogy has forged for this task are not fully adequate. There is an odd bias in critical pedagogy's account of what happens in the classroom, a "one-sided emphasis on critique" noted in the opening quotation from McLaren. Critical pedagogy has promoted a view of schooling as merely a site of "cultural exchange," rather than of genuine "cultural production." And rather than facilitate the task of constructing a theory of children's development in school, this view makes that task more difficult by viewing students as passive unless opposing the institution's goals.

Henry Giroux has noted the problem.

> Reproduction theorists have overemphasized the idea of domination in their analyses and have failed to provide any major insights into how teachers, students, and other human agents come together within specific historical and social contexts in order to both make and reproduce the conditions of their existence. More specifically, reproduction accounts of schooling have continually patterned themselves after structural-functionalist versions of Marxism which stress that history is made "behind the backs" of the members of society. The idea that people do make history, including its constraints, has been neglected. (1983, p. 259)[3]

The consequence of this is that "schools are often viewed as factories or prisons, teachers and students alike act merely as pawns and role bearers constrained by the logic and social practices of the capitalist system" (p. 259). Such accounts downplay human agency and resistance, and ignore the contradictions and struggles in schools, and they unwittingly justify neglect of teachers' and students' concrete interactions. "Radical educators . . . have generally ignored the internal workings of the school and have tended to treat schools as 'black boxes'" (p. 282).

Giroux believes this economic-reproductive model has helped illuminate the role of schooling in the reproduction of labor power and the relations of production, countered those who blame school "failure" on the individual rather than the institution, and exposed the ways in which class and power shape schooling. However it has done this with a "grimly mechanistic and overly determined model of socialization" and so leaves "little hope for social change and even less reason for developing alternative educational practices" (p. 266).

Giroux does acknowledge some exceptions to this generalization, especially work by "resistance theorists" such as Apple and Willis. Such workers have drawn upon cultural studies and ethnography to restore in both theory and method "the critical notion of agency" (p. 260). In such accounts schools are "contested terrains," marked by "collectively informed student resistance." The central messages and ideologies of schools are often refused, in "complex and creative fields of resistance." Schools, says Giroux, "provide spaces" for oppositional behavior, and have a degree of autonomy from the economy, often existing "in a contradictory relation to the dominant society" (ibid.)

These "resistance" theories focus appropriately on the culture of subordinate classes and groups, "constituted as much by the group itself as by the dominant society" (p. 261), self-produced as well as reproduced, "forged within constraints" that vary from school to school, and they, also appropriately, emphasize the importance of paying attention to "cultural production" and to the creative and active work that is accomplished collectively on this level. "In the concept of cultural production we find the basis for a theory of human agency, one that is constructed through the active, ongoing, collective medium of oppressed groups' experiences" (p. 284).

Willis has defined cultural production as real, collective processes at particular sites and at particular human stages. These processes involve agency and collective activity, including perhaps as their most specific activity not passive positioning in discrete kinds of Reproduction (i.e. class or gender), but profane combinations and inversions of resources taken from these things; not helpless inhabitation of contradictions but active work on them. (1981, p. 51)

Not surprisingly, Willis's analysis is more attentive than most to informal cultural production inside and outside the school, but he too submits to the bias McLaren and Giroux have identified. Genuine cultural production, writes Willis in his ethnography of working-class kids in the English midlands, takes place only *outside* the classroom, in the informal structure of the small group. At least for working-class youths in the circumstances in which Willis finds them, "the school and its formal time-table lies tangential to the real processes of learning and of the preparation of manual labour power" (1977/1981, p. 176). He grants that, like any institution, schools have a cultural level, as well as official and pragmatic levels (p. 177), but his emphasis is the way "an oppositional informal culture" (p. 178) achieves in an unintended manner the educational objective of directing working-class youths "voluntarily" into working-class jobs.[4] Willis describes the "basic teaching paradigm" (p. 63) as "essentially a relationship between potential contenders for supremacy" in which the teacher, lacking actual power, seeks "moral supremacy" through the "idea" of teaching as a "fair exchange—most basically, of knowledge for respect, of guidance for control" (p. 74). Knowledge will in turn be exchanged for qualifications, these for pay, and this for goods and services. While Willis does note phenomena such as students "seeking approval from an acknowledged superior in a very particular institutional form," as well as the prevalence of individual competition (p. 65), and the importance of "attitude" (p. 69), these are all interpreted as parts of "the exchange relationship in the educational paradigm" (p. 67) and as evidence of its coercive and controlling character. (Cf. Packer & Goicoechea, 2000 and Packer, 2001, for an alternative discussion of these phenomena.) In the background here of course is Marx's insight that value is created not in exchange in the marketplace, but in active production by labor. So when Willis describes the school classroom as merely a site of an "exchange" (of knowledge for respect), he implies that nothing of value is created in the classroom.

Willis has responded to criticism that he failed to appreciate the active stance taken by students other than "the lads." "Although the book did not focus on the conformists, ethnic groups, or girls, it seems unfair that the whole approach should be accused of assuming the passivity or invisibility of these groups when it turns so much analytically precisely on general qualities of *activity*" (1981, p. 61). But at the same time he grants, "The case of the 'ear'oles' (working-class male conformists in the Hammertown case study) is admittedly somewhat more complex, and they became—more as a stylistic device than as a theoretical necessity—somewhat of a foil for 'the lads' in the write-up of the book" (p. 62).

Even McLaren sees students as active only when they resist school's "hegemonic ideology." In statements of ostensible empirical fact like the following the interpretive framework of critical pedagogy will grant no creative activity in conformity:

> It was a rather grim paradox that when students were not working, they became active participants in resistance, and when they were at the mercy of the bleak self-effacement of instruction, they remained, for the most part, passionless observers and passive recipients of over-packaged (and over-cooked) information. (1989, p. 156)

In sum, critical pedagogy too frequently simply inverts the values of the typical school, viewing refusal to do what the school regards as learning, and rejection of its definition of success, as an active and creative stance; viewing success in the school's terms as becoming a passive victim. But this simplistic reversal makes no sense. While it is true that resistance is the occasion in which students' active, creative engagement is most evident, this does not mean that those students who don't show active opposition in the school are simply passively internalizing institutional messages. A working-class child who adopts middle-class, liberal democratic values and struggles to achieve in school and enter a profession may, from the viewpoint of a particular political stance, be faulted for abandoning their class of origin and supporting an inequitable system, but they cannot accurately be faulted for passive inactivity. Crossing a boundary between classes takes hard work, whether it is applauded or decried by others, whether or not it is a politically conservative move. Nor can this be ignored because it is not a "collective" enterprise, for, after all, the middle-class liberal notion that people can act as independent individuals is rightly held by critical theorists to be an illusion. In reality the children who choose to pursue a career of individual accomplishment are still members of a community, and can only act as they do as a consequence of this, even though they themselves are unaware of it.

When Giroux, for example, makes a parenthetical comment that the hidden curriculum is "internalized by (read imposed on) students," he and other critical pedagogists forget what cultural psychologists stress: that internalization is itself an active and creative process.[5]

Just as it is necessary to draw on the strengths of critical pedagogy to correct cultural psychology's tendency to neglect broader political and economic institutions and processes, it is necessary to draw upon the insights of cultural psychology to correct critical pedagogy's tendency to find agency only outside the classroom, and in those who oppose and resist the school's agenda. It is necessary, in other words, to draw on the strengths of cultural psychology and critical pedagogy to overcome limitations that each of them suffers from. We need to hold onto both the insight that all children are active agents, shaping their own fates, albeit without complete freedom or control, *and* the recognition that schooling is about the reproduction of society. We need to resist too quickly dismissing the classroom as a place where nothing of value is created.

Local Reforms and Fordism

In contrast to the paucity of critical pedagogy's theoretical conception of cultural production in the school classroom, the local reformers showed a practitioner's keen awareness that children bring needs and attitudes to school that shape their engagement in the classroom, and that the instruments of classroom assessment are actively taken up by students. This awareness was the basis for efforts to transform the classroom and so to transform children who were human products of Fordist capitalism.

The district's local reform efforts evinced a rich grasp both of the concrete realities of children's lives and of the community the schools served. When the staff and administration in Willow Run described their efforts to "make learning fun," to make teaching more "student-centered," they were guided by their familiarity with the needs and attitudes of the children in the local community. The kind of instruction in the "wire-a-building" project I have described is, of course, much the rage these days, going by the name "constructivist pedagogy." But the local reforms had a broader goal than this, and a deeper significance than is often the case with teaching "higher-order" thinking skills. Adoption of new kinds of activity was just one aspect of a larger reorganization of classroom life and of the kinds of relationship and recognition it permitted. To understand this we must consider how the children of Willow Run brought their class origins into the classroom; we must recognize how the needs and attitudes of such children stem directly from the fundamental organization of working-class life under Fordism. The schools' efforts at reform amounted to a riposte to the way in which capitalism shapes its human products.

The Fordist division of labor, the manual labor/mental labor split, is the origin of different class attitudes to forms of labor and knowledge. Working-class culture takes a critical attitude toward theoretical knowledge and book learning. Willis noted among manual workers in the English midlands,

> a massive feeling on the shopfloor, and in the working class generally, that practice is more important than theory. . . . The shopfloor abounds with apocryphal stories about the idiocy of purely theoretical knowledge. Practical ability always comes first and is a *condition* of other kinds of knowledge. Whereas in middle class culture knowledge and qualifications are seen as a way of shifting upwards the whole mode of practical alternatives open to an individual, in working class eyes theory is riveted to particular productive practices. If it cannot earn its keep there, it is to be rejected. (1977/1981, p. 56)

Willis adds, "The working class view would be the rational one were it not located in class society" where theory is disguised, its ties to material reality cut, turned into the currency of social advancement. Theoretical knowledge increases options for the middle class. For the working class it does nothing.

The economic conditions of the two classes reinforce these differences. Fordist production involved not just a division of labor; it rested on exploitation of working-class labor: the profit that flows from selling products of their labor belongs to the factory owner, not to the workers. The working class are unable to foster the "distance from necessity" (Bourdieu, 1979/1984) that the middle class enjoy. They must maintain a functional and pragmatic attitude, where the middle class can afford to be detached and indifferent. (Figure 4.1 sketches the class needs and attitudes that stem from the division of labor and economic circumstances of Fordism.) The poverty in Willow Run meant children came to school hungry and tired, starving for adult attention, with little experience of reading or being read to, expecting to fail. Many came from families in which parents had themselves often tasted failure in school. These parents expressed the hope their children would succeed where they had not, but at the same time few of them provided the preparation that middle-class families take for granted. The schools struggled to find ways to satisfy the children's needs and to address their attitudes. The local reform efforts were sanguine about the children's background, their families' lack of resources, and the poor self-esteem, low expectations, and everyday stress many of these children brought with them to school. The hands-on, student-centered pedagogy caught the attention of children born to a culture that valued manual labor and practical reasoning. The emphasis on practical activity with concrete products made sense to both children and parents. I came to see the local reforms as an important experiment at making schooling newly relevant to the lives of children of working-class culture. (Figure 2 illustrates how the local reforms dovetailed with the children's needs and attitudes.)

Aptitude and attitude

But the local reforms undertook more than introducing academic tasks likely to appeal to and engage children who saw knowledge as practical, and more than seeking to address the children's material and emotional

FORDISM		Division of Labor	
		mental	manual
Economic Conditions	purchased loyalty	Indirect, cognitive & symbolic relation. Distance from necessity; detachment, indifference, separation of form & function.	
	squeezed labor		Obedience, punctuality, strength & tolerance of monotony. Pragmatic, functional, sensual & immediate relation, due to scarcity of social & material resources.

	Attitudes Resignation to failure. Comfort in routine. Tolerance of domination: working for others. Skepticism about book learning & theoretical knowledge. Valuing practical expertise.
Needs Physical needs—for food and rest. Emotional needs—for attention and security.	

Figure 4.1. Fordism's Division of Labor and Economic Conditions, and Children's Needs and Attitudes

needs. The local reformers recognized that what the Willow Run schools had to do was not just teach new skills, but change children's attitude to learning. This involved touching not just their cognition but their motivation, even their personality. The task amounted to preparing the children for a new lifestyle, a new way of life, as their old one vanished. If the community was to be preserved this could only be done by transforming its children.

Central to this transformation was a change in the way in which students were assessed and evaluated in the classroom; a renunciation of central elements of the traditional classroom. Public schools, both in the United States and elsewhere, have been indicted for being institutions that read differences in culture, background, and attitude as differences, even deficiencies, in ability and aptitude. So-called revisionist or functionalist critics of schooling argue that it is class-biased; that both the skills taught and values promoted in schools are middle-class, so that working-class children find the habits and attitudes they have acquired at home provide little benefit or preparation when they enter the classroom. When schools, these critics suggest, make judgments of

Schooling Reforms in Kettering Elementary	
Attitudes & Needs	*Reforms*
• Resignation to failure.	• Removing the single axis of achievement.
• Comfort in routine.	• Novelty.
• Tolerance of domination: working for others.	• Knowledge as discovered, not dispensed by authority.
• Ethos of equality, not 'top-down.'	• Teacher as coach, not boss.
• Approval of conformity.	• "All children can learn"-no one stands out. • Recognition of multiple abilities.
• Valuing practical expertise.	• Practical, "hands-on, minds-on" projects.
• Skepticism about book learning & theoretical knowledge.	• "Learning can be fun."
• Needs for food and rest.	• Clean, predictable environment. • Free & reduced-price lunch.
• Needs for attention and security.	• Safe, cheerful environment. • Support, optimism. • Individual instruction.

Figure 4.2. How Children's Needs and Attitudes are Met—and Challenged—by Schooling Reforms in Willow Run

ability, as they do in the form of grades and test scores, they are in actuality measuring class or ethnic background, class or ethnic culture. Typically in school "a *social* gift [is] treated as a *natural* one" (Bourdieu, 1974/1982, p. 391).

For example, Bowles and Gintes in their classic study *Schooling in Capitalist America: Educational Reform and the Contradictions of Economic Life* (1976) argued that the "liberal goal" of turning to schools to compensate for the economic inequities of a capitalist economy is a "vain" one. Power and privilege have their origin in the economy, but they surface everywhere—in the family, in everyday interaction, and in school. Schools, they insist, inevitably draw young people into institutional relationships that reproduce the hierarchy and discipline of the workplace, and so reproduce the modes of consciousness required of workers.

The sociologist Parsons (1959) described the way in which the traditional elementary school classroom establishes a single "axis of achievement," along which students are sorted. Parsons noted that the moral and intellectual demands of classroom tasks are fused, in the early grades at least, so evaluation in effect measures "achievement motivation"—that is to say, willingness to work.

Parsons assumed that children differ naturally in ability, measurable as IQ, and that schools' sorting was functional, preparing children for appropriate positions in an organic social order. Schumpeter (1955/1951), an early analyst of modern capitalism whose work is still viewed with respect by economists, noted how a capitalist economy relies on differences in ability. What Schumpeter's and Parson's analyses failed to appreciate is that the abilities about which judgments of differences are made are social products, not natural properties. So they also neglected the transformative effect on children of such evaluation and sorting.

We now know that aptitude is not so neutrally observed and assessed—that what schools, for the most part, treat as natural and essential is in fact socially conditioned, the product of a particular social structure, and an unfair one at that. Sennett and Cobb (1972) described the result of schools' evaluation: how working-class people come to see themselves as less emotionally controlled and lacking the developed inner complexity of the middle class. These blue-collar workers see formal education as providing freedom—in the form of permission to control situations, and access to a greater set of social roles. Even those who cope and are relatively successful feel powerlessness—and judge themselves inadequate for this sign of their vulnerability. They feel they are less deserving of respect because they have failed to become individuals, instead remaining "average" members of the masses. Yet at the same time the work "educated" people do is regarded with revulsion, considered undignified, undeserving of respect, and in many respects immoral. There is keen awareness of white-collar corruption and crime.

As Sennett and Cobb insist, "What needs to be understood is how the class structure in America is organized so that *the tools of freedom become sources of indignity*" (p. 30, original emphasis).

The Willow Run teachers and administrators had good reason to be familiar with the phenomenon of children failing in school not because they lack ability but because of their cultural background. And so the new approach to pedagogy, the "hands-on, minds-on" learning, was coupled with moves away from the unitary axis of the traditional classroom. The slogan All Children Can Learn (part of the district's new Vision Statement; often repeated in meetings of the WRSI committee) asserted a belief in the equality of students, a belief put into action in the form of experimentation with portfolio assessments, attention to differences in learning style, celebration of differences in interests, mainstreaming, and elimination of tracking and ability grouping.

For example, Kettering's first-grade teacher was relinquishing elements of traditional instruction one by one. She had abandoned ability-based reading groups—the "Robins," the "Bluejays," and the "Buzzards"—because the children always knew "who could and who couldn't, who the haves were and who the have nots were." Instead she had begun whole-group instruction, had replaced workbooks with journals, added learning centers, and was exploring a whole-language approach with reading-through-writing, classroom projects, and collaborative group activities. Her expectations of students were now based less on notions of ability and aptitude and more on the assumption that every child was learning whether or not results were immediately apparent. She talked of children suddenly able to comprehend printed text and thereafter making continuous progress.

> And lo and behold it didn't matter that they couldn't read the first three books; all of a sudden they were reading the fourth book. Learning through osmosis or whatever, they had picked up all the way, and they hadn't been alienated, they hadn't been earmarked, "You're a dummy, you can't read, this is what you're going to do for the next twelve years." They just blended right in. Everyday there's another one that's jumping on the Reading Train, that's the way I look at it, and it's really amazing.

On one wall of her classroom was a literal Reading Train—a railroad made of construction paper, the students represented by bears in boxcars. This was still a linear representation of academic progress—as students worked through the sequence of reading books they advanced along the tracks—but differences in progress were not immediately interpreted as differences in ability.

These changes in the classroom were paralleled by changes in the relations among professionals throughout the district. Once the Willow

Run community schools received SSI funding a committee was formed to coordinate local reform efforts. The committee visited each of the district's schools. From the outset one central message was that we were not there to tell people what to do, or even to say that current practice was wrong. The committee's approach was to avoid any "top-down" imposition of new teaching approaches by those in authority, and instead to foster a climate in which staff and administration were equal partners, trying new approaches and taking risks together. They insisted that there was no "one best way" to schooling. As the district's curriculum coordinator, cochair of the WRSI committee, wrote in an e-mail to committee members:

> If we believe that student learning should be facilitated and not directed then we must have that same belief system for teachers and others. Then the question is, what are the questions that we must raise in order to have teacher and staff think more deeply about what it is they are doing, why they do what they do, what are some things they could do differently, and where can and should they go for more information and assistance?

In both cases—student learning and professional development—there was a tacit understanding that learning is not solely intellectual, and that evaluation is not simply an exchange of equivalents.

Schooling as Relational and Cultural

Elsewhere I have laid out in theoretical terms the understanding of learning and development that I came to see embodied in the local reforms (Packer & Goicoechea, 2000).[6] It is an understanding that schooling involves ontological change, change in the *kind of person* a child becomes. School is a social institution designed to transform children. Schools draw children from their families into new social contexts, new forms of social relationship, and situations in which new kinds of expertise are called for. The culture of the classroom is one in which children enter into relations that are abstract rather than personal, based not on personal characteristics but on role or position. "Student" and "teacher" are new, abstract subject positions. And the symbolic media of reading, writing, and arithmetic transform the child's attitude to objects and events that have hitherto been lived and grasped immediately.

Because human beings are reflexive, we actively take up the definitions others offer us. It is the desire for recognition that draws children into these abstract relations (cf. Packer & Greco-Brooks, 1999), and over time children adopt an attitude toward the sources of recognition and respect in the classroom, as these are granted or withheld. And this is how identity is forged in the culture of the classroom, in relationship and practical interaction with peers and teacher, through alignment with or against the available forms of recognition.

In such an account, what happens in the school classroom is, for all students, an active and creative process, an accomplishment, which teacher and students engage in together. A school can compel (or prohibit) attendance, membership in the classroom culture, and performance of academic tasks, but schools cannot, however, determine the attitude, the stance, children adopt within this social context. This is always an active choice on the part of the child. It is because schools cannot control the stance students adopt to the sources of recognition that "attitude" often becomes an issue. School is the site of important developmental transformation—whether children resist and drop out, or conform and graduate. Teaching and learning have a *cultural* and *relational* character without which problem-solving, skill-acquisition, and intellectual inquiry would not occur. To ignore this is to fail to grasp the interplay of the cognitive and social aspects of schooling, and to fail to see what is at stake in school reform initiatives.

In the traditional classroom, recognition is structured in terms of the single axis of achievement described by Parsons, and children either align with or against this axis. The resulting attitude is either faith in meritocracy or a resignation, a humbling, a wounding of dignity, as cultural differences are read as differences in natural ability. The whole arrangement serves to rationalize and legitimate the economic inequalities and exploitation facing the working class under Fordism, and to sustain its inequitable social order.

In the reformed classrooms sought in the Willow Run schools, the axis of achievement was being replaced with an expectation that all children would learn. The aim was to change the relationship between teacher and student so that recognition would be given to initiative, not to obedience. This in turn could change children's attitude to their learning, to their abilities, and to their own futures. The local reforms were a search—grounded in necessity as much as idealism—for a mode of schooling that would engage, not alienate, children whose background provided little preparation or incentive for the traditional school classroom, aimed at more than merely preparing the children to be workers in the "new economy." The reformers were attempting to change the kinds of person the children would become, and to improve their opportunities for a better life. The superintendent explained,

> All my life I've believed that there are certain parts of the population which are underdog for one reason or another, and it is up to all of us to work with them, and they should succeed. . . .
> They have to have the same chance as anybody else, maybe

more because they come from underprivileged homes which is
a disadvantage for them when they get to school.

The Willow Run Ethos

An important resource the local reform efforts drew upon was a community ethos of sharing and equality. Describing this ethos requires a
short retelling of the community's history, a story first told expressly for
the district's children, in a book titled *The Story of Willow Run,* com-
missioned by the school district in 1956. The community was described
then as one where "Everyone looked for a solution for the other fellow
as well as for himself" (Wilson, 1956, p. 88). The book told of how in 1941
the Ford Motor Company won a government contract to build B-24
bombers—the "Liberator"—using its new assembly-line technology, and
how a factory was built on a soybean farm that old Henry Ford owned,
on a stream known as Willow Run.

This factory was variously called "the most enormous room in the
history of man," "the arsenal of democracy," and "a sort of Grand Canyon
of the mechanized world." Floor space covered 67 acres—3.5 million
square feet (more than the office space of the Empire State Building).
The assembly-line itself was three-fifths of a mile long and, at the production peak, bombers rolled off the line and onto the runways behind
the factory at the astonishing rate of one an hour.

Bomber production needed many workers and Ypsilanti, the city clos-
est to the plant, had a population of only 12,000. In a matter of months
32,000 people—workers and their families—moved into the county from
all over the United States Ford was reluctant to provide housing for them,
and so a shanty town sprang up. When the Federal Housing Authority proposed construction of a permanent housing project the local residents were
horrified. The local Board of Commerce issued a statement.

> We welcome any growth that comes with due regard to normal
> peacetime life but dislike even to think of the effect of the loose
> aesthetic values almost sure to follow in the wake of an enter-
> prise so gigantic. Ypsilanti is a settled city with a definite char-
> acter, and we don't want the character to be changed. (Secretary
> of the Ypsilanti Board of Commerce, quoted in the *Washtenau
> Tribune,* Apr. 22, 1942. Cited in Roxanne Jayne and Susan
> Sachs, *Southern White Migration to the North: From Willow Run
> to Today.* University of Michigan, American Studies class 498,
> Apr. 25, 1973.)

Eventually the Federal Housing Authority financed "temporary"
housing, but the newcomers were still considered hillbillies, undesirable

white trash. This prejudice, together with the spartan conditions in Willow Village, caused the new arrivals to keep to themselves, making do as best they could.

Compare two statements. The first is by one of those war-time newcomers, quoted in "The Story of Willow Run."

> The whole secret of those glorious days was something actually quite rare in our world's society—kinship. Our problems were basically the same. Our ages and our goals were basically the same. No one could be selfish and survive. We needed each other. We needed encouragement and sympathy and help. Beyond this, we needed to belong. I think we were like a family, a good family. (Wilson, 1956)

The second is what a high school student, a tenth grader, told me when I went back to visit the schools in 1997. "If you go out in our community, our community is a community. It's not just people living in different areas. There is a community sense." She talked about the stereotyping of the community and its schools, then added: "Just because we don't have enough money, you know, doesn't mean that we're not as smart and we can't get the best education. We find our ways. And if you know how to survive without as much money you know how to live in the real world, cause in the real world you won't always have money; you won't always have people providing the best things for you."

Similarly, a recent letter from the district to parents referred to "the great Willow Run tradition of caring and commitment," and a recent report from WRSI to the Michigan State Systemic Initiative cited "a group cultural norm of support."

These statements point to an ethos of equality and mutual assistance special to Willow Run. I don't intend to debate whether this ethos is reality or myth; in either case it provided a resource for structuring relations among administrators and teaching staff, and for reorganizing the classroom. The local reformers drew on this ethos when they explicitly interpreted "systemic" to mean "not top-down," and when they encouraged ideas and initiatives for change from the teaching staff themselves, not imposed by administrators or outside experts. As a result, when some teachers expected to be told what to do, this was interpreted as their fear of taking risks, fear of failure, to be overcome by building community and support. And when the committee struggled with the difficulties of encouraging teachers to relinquish worksheets and textbooks, with limited funds for professional development, with fear of change, the Willow Run ethos was invoked to guide the actions taken.

Competing Logics of School Reform

The state and federal reform initiatives seemed at first to have goals congruent with those of the teachers and administrators in the Willow Run schools. The local reforms didn't seem to be fundamentally at odds with what Gerstner and others were demanding: for example, both valued "higher-order" thinking skills, as important preparation of children for adult life. Indeed, it seemed possible that this was a time when

> What is "best" for companies is also, more and more, "right" for people. . . . [F]or the first time in the history of industrial capitalism, the interests of businesses are consistent with those of citizens, consistent with the yearning for intellectual cultivation, self-direction, uniqueness, and zest in work. (Avishai, 1994)

Yet it turned out that neither of the large-scale reform initiatives did much to facilitate local reforms in Willow Run. On the contrary, they made these local efforts much more difficult. In part this was because they embodied very different *conceptions* of how schools work, in part it was because they were efforts to *rationalize* schooling.

The coexistence of the local reform efforts with not just one but two large-scale reform initiatives—and ultimately their clash—highlighted a divergence in underlying conceptions of schooling. The marketplace and systemic reform initiatives were organized by rhetorical/rational frameworks that were quite different from each other, and from the local reformers' conception of schooling. They both operated within one of society's two "systems of survival": "commerce" and "guardianship" (Jacobs, 1992) respectively. Products of society's economic and administrative systems, they each showed the relentless and incommensurate logics of their particular sphere.

On the one hand was an *economic* metaphor, with schooling understood as a process of production. Governor Engler sought to increase the efficiency of this process in order to improve the quality of its product: the schooled child. A quality index such as the MEAP test would ensure more efficient production by providing feedback to consumers, increasing accountability of teachers, schools, and districts, and introducing competition among schools that would break the monopoly of public schooling. The reform effort rested crucially on employing an adequate measure of "output" that could be put into play against the money and resources, the raw material, "input" to the schooling process.

On the other hand, the systemic reform initiative employed a *political* metaphor, with schooling viewed as a public service, an element of social infrastructure—like the post office, or the highway system—that distributes or delivers learning to students, its public. This reform initiative sought to ensure the equity of this distribution, through coordination of the delivery system. Central to this was the notion of "alignment": all the components of the delivery system must be appropriately coordinated—like getting water pipes lined up in the basement, or making sure the mail truck meets the plane on time and so gets the packages to the delivery person.

At first glance it might seem that these are simply trivial metaphors, barely relevant to the proposed reforms or their outcome. But I would argue that, on the contrary, these metaphors betray the fundamental logic underlying and organizing each of these large-scale school reform initiatives. This logic shapes the conceptualization of the problem facing public schooling, and of the appropriate forms of a solution, within each initiative. Each was a coherent logic, but together they were largely incompatible, for the two different rationalities clashed, one emphasizing competition and efficiency, the other coherence and equality. So while there was apparent convergence in these reforms' conceptions of the goals of public schooling, their conceptions of how to achieve these goals differed to the point of incommensurability, and these reforms' implicit conceptions of how schools work were significantly at odds.

Rationalization of Public Schools

There is a second feature to the two large-scale reform initiatives: their underlying motive of the *rationalization* of schooling. Habermas (1981/1984, 1981/1989) has drawn a distinction between *lifeworld* and *system* aspects of society. The first is the intersubjective, sociocultural field of social relations and face-to-face interaction; the second is the structural organization, integration, and differentiation of society's institutional components. Schools can be viewed as a component of societal systems, or as an aspect of the lifeworld. Viewed as a system, schooling requires strategic action in service of functionalist goals. Viewed as part of the lifeworld, what is called for is a debate to define and achieve shared norms. In terms of this distinction, the local reforms in Willow Run can readily be interpreted as a *lifeworld* response, in that they embodied detailed tacit knowledge about the particular needs and attitudes of the local children, and drew for resources on the practices and ethos of the local community. The large-scale initiatives, in contrast, are efforts to *rationalize* the organization and functioning of U.S. public schooling, seeking to apply an impersonal rationality to what was viewed as a dysfunctional social system.

Coleman has described the "rational reconstruction of society" that the social transformation of North America has brought about: the shift from a natural to a constructed physical environment; from a "primordial" to a "purposively constructed" social organization; from

a focus on the family to forms of social structure that include corporations and legal individuals, and from a face-to-face, organic community to rationalized, bureaucratic, impersonal interaction. In such
changes there has been a progressive transcendence of place, a move
from local to national economics and politics, and an erosion of primary institutions like the family with diffuse and multiple functions,
to narrow-purpose constructed organizations, especially the workplace and school.

As rationalization proceeds, the elements of social structure
become positions and offices, rather than persons, who are now
merely temporary occupants of these positions. In "primordial" organizations social control came mainly from norms, status, reputation,
and moral force, generated largely by informal consensus. "Closure
and continuity provide[d] a form of *social capital* on which the effectiveness of social norms depends" (1993, p. 9). But this social capital
has been so eroded that modern communities lack "the coercive power
on which the effectiveness of norms, status, and reputation depend,"
and new modes of social control must be developed, by means of new
entities: rules, laws, supervision, formal incentives, and sanctions by
designated agents.

Schools are a central institution in which children are prepared
for life in a rationalized society, and the large-scale reform efforts can
be seen as efforts at the further rationalization of this institution.

The School as Lifeworld

I've been building the case that the local reform initiatives embodied
a rich practical understanding of the nature of working-class life and
of working-class children's needs and attitudes, of the complex
dynamics of classroom interaction and evaluation, and of the ethos
of the Willow Run community. The local reforms were grounded in a
tacit understanding of the ways in which teaching and learning are
relational and cultural. This understanding informed a conception of
reform as a communal enterprise, which is both risky and challenging, in which there can be no single solution, and in which change
must be facilitated, not directed.

The Willow Run reformers believed that only by changing the
expectations in terms of which children were judged in school, and by
altering the relationship between teacher and students by, in turn,
transforming the community and culture of the classroom (and of the
school, indeed the district), could these children not only come to learn,
but become "lifelong learners."

In all these ways, the local reform efforts were surely grounded in
the lifeworld of schooling, not in its institutional structures.

A Critical Stance

The interpretation of the large-scale reform initiatives as arising from society's two "systems of survival" and as aimed at rationalization, while the local reforms are grounded in the lifeworld, aimed at facilitating cultural change, raises a number of questions. Is a political or an economic logic more appropriately applied to public schooling? Is a "monstrous hybrid" (Jacobs, 1992) created by their conjoint application? Indeed, is any rationalization effort detrimental to the lifeworld of schooling? After all, Habermas has suggested that rationalized systems tend to displace communicative action and language, the "genuine and irreplaceable medium of reaching understanding" (1981/1989, p. 342), and undermine the structures of intersubjectivity of the lifeworld. In the "irresistible irony of the world-historical process of enlightenment" (p. 155), rationalization makes possible heightened complexity of societal political and economic systems, but this engenders hypertrophy and the imposition of "system imperatives" that "burst the capacity of the lifeworld."

I consider these empirical rather than conceptual questions. But where should the critical researcher of public schooling stand to try to answer them? How should one judge the adequacy and appropriateness of these competing demands of schooling, these competing goals for what society should seek to accomplish with its schools, and competing conceptions of teaching and learning? If one grants that value-neutrality is not an option, what viewpoint does one adopt, and how does this influence one's inquiry? Feinberg points out that reproduction historians of education (he calls them "revisionist") have typically neglected to acknowledge the basis of their own critical stance. He sees "two independently critical pivots" operating in most analyses of educational reform: "a commitment to upward mobility and equality of opportunity for all members of the society," and "a commitment to local authority and community participation in the affairs of education," and notes that these two may clash, leading the researcher into contradiction (1983, p. 142). And Gutmann (1987) considers these reproduction theories (she calls them "functionalist") apolitical, in the sense that in assuming that schools deterministically serve the interests of capitalism they discourage discussion of how citizens resolve debates over schooling, and also action along such lines. My decision was to allow critique to emerge immanently from the local setting: to view the state and federal reforms through the lens of the local practices of the lifeworld; and to listen to the voices of children, teachers, and parents in order to hear how their concerns were fostered or thwarted. And in May 1997 I returned to the district to discover how things had turned out.

The systemic reform approach ostensibly sought a combination of "top-down" and "bottom-up" elements, but in practice the Willow Run staff found themselves on the receiving end of "top-down" mandates for "bottom-up" change. They perceived in these a failure to "walk the talk" on the part of systemic reform. In addition, bureaucratic requirements— annual reports, yearly plans, and progress assessments, all in prede- termined categories and formats—sapped energy from the local efforts and forced upon them a homogenous and stultifying vocabulary.

The official evaluations of systemic reform started to appear after the first couple of years of the five-year program, first from the states, then from the feds. There was quick acknowledgment that reform is harder than it seems—in particular that the school system needs not just "alignment," but also "capacity building." It is, after all, not suffi- cient to get the water pipes lined up if they're not large enough to sus- tain an adequate flow. Ironically, the "capacity" the SSI reports appealed to, was pretty much the very things the local reformers in Willow Run had attended to from the outset. The evaluation reports defined capac- ity first in individual terms, in terms of dispositions, views of self, and the persona adopted in the classroom—"the new standards for students require everyone in the educational system to change their role and rela- tionships" (Goertz, Floden, & O'Day, 1995)—and then in terms of the culture of school and community, including outside networks and rela- tions. Individuals operate within "communities of practice," the report declared. Systemic reform had, it concluded, insufficiently targeted this element. But the report didn't question the adequacy of systemic reform's underlying conception of schooling.

If SSI *neglected* community and relationship in the schools, Engler's reforms were *destroying* them. Engler was getting national visibility as a result of his actions: President Clinton arrived in Michigan a few days after I did, because Engler had offered Michigan as a proving-ground for the national achievement tests Clinton had been promoting.

Yet local opinions about what Engler had done were unmixed. "He is ruining public education in this state," one teacher told me. Several people pointed out that the MEAP test had become the overriding con- sideration in school reform: it was the measure of both student achieve- ment and school performance, the basis for school accreditation, and drove the curriculum because although no curriculum content was man- dated, the test items were linked to specific materials. And it was now also the basis for the state to justify seizing control of "failing" schools. There was an appearance of local control and choice, but in actuality everything was now driven by a single measure of quality.

> This sure feels like a mandate, but there's nothing I can do with it; there's no way I can change it; I can't protest it. If you [have] a mandate, there's usually a process that you can impact it. You can't impact this kind of system! They'll still be messing with you, but it's not official so therefore you can't do

anything with it. You can't even tell people that it's happening, because it's not official. (Interview with county administrator, May 1997)

Scoring of the test was drawing attack from many districts, both rich and poor. The category cut-points—defining students as "proficient," "novice," or "not yet novice"—were seen as arbitrary, and as designed to fail kids, because the test was intended to "pull instruction." The director of the Michigan principals' association pointed out that "If 96 percent of students were scoring proficient on this, it [the test] would be considered a failure."

Everything that I have seen indicates to me that there's every intention of creating—and they're doing a darn good job—of increasing the distance between the haves and the have-nots. They absolutely do not want to see what they consider to be kids in the underclass succeed. (Interview with district administrator, May 1997)

Despite these criticisms, the Willow Run school board, disappointed by the district's low MEAP scores, had threatened to fire school principals, and this had led in turn to plans to hold teachers individually accountable for their students' scores. This was creating a climate of fear and anxiety, and splintering the culture the local reformers had been working to build. The board chair was quoted in the local paper.

I'm not threatening anybody. I'm just telling people to do their job. You can't come back here year after year with the same scores. There are no excuses. In private industry, if you have results like this, you wouldn't have a job. (Miller, 1997)

So although the marketplace reform initiatives claimed to foster, indeed to depend on, local initiatives for improved instruction, they had the effect of stifling these initiatives and narrowing curriculum and instruction. Willow Run found itself pushed to choose curriculum materials that would match those upon which the achievement tests were based, and the school board demanded that instruction focus on the test. More dangerously, the tests were being used in a manner that had the effect of labeling poorer school districts lower in *quality,* even though their students arrived at school less prepared by family and community (more accurately, *differently* prepared) than in wealthier districts. Long-standing differences in resources became read as differences in the "quality" of schooling, just as differences in children's cultural background have so often been read as differences in "ability."

Conclusions

The typical story we are told about U.S. public schools is that changes in the economy are leading to a "workplace 2000" (Boyett & Conn, 1992; Johnston & Packer, 1987) that requires new problem-solving and communication skills. This means that students must be taught "higher-order" competencies, which necessitates that the school classroom implement reformed curriculum and pedagogy. But this story is incomplete. The economy is certainly changing, but in addition to new kinds of work there is an altered social contract, one in which workers are being forced to adopt what amounts to a new way of life, to abandon as unworkable the stable, relatively affluent lifestyle of the "blue-collar middle class." This means that preparing students for the workforce requires inculcating attitudes to work and learning different from those of their parents.

Is the "new economy'" really something new? The economic exploitation of fordism continues in postfordism. Its basis is no longer the division between blue- and white-collar work, but the distinction between a small inner core of employees with secure employment and an outer core of part-time and temporary workers. From both, "flexibility" is demanded: the inner core are expected to work long hours if salaried, to work mandatory overtime if paid hourly. The outer core are hired only when and as needed. Flexibility means willingness to work long hours, in temporary positions, with stagnant wages, and to accept relocation and downsizing. Unemployment is at an historical low today, productivity extraordinarily high, and capital returns are startling. But there is a hidden dark side to the economic boom of the 1990s. A silent majority are not benefiting. Six hundred thousand jobs were lost in 1998 alone, and while the majority of those laid off found new employment, generally pay was lower, benefits fewer, and security less.

If economic exploitation continues (albeit with the new name of flexibility), it must still be rationalized and legitimized. It would be no surprise, then, to find public schooling pressured to continue to sort children and attach to them what Sennett and Cobb called "badges of ability." The school reform initiatives with the greatest impact in Michigan, the marketplace reforms, seemed directed more toward "increasing the distance between the haves and the have-nots," than improving the quality of education for all. The "interests of business" and "those of citizens" do not coincide, nor do they share the same "vision of the kind of human beings" children will become. A cynical interpretation of the situation in Michigan would point out that if marketplace reforms have the effect of labeling poor districts and poor children as *second-rate,* then this reform has indeed served the needs of the economy for newly "flexible" workers. A workforce that has been led to see itself as inadequate is more likely to accept the terms of the new social contract.

The question, then, of how to reform the school and classroom so that children from working-class families have an equal opportunity to learn is an important and contentious one. It is not simply a technical question, nor one of alternative means to a common end, because schools can operate to legitimate the economic relations of post-Fordist production, or to challenge them. The "new economy" makes new demands of workers, and these are not just intellectual demands. "Attitude" is the quality employers regard as most important when they hire a new worker (Applebome, 1995). And schooling, I suggest, is in a sense all about attitude.

What does this tell us about the developmental processes in school? I've argued that development and learning entail *ontological* change; change that cuts deeper than the epistemological constructions developmental psychologists have typically considered. The processes that bring about such ontological change in the institutions of school are, I have suggested, relational and cultural ones. But these processes are themselves not unchangeable: they are subject to transformation, in the process we call "history."

The Willow Run community schools found themselves on the edge of history, caught up in the structural transformation of the nation's economy, in a national program to make schooling more equitable, and a statewide effort to improve its efficiency and quality. Far from being passive in the midst of these forces, the Willow Run staff and administration took the initiative, drawing on available resources and working around obstacles. The larger reform initiatives sought to rationalize public schooling, bringing to bear on one hand a political and bureaucratic rationality, on the other a business and economic rationality. They are exemplars of a general historical trend that increasingly draws local communities and local action into larger institutional webs. The larger reform initiatives operated without an adequate understanding of the cultural and relational character of learning and teaching—but this didn't diminish their impact. The rationalization efforts depended for their effect on the continued operation of the lifeworld of the school, without having an adequately conceptual grasp of the lifeworld's character.

This rationalization is, consequently, an important aspect of the developmental processes of schooling. Failure to consider its existence and impact blinds us to the political and economic influences on children's growth to adulthood. It seeks to define and impose the ends of development, and often its means; the product and the process of development. In short, it seeks to shift the trajectory of development. Both the "economic" and "political" school reform initiatives touched and tried to alter the relationship between lifeworld and system: the local and the distal, the neighboring and the remote. Each had something to say about the roles that distant centers of power—state government, business conglomerates, national and multinational industries, and the federal government—should play in the day-to-day life of public schools, and the degree of autonomy local communities should have in running schools. The classroom is less and less the primary context defining who students are. In Habermas's terms, the lifeworld of the classroom is being penetrated by the system and by its imperatives, and this threatens a "bursting of the capacity of the lifeworld."

This means that children's development in school is increasingly shaped by the larger webs in which schools are located, rather than by purely local exchanges among teacher and students. These webs exert a mediated, indirect action, so that it is easy to mistake the classroom for a self-contained unit when it is in actuality a node in a wide-ranging social network. The extended networks exert a "relationist ontology" (Latour, 1997): they provide the recognition—positive or negative—in relation to which children forge their identity.

We must grapple here with the complexities of developmental processes on several scales: schools seek to change children; the reform efforts aim to change the institution in which children change. And altering the trajectory of development becomes necessary when a way of living proves no longer tenable, due to changed political or economic circumstances. This "development of development"—that is to say, innovations in the institutions that define specific developmental pathways—is not a simple matter, especially when there is a political struggle to define who children should become. But for the developmental psychologist, or for anyone interested in the future of our children and our society, understanding what is at stake, understanding the social relationships and practices within which children become adults, and identifying and understanding the factors and forces that hold current developmental trajectories in place while generally going unnoticed and unquestioned, is a crucial enterprise.

Notes

1. The adjacent hydramatic plant is still operating, producing automatic transmissions.

2. Strictly speaking, NSF is not a federal agency but an independent U.S. government agency.

3. Giroux agrees on this last point with Willis's (1981) criticism of Althusser (1972), almost word for word.

4. As Willis sees it, this cultural production involves an ironic reproduction of the exploited positioning of the working class, because the small group of "lads" valorizes labor power, that is their capacity for manual labor.

5. Cf. Packer, 1993. Giroux perhaps get close to my view when he suggests that reproduction and resistance theories "share the failure of recycling and reproducing the dualism between agency and structure" rather than linking these "in a dialectical manner."

6. The empirical investigation described in this chapter and the theoretical reading and reflection leading to that paper occurred simultaneously. The notion that school involves ontological change through relationship and culture developed as reading informed empirical inquiry and vice versa. The paper and this chapter thus each flatten out what was a circular and dialectical process of discovery, and in this respect misrepresent its character. I can find no more adequate form of exposition, however.

References

Althusser, L. (1972). Ideology and ideological state apparatuses. In B. Cosin (Ed.), *Education: Structure and society*. New York: Penguin.

Applebome, P. (1995). Employers Wary of School System. *New York Times,* (Feb. 20), A1, C8.

Avishai, B. (1994). What is business's social contract? *Harvard Business Review*(Jan.-Feb. 1994), 38-48.

Bourdieu, P. (1974/1982). The school as a conservative force: Scholastic and cultural inequalities. In E. Bredo & W. Feinberg (Eds.), *Knowledge and values in social and educational research* (pp. 391-407). Philadelphia: Temple University Press.

Bourdieu, P. (1979/1984). *Distinction: A social critique of the judgement of taste*. (R. Nice, Trans.). Cambridge: Harvard University Press.

Bowles, S., & Gintes, H. (1976). *Schooling in capitalist America: Educational reform and the contradictions of economic life*. New York: Basic.

Boyett, J. H., & Conn, H. P. (1992). *Workplace 2000: The revolution shaping American business*. New York: Penguin.

Bruner, J. (1996). *The culture of education*. Cambridge: Harvard University Press.

Carr, L. J., & Stermer, J. E. (1952/1977). *Willow Run: A story of industrialization and cultural inadequacy*. (Original work published by Harper.). New York: Arno Press.

Coleman, J. (1993). The rational reconstruction of society. *American Sociological Review, 58,* 1-15.

Feinberg, W. (1983). *Understanding education: Toward a reconstruction of educational inquiry*. Cambridge: Cambridge University Press.

Gerstner, L. V. Jr. (1994). Our schools are failing. Do we care? *New York Times,* (May 27).

Gerstner, L. V. Jr., Doyle, D. P., & Johnston, W. B. (1995). *Reinventing education: Entrepreneurship in America's public schools.* New York: Penguin.

Giroux, H. A. (1983). Theories of reproduction and resistance in the new sociology of education: A critical analysis. *Harvard Educational Review, 53,* 257-293.

Goertz, M. E., Floden, R. E., & O'Day, J. (1995). *Studies of education reform: Systemic reform. Vol. 1. Findings and conclusions.* Newark: Rutgers, the State University of New Jersey, Center for Policy Research in Education.

Gutmann, A. (1987). *Democratic education*. Princeton: Princeton University Press.

Habermas, J. (1981/1984). *The theory of communicative action. Vol. 1. Reason and the rationalization of society*. (T. McCarthy, Trans.). Boston: Beacon.

Habermas, J. (1981/1989). *The theory of communicative action. Vol. 2. Lifeworld and system: A critique of functionalist reason*. (T. McCarthy, Trans.). Boston: Beacon.

Jacobs, J. (1992). *Systems of survival: A dialogue on the moral foundations of commerce and politics*. New York: Random.

Johnston, W., & Packer, A. H. (1987). *Workforce 2000: Work and workers for the 21st century*. Washington, DC: U.S. Department of Labor.

Latour, B. (1997). On actor-network theory: A few clarifications. www.keele.ac.uk/depts/stt/stt/ant/latour.htm.

McLaren, P. (1989). *Life in schools: An introduction to critical pedagogy in the foundations of education*. New York: Longman.

McLaren, P. (1995). *Critical pedagogy and predatory culture*. London: Routledge.

Michigan Future, Inc. (1992). *Crossing to the New Economy: A citizen vision for a prosperous Michigan and a strategy for getting there.* Michigan Future.

Miller, J. (1997). Principals urged: Improve test scores. *Ann Arbor News,* (Jan. 17).

O'Day, J. A., & Smith, M. S. (1993). Systemic reform and educational opportunity. In S. H. Fuhrman (Ed.), *Designing coherent educational policy: Improving the system* (pp. 250-312). San Francisco: Jossey-Bass.

Packer, M. (1993). Away from internalization. In E. A. Forman, N. Minick, & C. A. Stone (Eds.), *Contexts for learning: Sociocultural dynamics in children's development* (pp. 254-265). New York: Oxford University Press.

Packer, M. (2001). Changing classes: School reform and the new economy. Cambridge: Cambridge University Press.

Packer, M. (In press). The problem of transfer, and the sociocultural critique of schooling. *Journal of the Learning Sciences.*

Packer, M. J., & Goicoechea, J. (2000). Sociocultural and constructivist theories of learning: Ontology, not epistemology. *Educational Psychologist, 35,* 227-241.

Packer, M., & Greco-Brooks, D. (1999). School as a site for the production of persons. *Journal of Constructivist Psychology, 12,* 133-149.

Parsons, T. (1959). The school class as a social system: Some of its functions in American society. *Harvard Educational Review, 29*(4), 297-318.

Schumpeter, J. A. (1955/1951). *Imperialism and social classes.* (H. Norden, Trans.). New York: Augustus Kelley.

Sennett, R., & Cobb, J. (1972). *The hidden injuries of class.* New York: Vintage Books.

Serpell, R. (1993). Interface between sociocultural and psychological aspects of cognition. In E. A. Forman, N. Minick, & C. A. Stone (Eds.), *Contexts for learning: Sociocultural dynamics in children's development* (pp. 357–368). New York: Oxford University Press.

Smith, M. S., & O'Day, J. (1990). Systemic school reform. In S. H. Fuhrman & B. Malen (Eds.), *The politics of curriculum and testing: The 1990 yearbook of the Politics of Education Association* (pp. 233-267). London: Falmer.

Willis, P. (1977/1981). *Learning to labour: How working class kids get working class jobs.* New York: Columbia University Press.

Willis, P. (1981). Cultural production is different from cultural reproduction is different from social reproduction is different from reproduction. *Interchange, 12*(2-3), 48-67.

Wilson, M. F. (1956). *The story of Willow Run.* Ann Arbor: University of Michigan Press.

II. CULTURE AS THE OPERATION OF POWER

CHAPTER 5

Critical Inquiry and Children in Day Care

Robin L. Leavitt

The child as a conscious becoming being pursues a "project" of freedom in order to become some-one herself and not a being-for-others.
—Polakow, *The Erosion of Childhood*

Critical inquiry has focused primarily on older children and adults, who are considered to be competent dialogic participants, able to actively participate in their own emancipation. The experience of early childhood has been virtually left out of this discourse. All too often the relevance of scholarly attention to young children is dismissed, as they themselves are. Likewise, child care centers have not been considered as sites of struggle by critical scholars focused on schooling. Yet, it is within the social world of the day care center that the young child appropriates, and is subject to, adult systems of meaning and patterns of interaction. These settings, and those persons within them, are subject to, and contribute to, the political, economic, historical, and cultural forces of the larger society. The institutionalization of child care, as a phenomenon with developmental and social-political implications, should not be overlooked by those claiming the concerns of critical perspectives. The major question I pose here, then, is, To what extent can a critical perspective be applied to understanding the experiences of our youngest children in day care—those children under five years of age? This question encompasses the research endeavor itself, the interpretation of children's experience, and the boundaries of critical inquiry. I conducted a critical inquiry focusing on children in day care and re-examined my previous interpretations.

Critical Inquiry and Young Children: The Researcher's Stance

How do we understand children from a critical perspective? I begin with the assumption that children, from infancy, are active, intentional, reflective, interpreting participants in the social world (Denzin, 1977; Packer & Mergendoller, 1989; Polakow, 1992). This assumption derives not from critical theory alone, but builds on interpretive and symbolic interactionist views of human development (e.g., Berger & Luckmann, 1967; Blumer, 1969; Cooley, 1922; Goffman, 1959; Mead, 1934/1962; Packer, 1987). Together, these theoretical perspectives suggest that children are not passive recipients of adult care, or entirely subject to maturational and environmental processes. Children have active roles in their development as they are encompassed in human relationships and engaged in symbolic interaction. Child development, then, is a reciprocal, dialectical process of construction and constraint (Power, 1986), as the child both "creates and is created by the social universe of which he/she is a part" (McLaren, 1989, p. 166). Given these assumptions, the researcher is confronted with the dialectic of the child's developmental capabilities and limitations, or, in the terms of critical pedagogy, the child's potential to create and resist.

A critical investigation of children's lived experience, then, is an investigation of their position in the social world—what they are allowed to do and how they are understood, defined, and treated by adults. Recognizing that children's identities, like our own, are constructed in relations of power, the researcher's task is to describe the dynamics, contradictions, and asymmetries of power in these settings, and look for places of resistance. Following Foucault (1980), I understand power as exercised, rather than possessed, and embedded in the microrelations of everyday life, present in the everyday routines, rituals, and interactions of the setting under study. This everyday "terrain of conflict and struggle" (Giroux, 1991) is my focus of inquiry. The researcher's commitment is to describe, understand, confront, and transform unjust, oppressive power relations.

The task, then, is primarily phenomenological and interpretive, or ethnographic, as reconceptualized by postmodern thought. In making sense of child care, I draw from multiple, diverse texts. As just noted, critical theory is only one perspective at play in the interpretive endeavor. In this study I applied Foucault's (1975/1979) postmodern concept of disciplinary time; Goffman's (1959, 1961, 1967) interactionist concepts of total institutions, collective regimentation, and nonpersons; Polakow's (1992) phenomenological description of temporal rigidity; Sartre's (1939/1962, 1943/1956, 1960/1963) phenomenology of objectification, serialization, and alienation; Hochschild's (1979, 1983) interactionist studies of emotion work and emotional labor; Gordon's (1989) sociological explication of emotional culture; and feminist texts challenging traditional methodologies (e.g., de Lauretis, 1986; Harding, 1987), addressing problematic relations of power and gender, and focusing concerns for reciprocity and being-in-relation (e.g., Gilligan, 1982, 1988; Noddings, 1984). (See Leavitt, 1994, 1995a for elaboration.)

Tales from the Field

From this critical positioning, I engaged in a long-term study of child care. Drawing from my field notes and from this diverse body of literature, I constructed and published several narratives illuminating the children's and caregivers' shared occupation of, and confinement to, the day care center (Leavitt & Power, 1989; Leavitt, 1991, 1994, 1995b; Leavitt & Power, 1997). Emerging themes highlighted issues of autonomy, reciprocity, authenticity, power, and resistance. Particularly relevant to this discussion, I looked for the ways in which the children's world was shaped, controlled, and constrained by the decisions and actions of the adults who cared for them. I actively searched for indications of freedom young children had, in order to comply with or resist adult imposition.

Throughout my immersion in the field and in the interpretive process, I view the day care center as an emotionally alienating institution imposing a temporal and spatial regime on the lives of children. While space does not allow full elaboration, the following field notes provide the reader with the flavor of my accounts:

It was nap time, and nineteen-month-old Emily was having trouble getting settled as she often did. The caregiver walked over to Emily's cot, grabbed her arm, and roughly turned her on her stomach. She then rubbed Emily's back very hard, while Emily cried. When Emily tried to move, the caregiver pushed down on her back a little harder to stop her from moving.

The preschoolers were sitting in a circle on the floor as nap time ended. Ned, still sleepy, was sitting next to me, resting his head on my arm, while he listened to the teacher talk. The teacher noticed Ned leaning his body on me and said, "Ned, you need to sit on the line. Sit up now." Ned responded, "I wanna sit by her!" But he did scoot a little away from me. A second adult, observing, went over to Ned, put her hands under his armpits, and moved him about six more inches away from me. Ned, resigned, put his arms in his lap and let his head fall forward toward his chest.

Four preschoolers had been waiting at the table about five minutes for their afternoon snack to be served. Other children were washing their hands or waiting for their snack at other tables.

The four children at this table talked with each other while they
waited. Then they began to blow their napkins off the table and
to giggle loudly at their actions. All four children jumped up to
pick up their napkins, creating a loud noise as Lily's chair fell
over. The teacher turned to the children and said sternly, "I think
this table needs to have some quiet time." All four children qui-
eted immediately. As they did so, the caregiver said, "That's good
sitting. I like how quiet you are. Let's have silence."

"We're going to go outside," the teacher announced to the four-
year-olds. "Let's get our coats." She helped some of the children
with their coats. "Dennis, here's your coat. When you get your
coat on, come back so I can zip you up." While the children were
busy with their coats and talking among themselves, the teacher
said, "When you get your coat on . . . listen! You're not listening!
When you get your coat on, sit on the rug so I can count who's
here." Some children complied, and sat on the rug. "Sit on the
rug," the teacher repeated to the others. "I like the way some of
you are sitting right now. Know what, boys and girls? You need
to listen more. It'd be nice if you'd be quiet so I can tell you what
we're doing next. We're going to go outside. We're going to walk.
We're not going to run; we're not going to gallop; we're going to
walk." The children lined up and walked outside with the teacher.

The interpretive task of the critical researcher is to undermine and
question what appears natural (Kincheloe & McLaren, 1994) in these all
too typical situations. Interpreted through a critical lens, these field
notes, and countless more like them collected over a decade, revealed the
extensiveness of the adults' power over the children. The caregivers' command over the children appeared as a pervasive source of social power
in and over the children's everyday lives. The children sometimes "resisted" by ignoring the adult, or by actively protesting, but these attempts
were always undermined and repressed. There was no choice but to comply. This conclusion is consistent with the critical theory premise that
"the oppression that characterizes contemporary societies is most force-
fully reproduced when subordinates accept their social status as natural, necessary, or inevitable" (Kincheloe & McLaren, 1994, p. 140). In
these incidents, the "subordinates" were the children, as they almost
always eventually accommodated and accepted the adults' authority.

Three-year-old Amanda was sitting at the table and cutting paper
as she participated in the morning's "art" activity. After awhile,
she put down her scissors, stood up from the table, and quietly
stated, "I don't want to do this anymore." The caregiver's response
was to ask, "Are you ready to glue?" She stopped Amanda from

leaving the table, sat her down, and handed her the glue. Amanda sadly resigned herself to continuing the activity.

Reinterpreting Power and Resistance

The adults' overwhelming suppression of the children's initiative and fundamental agency to be self-directed glared at me from these field notes, and from many more like them. It seemed clear that the caregivers' incessant and intrusive controlling behaviors undermined children's attempts to assert their own power. I have published, therefore, largely negative accounts of child care. Reflecting over the years, though, I have been perturbed by the notion that the lines distinguishing the adults' absolute oppression of the children, and their ability to resist, blur in these stories. Consider how situations such as the following contributed to my need to reexamine the children's experiences:

> The caregivers arranged twelve infants, between twelve and twenty-four months, on the floor for "story time." One caregiver sat before the children and flipped through the pages of the book, pointing to the pictures while repeatedly asking the toddlers, "What is it? What is it?" A few children in the back of the group stood up in order to better see the pictures. They were pushed down by a second caregiver who had been standing behind them. "Sit down, Tyler!" she commanded, as she took her hand and firmly pressed it into his shoulder, pushing him to the floor. A few other children attempted to stand up. The caregiver then grabbed each of their arms and pulled them back down to a sitting position. Meanwhile, the first caregiver continued to question the children about the pictures in the book.

Now, ending the account at this point, the researcher could focus on the adult's manipulation of children's bodies as she forced them to comply with her demands. The adult constrains; the children are constrained. But more was noted in this situation:

> Unable to see the pictures, the children's attention wandered, as they watched a third caregiver, who was engaged in custodial tasks, wiping tables and stacking chairs.

How does the researcher now interpret this account in its entirety? At first consideration the observation suggests only that the activity is not holding the children's attention and that they require redirection on the part of the adults. Applying a critical lens, however, poses this question for the researcher: Can the toddlers' wandering attention be considered resistance? Recent perspectives in developmental theory tell us that, from earliest infancy, children can control their environments to some extent. For example, they turn their heads away from excessive stimulation such as light and sound; they cry to elicit adult attention. To answer thid question, another must be posed for critical theorists, How much intentionality is required by the concept of resistance? And to what extent might we consider intentionality a part of these children's actions?

Additional field notes highlight these theoretical complexities with respect to interpretations of power and resistance. The italicized text indicates what might be interpreted as children's intentional, if ineffective, attempts to resist their caregivers.

> Three-month-old Corrine's fussiness suggested to the caregiver that she might be hungry for her afternoon bottle. When it was ready, the caregiver held Corrine in her lap while sitting on the floor. Corrine took the bottle readily, but after she had drunk about three ounces she began to refuse the bottle, *turning away her head*. The caregiver spoke to Corrine and jiggled the bottle, as she tried to get Corrine to take more, but Corrine *fussed and cried*. The caregiver removed the bottle from Corrine's mouth, waited a minute or so, and then tried again, reinserting the bottle. It seemed at first that Corrine had begun to drink again, but I noticed that she was *not swallowing,* as formula was running down the side of her face toward her ear. I pointed this out to the caregiver. She responded, "Oh, well, I'm not stopping now." She continued to hold the bottle in Corrine's mouth. After a few more minutes, the caregiver stopped; the bottle was just about empty.

> There are times when a toddler resists sitting in his or her chair during mealtime. Several of them like to *get up* in the middle of snack and *leave the table,* so the caregivers decided to strap the toddlers to their chairs during meals and snacks. The caregivers used either a blanket or an elastic cord to wrap around the child and the back of the chair. Or, they took the child's shirt and put it over the back of the chair while still worn by the child; this put the chair between the child's skin and shirt. Within a week after the caregivers started strapping the toddlers in, fifteen-month-old Troy deduced that being belted to the chair didn't mean *he and the chair couldn't move, and he and his chair walked (or rather, scooted) away from the table*. Troy and the other children thought this was very funny, and it became even harder for the caregivers to get the toddlers to stay at the table during snack time.

> The caregiver asked the children to sit in a circle so that she might read them a story. Initially a few children demonstrated

a lack of interest, but eventually all the four-year-olds sat down to listen. During the story, Seth got up to climb on the nearby jungle gym. The caregiver directed him to return to the circle and sit down, which he did. Soon after, though, he got up again. The caregiver again directed him to return to the circle and sit down. This time, however, Seth *ignored her and continued to climb* on the jungle gym. While the other children watched and waited, the caregiver asked Seth if he would like to go to the "sick room" for "time out." Seth *shook his head "no,"* but did not return to the circle. The caregiver then threatened, "I'm going to take you to the sickroom and close the door." to which Seth calmly responded, *"I'm going to kill you."* The caregiver shook her head, rolled her eyes, and said, "Well, that's not a very nice thing to say." She did not, however, follow through with her threat.

It was "free play" time. The two-year-olds had two play choices: blocks or legos. A few of the children put some legos together and made gun noises ("bang, bang!"), pretending to shoot each other. When the caregiver asked the children what they were doing, Derek responded, "This is a gun." The caregiver replied, "We don't have guns in here; do we?" The children did not seem to mind her comment; *they just changed the names of their constructions to "hair spray" and "brushes," but continued to "shoot" each other.*

Corrine, Troy, Seth, and the other toddlers appeared to purposely resist the adults' impositions. In Corrine's case, the parameters for resistance were very narrow, and the reader may be appalled at the unceasing insensitivity of care, as the adult failed to recognize and respond to Corrine's "voice." On the other hand, the reader may be amused by, or even applaud Troy's, Seth's, and the lego-toting toddlers' subversive efforts, and be generally unconcerned about the extent of their oppression. Such a reaction may reassure us as to children's power to resist, or it may deflect the seriousness of the adults' exercise of power, insofar as it may be repeated and arbitrary, continually requiring children to either accommodate or subvert. The following situation illustrates again how children's attempts to resist are deflated by the adult, but the last sentence suggests neither adult or child "won" the power struggle:

The caregiver gathered the toddlers together on the carpet for a story before lunch. About halfway through the story, she stopped reading and told Caleb to go wash his hands and face. He shook his head and said, "No!" The caregiver told Caleb he *had* to go. He protested again. Faced with Caleb's opposition, the caregiver then put down her book, picked up Caleb, and carried him to the bathroom, as the other children watched. Caleb cried and struggled throughout this process, during which I suggested to the caregiver that Caleb might want to hear the rest of the story before washing up. She responded, "His face is dirty. He has to wash up." The other children waited for the caregiver to return. When they returned to the group, the caregiver resumed reading the story, interrupting herself periodically to call on children one by one to get up to wash . . . . Meanwhile, Caleb sat with a frown on his face and did not show interest in the story.

These field notes suggest that there is a dialectic, or a continuum, of power relations between adults and the children in their care. A close look reveals what room children have to resist, from seemingly simple communicative behaviors such as turning their heads away, to overt exclamations of "No!" and, of course, physical resistance to caregivers' manipulation of their bodies. Despite these expressions of resistance, adults appear unyielding, as they hold the balance of power.

Who is the Oppressed in Child Care?

In the narratives I constructed, my primary concern was always for the children, whom I viewed as more vulnerable and powerless due primarily to their age, their attempts at resistance notwithstanding. I could not fathom why caregivers allowed Caleb and his peers such minimal self-direction and determination, or why the children's agency seemed so threatening to the caregivers. Clearly, though, understanding the complexities of power relations in day care centers requires that some of the same questions posed earlier on behalf of the children also be applied to the caregivers. That is, what are the ways in which *the caregivers'* world is shaped, controlled, and constrained by *the children*? Consider these field notes:

The toddlers were playing, except for fifteen-month-old Kyle, who was crying. As he approached the caregiver, she knelt down, put her hands on his shoulders, and said, "You must learn to smile. You're always crying. I'm not picking you up." The caregiver walked away from Kyle. He followed her and reached out to hold onto her leg. The caregiver, exasperated, said, "Will you just go away? Turn it off. I don't want to hear it." Kyle continued to stand there and cry. The caregiver cried out, "someone take me out of here!"

(No one did relieve her, and she stayed in the room with the children.)

Now, who is the oppressed in this situation? Certainly Kyle was oppressed—he reached out for what he needed and was denied that comfort. Moreover, he was subjected to the adult's whims and inclinations as she rejected him physically and emotionally. But the reader must see that the caregiver was also oppressed, as she also was confined to the setting, and she really *could not* control Kyle's crying, or the general neediness and dependency of his toddlerhood.

And so, the task of analyzing unjust, oppressive power relations is not uncomplicated. In the search for asymmetries of power, the researcher is challenged to refrain from dichotomizing power relations into simplistic portrayals of oppressed (children) and oppressor (caregivers). Critical scholars focused on any setting, but particularly child care centers, must concern themselves with *all* persons in the setting. This widens the research question, What freedom does the *caregiver* have to project herself into the organization of the day care world?

Caregivers are not only constrained by children's unpredictability and innate and seemingly unceasing dependency. They also are oppressed by the decisions and actions of other adults to whom they are subordinate (e.g., parents, supervisors, and corporate directors of franchise centers). Caregivers lack considerable control over their labor, for example, they have no say in the number of children, or what age children, for whom they will care, or how they are grouped. They also provide the largest subsidy to day care in their undervalued and underpaid labor. Caregivers, generally, are one group of women caring for another group of women's children; the conditions of their work is, then, gendered and class-based. Clearly, the institutional structure of day care centers, and the political, economic, and cultural assumptions governing their existence and operation within our society play a significant and complex role in both the caregivers' and children's oppression experience of oppression. Understanding the complexity of the power relations within day care centers, then, requires the critical researcher to see that caregivers' oppressive practices may be, in part, expressions of *their own resistance* to their lived and felt constraints and conditions. The idea that oppression might be a form of resistance, strange as it may seem, is as yet unexplored by critical scholars.

The scenes described in my field notes, consequently, are ones where *both* children and adults are attempting to resist the oppression, in its varied forms, that they experience. This oppression occurs within a postmodern, commodified culture of child care, which in turn, is grounded in our ideological assumptions about children, adults, and childrearing. Further work, beyond the disciplinary confines of traditional child psychology and development, is needed to understand the contradictory definitions of childhood at large in our society and at play in the child care center. For example, caregivers are confronted with conflicting portrayals of children as innocent and passive, but also untamed, and willfully disobedient. That our society tends to take an instrumental view of children, that is, to value their future as adults over their present experience as children, and to resist the notion of communal or shared responsibility for children, creates, in part, the caregiving conditions and practices I have described. These intersections between cultural ideology and daily practice must be addressed by critical scholars, and it is no easy task. Furthermore, transformation of any unjust power relations within day care centers requires attention to caregivers' own interpretations of their experience, and to their task of conscientization (Freire, 1970, 1985). This focused attention on caregivers is necessary to understand their relations with children and the dynamics of the power relations within child care centers.

Expanding the Boundaries of Inquiry

In the "fifth moment," scholars are increasingly engaged in self-conscious critiques of their endeavors (Lincoln & Denzin, 1994). The description, interpretation, and understanding of child and human development is, frankly, messy, as we attempt to link seemingly disparate theoretical and methodological disciplinary boundaries. I will now summarize some of the tensions I've experienced in my studies of young children.

Child development theory

The editors of this volume acknowledge that the interpretive frame in terms of which we now understand child development has changed. While the role of social and historical context may be more appreciated by scholars, a cognitive-development orientation persists in texts on child development. Moreover, whatever the advances made by researchers broadening the boundaries of our understanding, they have yet to meaningfully reach the level of everyday practice.

There is a need to reinterpret what we think we understand about the process of child development. Applications of critical theory to understanding children's everyday experiences suggest, for example, that the literature on children's social development and "prosocial" behavior be reexamined and reinterpreted. In particular, terms such as *noncompliance* and *disobedience* and the taken-for-granted assumption of adults that child compliance is most often an indication of developmental growth, or maturation, need to be reassessed.[1] Interpreted through a critical lens, the field notes I've shared suggest that child compliance may sometimes be seen as submission and subordination, and is not wholly desirable. To "accommodate," is, in a sense, to be neutralized.[2] Likewise, recognition of the dialectical nature of child development and children's agency can help scholars and caregivers alike better understand child opposition, and moreover, *legitimate* such opposition as oft-called for resistance.

Critical theory

Attempts to apply a critical perspective to understanding children's development in social contexts raises questions pertaining to some of the most fundamental premises and constructs of critical theory. Critical scholars posit that human beings are active agents in the construction of our social worlds. What are the ways in which this is true for young children? Still unclear, is the meaning of *resistance* when the term is applied to children's lived experience. Consider one more example: is it "reproduction" or "resistance" when young girls persist in dramatic housekeeping play, and young boys in block play, despite a generation of conscientious and explicit redirection of gender-based play intended to liberate both sexes from behavioral prescriptions?

Critical scholars typically focus on conflict, inequity, and the imbalance of power. When focusing on the relations between adults and young children, what imbalance of power ought to concern the researcher? The fact is, there will *always* be asymmetrical relations of power between adults and children. How should critical scholars account for this lived reality, and what, then, should be our focus when examining the shared experiences of children and their caregivers? That is, to what extent is children's marginalized otherness simply developmental, and thus unavoidable? Certainly we would not ask caregivers to abandon what we might think of as their *protective* authority over children, in their task to socialize them. For example, restraining a child from running into the street is certainly controlling, but it is also empowering for the child.

This example may seem to be trivial or obvious, but it poses this question for critical scholars: How are adults to balance the seemingly conflicting missions of child socialization and child empowerment? In other words, what forms of child socialization are empowering or disempowering, given children's emerging competencies and developmental limitations? To illustrate, some scholars distinguish between "developmental power" and "extractive power" (Smith, 1983). Developmental power is *responsive,* supports a child's developing capacities, and recognizes, respects, and validates the child's agency. Extractive power treats children as things to be managed and controlled; the power exercised is the goal rather than the means. Studies of children and adults in varied contexts, and that link critical perspectives with interpretive, interactionist, and psychological perspectives on human development, are needed to illustrate what these different forms of power look like in everyday practice.

The researcher endeavor

The critical researcher claims a particular political stance: a commitment to ameliorate imbalances of power and to emancipate the oppressed. If it is indeed the responsibility of critical scholars "to empower the powerless and transform existing social inequalities and injustices" (McLaren, 1989, p. 168), the researcher must ask where she fits into the power equation. That is, how do we extend the ethics of critical research to our studies of young children and their caregivers? For example, insufficient attention has been paid to objectifying research tactics such as the "Strange Situation" that deliberately focuses on our youngest children in an attempt to measure attachment and the effects of day care (see this discussion in Leavitt, 1994, 1995a). How can our youngest children be included in the process of research, so that they are not objectified, again, this time by the researcher?

As well, if "true critical research is a collaborative endeavor" (Carspecken & Apple, 1992), what do I, as a critically stanced researcher, do with my outrage over the caregivers' care? How do I collaborate with children's caregivers and reach shared understandings of lived experience? Whose story am I to tell and with what consequences? As I noted earlier, it is too simplistic to identify one group as oppressed (children) and the other as oppressor (adults). But in the process of attempting to interrupt the othering of marginalized children, I took sides and othered (betrayed) their caregivers (see Leavitt, 1998, for elaboration of this dilemma). How the critical researcher deals with these multiple relationships, contextual complexities, and conflicting interests in the endeavor to engage in dialogic praxis is a constant challenge. It requires the researcher to look at the institution of day care beyond the microlevel of power relations (my focus), and to see how these places work in terms of the larger political and social framework of which they are a part. In other words, the asymmetrical power relations in day care centers that I've described are embedded in particular historical/cultural/structural conditions that need to be addressed—again, no easy task.

Conclusion

Critical scholars, as our volume editors explain, are "concerned with understanding and combating oppression based on gender, race, class, culture, and sexual orientation." I have attempted to bring into the discussion the factor of *age,* as I consider the fact that young children are also subject to oppression. As a researcher studying the experiences of children and their caregivers, I am grappling with many contradictions and interpretive ambiguities in making sense of the power relations in day care programs. The questions I pose here cannot be answered a priori, or out of context, but must be addressed through ongoing immersion in, and reflection on, the life-worlds of children and their caregivers, and within the context of our critical concerns. Critical studies of young children have the potential to deepen our understandings of core critical theory concepts such as "agency," "power," and "resistance." At the same time these constructs help us to look at and think about children, ourselves, and adult-child relations in new ways. They challenge traditional perspectives on child development, and legitimate alternative views of children and our adult relations with them. This interplay of developmental and critical perspectives might be empowering of both children and their caregivers.

Notes

The writing of this paper was supported by an Illinois Wesleyan University research grant awarded to the author.

Many of the field notes herein were provided by students at Illinois State University and the University of Illinois under the supervision of Martha Bauman Power and myself.

1. Students in my child development classes tend to ask questions about how to "control" children, and about how to get them to "listen."

2. Here I can't help but think of children as being "assimilated" into the "Borg," for which the non-Star Trek parallel would be the collective of perfectly obedient and controlled children. Thus, as Packer suggests, it is interesting to recast the Piagetian functions of accommodation and assimilation into more political terms of accommodation and resistance.

References

Berger, P., & Luckmann, T. (1967). *The social construction of reality: A treatise in the sociology of knowledge*. Garden City, NY: Doubleday.

Blumer, H. (1969). *Symbolic interactionism: Perspective and method*. Englewood Cliffs, NJ: Prentice Hall.

Carspecken, P. F., & Apple, M. (1992). Critical qualitative research: Theory, method, and practice. In M. LeCompte, W. Millroy, & J. Priessle (Eds.), *The Handbook of Qualitative Research in Education* (pp. 507–553). New York: Academic.

Cooley, C. H. (1922). *Human nature and the social order*. New York: Scribner.

de Lauretis, T. (1986). *Feminist studies / Critical studies*. Bloomington: University of Indiana Press.

Denzin, N. K. (1977). *Childhood socialization*. San Francisco: Jossey Bass.

Foucault, M. (1979). *Discipline and punish: The birth of the prison*. New York: Vintage. (Original work published 1975.)

Foucault, M. (1980). *Power/knowledge: Selected interviews and other writings 1972-1977*. New York: Pantheon.

Freire, P. (1970) *Pedagogy of the oppressed*. New York: Seabury.

Freire, P. (1985). *The politics of education: Culture, power, and liberation*. South Hadley, MA: Bergin and Garvey.

Gilligan, C. (1982). *In a different voice: Psychological theory and women's development*. Cambridge: Harvard University Press.

Gilligan, C. (1988). Remapping the moral domain: New images of self in relationship. In C. Gilligan, J. Ward, J. Taylor, & B. Bardige (Eds.), *Mapping the moral domain* (pp. 3-19). Cambridge: Harvard University Press.

Giroux, H. (1991). Modernism, postmodernism, and feminism: Rethinking the boundaries of educational discourse. In H. Giroux (Ed.), *Postmodernism, feminism, and cultural politics* (pp. 1–59). Albany: State University of New York Press.

Goffman, E. (1959). *The presentation of self in everyday life*. New York: Doubleday.

Goffman, E. (1961). *Asylums: Essays in the social situation of mental patients and other inmates*. Garden City, NJ: Anchor Books/Doubleday.

Goffman, E. (1967). *Interaction ritual: Essays on face-to-face behavior*. New York: Random.

Gordon, S. L. (1989). The socialization of children's emotions: Emotional culture, competence, and exposure. In C. Saarni & P. L. Harria (Eds.), *Children's understandings of emotions* (pp. 319-349). Cambridge: Cambridge University Press.

Harding, S. (1987). *Feminism and methodology*. Bloomington: Indiana University Press.

Hochschild, A. (1979). Emotion work, feeling rules, and social structure. *American Journal of Sociology, 85*, 551-575.

Hochschild, A. (1983). *The managed heart: The commercialization of human feeling*. Berkeley: University of California Press.

Kincheloe, J., & McLaren, P. (1994). Rethinking critical theory and qualitative research. In N. K. Denzin & Y. S. Lincoln (Eds.), *Handbook of Qualitative Research* (pp. 138-157). Thousand Oaks, CA: Sage.

Leavitt, R. L. (1991). Power and resistance in infant-toddler day care centers. In S. Cahill (Ed.), *Sociological Studies in Child Development*. (Vol. 4) (pp. 91-112). Greenwich, CT: JAI.

Leavitt, R. L. (1994). *Power and emotion in infant-toddler day care.* Albany: State University of New York Press.

Leavitt, R. L. (1995a). Infant day care research: Limitations and possibilities. In S. Reifel (Ed.), *Advances in Early Education and Day Care,* (Vol. 7) (pp. 155-178). Greenwich, CT: JAI.

Leavitt, R. L. (1995b). The emotional culture of infant-toddler day care. In Hatch, J. A. (Ed.), *Qualitative research in early childhood settings* (pp. 3-21). Westport, CT: Praeger.

Leavitt, R. L. & Power, M. B. (1989). Emotional socialization in the postmodern era: Children in day care. *Social Psychology Quarterly, 52* (1) 35-43.

Leavitt, R. L., & Power, M. B. (1997). Civilizing bodies: Children in day care. In J. Tobin (Ed.), *Making a place for pleasure in early childhood education* (pp. 39-75). New Haven, CT: Yale University Press.

Leavitt, R. L. (1998). Webs of trust and deception. In Graue, M.E. & Walsh, D. (eds.), *Studying children in context: Theories, methods, and ethics* (pp. 62-69). Thousand Oaks CA: Sage.

Leavitt, R. L. (1998). Lincoln, Y. S. & Denzin, N. K. (1994). The fifth moment. In Denzin, N. K. & Lincoln, Y. S. (Eds.), *Handbook of qualitative research* (pp. 575-586). Thousand Oaks, CA: Sage.

McLaren, P. (1989). *Life in schools: An introduction to critical pedagogy in the foundations of education.* White Plains, NY: Longman.

Mead, G. H. (1962). *Mind, self, and society.* Chicago: University of Chicago Press. (Original work published 1934.)

Noddings, N. (1984). Caring: *A feminine approach to ethics and moral education.* Berkeley: University of California Press.

Packer, M. (1987). Interpretive research and social development in developmental psychology. Paper presented at the biennial meeting of the Society for Research in Child Development, Baltimore.

Packer, M., & Mergendoller, J. (1989). The development of practical social understanding in elementary school-age children. In L. T. Winegar (Ed.), *Social interaction and the development of children's understanding* (pp. 67-94). Norwood, NJ: Ablex.

Polakow, V. (1992). *The erosion of childhood.* Chicago: University of Chicago Press.

Power, M. (1986). Socializing of emotionality in early childhood: The influence of emotional associates. In P. Adler & P. Adler (Eds.), *Sociological studies of child development* (Vol. 1) (pp. 259-282). Greenwich, CT: JAI.

Sartre, J. P. (1956). *Being and nothingness*. (H. E. Barnes, Trans.) New York: Simon & Schuster. (Original work published 1943.)

Sartre, J. P. (1962). *Sketch for a theory of the emotions*. (P. Mariet, Trans.). London: Methuen. (Original work published 1939.)

Sartre, J. P. (1963). *Search for a method*. (H. E. Barnes, Trans.) NewYork: Knopf. (Original work published 1960.)

Smith, J. F. (1983). Parenting and property. In J. Trebilcot (Ed.), *Mothering: Essays in feminist theory* (pp. 198–212). Totowa, NJ: Rowman & Allenheld.

CHAPTER 6

Engendering Subjects:
A Foucauldian Analysis of
Developmental Gender Differences

Elizabeth Debold

Introduction

I am tired of gender differences. I am tired of the way gender has become a category of excuse or blame, tired of binary arguments about women as cultural victims and men as cultural perpetrators, tired of living on different planets. A woman philosopher, who I approached about my inquiry into gender, spent half an hour arguing with what she thought I stood for before turning her head away from me to say softly, "I just don't understand why gender is an interesting category of experience." Really, why should it matter? Aren't we working toward equality anyway?

These issues aren't simply academic—For instance, discourses of the subaltern. They critically affect lives; they provide the cultural context within which we each must find our way. I was surprised that, in response to a relatively benign question about the image of the "ideal woman," adolescent girls revealed their hopes and anxieties about gender equality. Lucy, a white seventh-grader at the Laurel School for Girls in Cleveland in the late 1980s, describes her "ideal woman," by saying, "Really no different than a man." Assuming a negative implication about difference in the question she is asked, Lucy continues: "I think that we could do like anything that they do, or the other way around; neither of us should be stereotyped." Two years later, Becca, a classmate of Lucy's, says firmly, "I think everyone should just be equal. It's ridiculous that people think differently."

Ridiculous or not, somehow, gender, and our sense of difference, don't go away. Why? It's not simply that biology is destiny. Gender holds the heart of culture, literally and figuratively. Gender—the countless ways in which we culturally and psychologically play out and play upon the biological differences between the sexes—is the foundation of our most basic understandings of ourselves and each other. Gender shapes our fundamental social arrangements from the family to the workplace. A deep look into how our sense of ourselves as men and women—our gender identities—comes about is positively dizzying. It's a gaze into the labyrinth of our culture, into the very mechanisms by which culture comes into being generation after generation. To question our gender identities is to question the foundation of society itself.

This elaboration, the ways in which fundamental differences in our procreative functions have been gussied up within culture, masks questions of equality in the dress of difference. "The first thing that strikes the careless observer is that women are unlike men. They are 'the opposite sex' (though why 'opposite' I do not know; what is the 'neighboring sex'?)," wonders Sayers. "But the fundamental thing is that women are more like men than anything else in the world" (1971, p.37). My argument is grounded on this basis—that women and men are fundamentally alike (or equal)—in that we are both embodied as human beings in human bodies, but the way in which we come to know and experience our embodiment within culture creates difference. I am looking at how masculine and feminine persons are created through the interaction of psyche and culture. In this chapter, I present a preliminary exploration of a thesis that explains how masculine and feminine subjects are (en)gendered through the relationship among culture, the psyche, and knowledge in early childhood and early adolescence. By subjecting Gilligan's (1990, 1991a, 1991b, 1996) working theory of a gendered asymmetry in human development to a Foucauldian analysis, I propose that the "power/knowledge" about gender that children incorporate at these two ages affects boys' and girls' most primary reality—their lived sense of self. I argue that who they are at a psychophysical level transforms as cognitive development makes available new knowledge about themselves as male and female within culture. Differences in the way in which men and women perceive the socioemotional and relational realities of their worlds are the result of boys' coming to know themselves as male when they are concrete thinkers and girls' coming into womanhood when they are beginning to think abstractly.

I begin this chapter with a presentation, in adolescent girls' voices, of common explanatory discourses relating to gender difference. Then I follow with a discussion of how I bring Foucault's theory from cultural development into human development. From here, I present the grounding of a Foucauldian analysis, first with a very brief historical perspective on the creation of the middle-class masculine and feminine followed by an exploration of the sensitivity of the human body. Then I explore the phenomenon of gender differences in psychopathology and use this to frame my explanation of Gilligan's working theory and the development of masculine and feminine subjects.

Explanatory Discourses

Our common explanations for the systematic differences between groups of people—gender differences but also racial and economic—have bounced between an underlying premise relating either to nature and biology *or* nurture and culture. Maccoby and Jacklin's groundbreaking 1974 analysis of sex differences has held to the present day. Their inquiry demonstrated that there are very few significant differences in the abilities and aptitudes of boys and girls (Golombok & Fivush, 1994; Lytton & Romney, 1991; Maccoby, 1988, 1990). When individual differences are looked for between boys and girls, they are difficult to find with any consistency. The differences that do exist, such as girls' higher performance in verbal abilities and boys' in math and spatial ability, are minor and the differences in math and spatial ability have been diminishing over time (Baennenger & Newcombe, 1989; Hyde & Linn, 1988). Despite this evidence, readily available cultural explanations for the root of gendered differences tend to dichotomize culture and nature—resorting to one or the other as if they were separable—to argue that difference grows either from cultural oppression or from women's desires and nature.

"What do you think society values in women today?" a woman interviewer asks Joan, a classmate of Lucy and Becca's. "I don't know," Joan answers, "I don't think they like women too much. I don't know but we are really good." The argument that male cultural authority—the ubiquitous, impersonal "they"—is the cause of women's oppression and, therefore, of inequity presents an explanatory discourse about gender available to Joan. Joan continues, "I don't know what they think but in the past they didn't think very well of women. I hope they do now." Joan's knowledge of being in a hostile relationship with cultural authority—which may relate to her not being able to know, as her repeated "I don't knows suggest—resonates with the study on women and epistemology conducted by Belenky, Clinchy, Goldberger, and Tarule (1986). Their "women's ways of knowing" project pointed to the relationship between cultural authority and the struggles women must endure in order to authorize themselves and their knowledge. For women, as *Women's Ways of Knowing* found, coming into a more self-defined epistemology requires questioning culturally authorized knowledge and Authority. Asking the question, What do They want from me? in relation to typically male authority or Authority is often problematic for women, too often carrying an implication of male sexual desire and aggression. The historical relationship of women to a male-voiced cultural authority creates specific forms of epistemology and subjectivity—so clearly defined by Miller (1976) as a psychology of subordination.

Side by side with discourses circulating about cultural oppression are explanations of difference rooted in natural desire. Arguments about what girls—and women—do and do not want are often arguments about natural or essential differences between women and men dressed up in the language of individualism and free choice. In a recent study by Taylor, Gilligan, and Sullivan (1995), working-class and poor girls report the same dreams for success held by girls at the elite Emma Willard School (Gilligan, Lyons, & Hamner, 1988) and at the Laurel School. Linda, a Portuguese girl who dreams of being a pilot, says, "It's people, they say girls, they don't fly; you know . . . it's like, they kind of think that guys are more than girls—I don't think that. I go against that 100 percent; I think I can be anyone I want. And no one is stopping me. I just go off for what I dream for and if I really try hard, maybe I'll do it" (p. 245). Linda's "maybe" plays the edge between free choice and natural desire. She believes that success is up to her, her hard work, and her drive. For Linda and most of her poor and working-class peers in the study, it is already apparent that the material and relational realities of their lives are daily and rapidly eroding their dreams. As much as they have resisted, they seem to be headed for lives very much like their mothers. Even the privileged Laurel girls' doubt that they can achieve the difficult balance between work and home. These privileged girls, like their poor and working-class peers, may also find their dreams of work and love diverted to either full-time motherhood or part-time work and motherhood. They, too, appear to be on a path that may lead them to replicate their mothers' lives. The reproduction of a similar set of choices, generation after generation, where women appear to *choose* to mother and, often, to abandon a full role in the public sphere, ends up supporting the premise that women's desire to nurture is simply natural.

In late capitalist America, conflicting discourses of free choice and natural desires clash against each other: these girls dream of living beyond their mothers' wildest imaginings only to find that they often have gone just around the corner from home. While the statements from the girls that I have selected are representative of their classmates, I am using the words of these girls to "ventriloquate," in a naive dialogic (Bakhtin, 1981; Brown 1992), centuries of debate and discourse to demonstrate how nearly commonsensical and readily available are conflicting understandings of the source of human inequality. The girls' expressions of faith in meritocracy and free choice, their belief in human equality, and their concerns about male cultural domination neither eliminate the nagging question of essential differences between men and women nor do they explain why it is that girls tend to become certain kinds of subjects, embodying a certain subjectivity. Ironically, within the classic liberal feminist argument where "everybody's equal" and how we live is a matter of free choice, the common sense reason why men usually end up manly, and women womanly—or why any cultural group tends to exhibit certain characteristics—is left open to an interpretation of nature; that it's just the way things are and should be.

The tacit refusal of liberal feminism to engage with the physical body only reinforces the concept of the body as the landscape of nature.

As Holland and her colleagues comment, "there has been a tendency to associate any sense of bodies as material with a naive biological essentialism" (1994, p. 21). Despite all of the brilliant feminist research and analysis that demonstrates the lack of meaningful difference in so many domains of human capability and the effects of cultural subordination on limiting human expectations, the historical persistence of gendered differences between men and women, particularly in terms of social, political, and economic power, leaves the question of "nature"—Freud's "biology is destiny"—unanswered. While arguments for bodies as social constructions, following Foucault and others, begin to erode the bedrock of biology, such arguments unwittingly tend to make human beings cultural dupes, voicing or expressing aspects of culture that are, arguably, often not in their best interest. Furthermore, the extreme social constructivist position often posits a postmodern, unfixed, ever-changing body that denies the constraints posed by material embodiment (see Suleiman, 1986). By pushing the body aside, an extraordinary body of knowledge on differences between women's and men's mental and physical health is left to be rationalized as evidence of essential differences.

Research indicates that "at least twice as many women as men receive a diagnosis of psychiatric disorder" with women more susceptible to emotional trouble (Golombok & Fivush, 1994). Women are far more likely to suffer from affective disorders (e.g., depression) and anxiety disorders than men (while men are more likely to engage in substance abuse or exhibit antisocial personality disorders). Even though the historical creation of the male medical establishment constructed women as a patient class (Ehrenreich & English, 1978), this difference cannot be simply accounted for as evidence of bias or of women's socialization toward seeking help (Golombok & Fivush, 1994; Nolen-Hoeksema & Girgus, 1994; Petersen, Sarigiani, & Kennedy, 1991). In an earlier century, these facts underscored something essential about the pathology that was woman. Current arguments that women speak their resistance to patriarchal culture through disorder (see, e.g., Bordo, 1993; Gilligan, 1991a, 1991b; Steiner-Adair, 1986) implicitly rest in an assumption about the interrelationship of mind and body. The fact that the body is material means neither that it is immutably, ahistorically "natural" nor that it is *not* a cultural palimpsest. The possibility of change and transformation of the sentient body—of rewriting and revising the psyche—is the hope both of therapeutic practices and of Foucault.

Embodying Foucault

Foucault's (1979, 1980, 1986) analyses of the relation between power and knowledge present a challenge to how we understand human development. Foucault argues that power is not simply the prohibitive force of law nor an oppressive hierarchical structure but is omnipresent, invisible, and inescapable. It is manifest in *what* we are able to know and accept as "knowledge" and in *how* we feel and experience our very bodies. Foucault similarly argues that knowledge is neither the sum total of the culture's recorded achievements nor the measure of an individual's acquisition of those achievements but is a living discourse through which the relations of power are incorporated into individual and social bodies. "Knowledge and power are integrated. . . . It is not possible for power to be exercised without knowledge, it is impossible for knowledge not to engender power" (1980, p. 52).

Foucault sees these "relations of knowledge in relations of power" as providing blueprints that direct our construction of reality (1979, p. 305). He called this web of relations "power/knowledge" to maintain an equation between power and knowledge. To paraphrase Rich (1979), power is evident in the assumptions in which we are drenched. Foucault does not dichotomize the material reality of the body and the subjection of the body to cultural power relations through knowledge. "In other words, individuals are the vehicles of power, not its point of application. . . . The individual is an effect of power, and at the same time, or precisely to the extent to which it is that effect, it is the element of its articulation" (1980, p.98). The "netlike organization" of power creates certain forms of subjectivity through the creation of knowledge and the circulation of discourses that tell us what is desirable, normal, and true about our experience.

Foucault's project has been "to create a history of the different modes by which, in our culture, human beings are made subjects" or, more simply, to ask, "who are we?" (1983, pp. 208, 212). Foucault observes that "there are two meanings of the word *subject*: subject of someone else by control and dependence, and tied to his own identity by a conscience or self-knowledge. Both meanings suggest a form of power which subjugates and makes subject to" (p. 212). As Sawicki explains, "power grips us at the point where our desires and our very sense of the possibilities for self-definition are constituted" (1991, p. 10). Our self-knowledge is a form of social control: what we come to know as our selves within a social context is experienced as our "chosen" identity.

Foucault's project ostensibly seems similar to that of the developmental psychologist. However, developmental theories that assume that all knowledge is constructed also assume that the child's construction of knowledge is politically neutral. Normative development of "the" child as subject is frequently considered as if development were outside of the socio-politico-cultural context in which a child develops. I am referring to universalist, context-free theories of cognitive development in the tradition of Piaget and Kohlberg. Foucault's analysis suggests that the relations of power that inhere in what the disciplines of human science value as knowledge will provide blueprints for directing a child's construction of reality. Development, then, can be considered as the process by which we become drenched in, and shaped by, culture-bound assumptions of power/knowledge. In order to consider the study of human development as a process of incorporating and being incorporated by power/knowledge, we need to explore humans as subjects and objects of the relations of power that inhere in our construction of knowledge. So, to take Foucault's statement that "the individual . . . is the product of a relation of power" (1980, p. 74) into psychological research means to ask if there is evidence that the course of an individual's development is a process by which power/knowledge is incorporated in our embodied being.

My interest is in the ways in which human beings incorporate knowledge relating to being male or female in our culture such that we fashion masculine and feminine identities. Within most cultures, including our own, individual and social identity are fundamentally shaped by conceptions of gender that are associated with the biological differences between male and female. While one could argue whether the dichotomous dimorphism that we typically attribute to gender is actually a natural category, the *understandings* that we hold about what is normatively male, and therefore masculine, and normatively female, and therefore feminine, are cultural elaborations of sex differences.

The categories *masculine* and *feminine* imply norms of behavior for each sex that are related to male and female identity within white or middle-class culture. Femininity and masculinity are the social and cultural attributes of gendered identity. The establishment of these norms hierarchically distinguishes types of behavior and categories of persons (i.e., "feminine" and "masculine") while, simultaneously, inciting the desire of subjects to be normal. Foucault explicates this "normalization" as an effect of power (1983, p. 208). The normative engages subjects in a willing subjugation to identities that typically maintain social control.

Gendered knowledge offers the individual subject "specific kinds of solutions to problems . . . [subjects] face" that allows the subject to discipline herself according to established power relations inherent in the knowledge itself (Sawicki, 1991, p. 85). This effect of power/knowledge is "disciplinary power" (p. 22). Disciplining practices—relating to dress, behavior, and so forth—that divide and classify the subject by gender are objectifying processes as well as subjectifying because they create out of subjective experience ways of seeing oneself as an object within social discourse. "In this process of social objectification and categorization, human beings are given both a social and a personal identity" (Rabinow, 1984, p. 8). Through "addressing real needs," the subject often willingly finds himself embodying modes of being and behaving that constrain and narrow human subjectivity even when "there may be better solutions; and there may be better ways of defining the problems" (ibid.). Knowledge of masculine and feminine standards of behavior—what is normal or socially desirable—helps children to construct identities that allow them to participate as male and female members of society. It solves a fundamental problem of human being, Who or what am I? How am I to be or to act? What does it mean to be the creature that I am?

"Gender" is a dichotomizing field of knowledge and power relations critical to creating an identity in this culture (Debold, 1994). How does this dichotomizing knowledge become incorporated into the human psyche or, in other words, attached to us as an identity? Foucault began his historical analyses through an investigation of times of resistance, outbreak, or struggle "using this resistance as a chemical catalyst so as to bring to light power relations" (1983, p. 211). From these times of struggle, he then explored what knowledge, embodying which relations of power, related to these historical moments. Thus, to analyze power and its effects on individual subjects, I need to

> a. locate times of *resistance:* Are there times in human development that can be identified as struggle or outbreak? If so, does this resistance relate to gender? What knowledge relating to gender is available to children at these times?

> b. identify *relations of power:* What do children learn about gender that divides them hierarchically from themselves and from others? What do they learn that gives permission to some to act on the actions of others?

> c. explore how *the exercise of power* happens: How is this dividing knowledge tied to identity? What problems does it solve? What threats are used to elicit obedience and conformity? What rewards are similarly offered?

> d. point to *forms of rationalization* and *institutionalization* for these gender differences: What and whose interests do they maintain and protect? What rationales are given for those norms? What institutions do these norms legitimize?

To begin this analysis of individual developmental history from a Foucauldian perspective, I first need to establish the larger historical context that has created the cultural norms in which children now develop and fashion identities. From this, I will explore what psychology understands of the psyche's sensitivity to distress and present Gilligan's theorizing about gender development. With this grounding, I take up the questions just raised to explore developmental gender differences as an effect of power.

Historical Developments

We develop as gendered beings along two axes of history—cultural history and the individual life span. The process of becoming a gendered

subject during the course of one's life span intersects with the historical creation of gendered subjectivity. Research in the various disciplines
of history (Foucault, 1970/1973; Laqueur, 1990), literary criticism (Armstrong, 1987) and philosophy (Bordo, 1987; Rorty, 1979) points to the
early modern period as engendering institutional systems of knowledge
and desire that continue to shape middle-class masculine and feminine
subjectivity. A close look at this point in history reveals how transformation of culture transforms subjectivity.

As diverse historical explorations show, the early modern period
marked a dramatic change in the organization of human life and human
identity. Descartes's private pursuit of reason through pure mental reflection helped to legitimate and create the private, psychological self understood since then as the basis of human subjectivity (Armstrong, 1987;
Bordo, 1987). Before the seventeenth century, writes Laqueur, "To be a
man or a woman was to hold a social rank, a place in society, to assume
a cultural role, not to *be* one or the other of two incommensurable sexes"
(1990, p. 8). To be a man or woman, then, was not to consider one's self to
be "masculine" or "feminine" or even a private psychological being, but to
be a member of a sociopolitical class. As the rise of the middle classes by
the mid-eighteenth century upset the historic social and moral order
based on genealogy, a new social and moral order was defined on the basis
of sex difference, thus engendering middle-class Western culture (Armstrong, 1987) and creating a "psychology" for each gender. The understanding of gender difference was intrinsic to the development of middle-
class life in which a boundary was created between the private life of home
and the public sphere of commerce and politics.

The creation of the middle class within a new capitalist economy
led to a fundamental problem, Who was available to marry these newly
prosperous men? This question needed to be answered out of individual
necessity—who am I?—and cultural imperative—how does the culture
continue? According to the rules of the old social order, middle-class men
did not have the status to marry noble women (see ibid.). This new middle-class male subject, like his noble predecessors, was defined by his
wealth, status, and role within the political economy. The first conduct
books were written in the seventeenth century to develop the manners
and styles of these men to enable them to engage in commerce with nobil-
ity. As more and more men became free to create their own place in the
world, rather than inherit it, new social rules arose that divided the world
outside of the home—once the site of most meaningful social and economic activity—from home life. Viewed increasingly as less morally high-
strung than women, men's lack of scruples became viewed as necessary
for them to survive and to have the possibility of thriving within a changing capitalist economy. This new division of the world entailed a loss for
men. As the domain of care and nurturance became exclusively feminine,
men lost close connection with the dailiness of family life, childrearing,

and education that were once part of the seamless fabric of their family and work lives. Men compensated for their loss of a working homeplace, a daily experience of ordinary connections, through an increasing idealization of a sanitized middle-class homelife ruled—in the man's absence— by a feminine vision of order and calm. While there is little doubt that men were dominant within premodern and early modern households (see Lloyd, 1984/1993), within the early modern home an ideal of living was made widely available in popular, cultural discourse which, increasingly over the decades, depended on women shaping their selves—emptying them out, actually—into a subjectivity that valorized as moral goodness a passive submission oppositional to masculine capitalist activity. Through this division, a mate for the middle-class man was created: the passive, nurturant middle-class feminine subject.

Middle-class hegemony intrinsically required a reconfiguring of women's desires to conform to a gendered ideal of feminine subjectivity that men came to desire. Laqueur (1990) observes that women's sexual desires, previously assumed to be similar to, if not greater than men's, were transformed into passivity and ignorance of sexual desire. This new passivity served to legitimate women's exclusion from public life on the grounds of their being too delicate, too refined for vulgar commerce. "Woman," the psychologically feminine subject, became increasingly privatized and idealized. In an extraordinary tension, women's domestic sphere of knowledge became the body—its feelings, appearance, comportment, acculturation, and nurturance—even as the desirable woman became disembodied through ideals of bodiless purity and domesticated goodness. By the Victorian era, women's psychological connection with the body, within a culture that deeply embraced splitting passive body from active reasoning mind, led science (and medicine) to question whether women should engage in intellectual activity (Russett, 1989) or were even capable of the activity of orgasm (Laqueur, 1990). "Woman," then, as a body of knowledge, became sanctioned—and desired by middle-class men and women alike—as the passive subjective, outside the realm of active, objective rationality.

The essentially feminine subject, outside authorized knowledge and political authority, was created by inciting women's desires for power and security. Armstrong observes that middle-class women (and those that aspired to middle-class life) actively embraced and created the proffered domestic sphere of influence and power separate from male authority in the workplace, academy, and government. Women's eagerness to claim this social space may be due to the fact that up until that time the home had been the locus of social and economic power. The creation of the private sphere also gave women security. With the anxiety raised by the dissolution of the genealogical order, the question of how women could obtain security and avoid victimization was increasingly answered through the achievement of this newly "natural" feminine subjectivity (ibid.). Through increased literacy, conduct books and the novel, a subjectivity was authorized that granted safety and security through a sexual and economic exchange of a woman's virtue for a man's economic security (ibid.). Throughout the early modern period, women were instructed to prove their true moral goodness by denying any motivation to marry for economic gain and thus, ignore, that is, not know, their economic vulnerability within a changing socioeconomic order (Grieco, 1993; Armstrong, 1987). While there had previously been an historical relationship between women and the material body (due both to childbirth and men's projections), this relationship was rewritten as oppositional to maleness and became a basis for aligning women's psyches and essential subjectivity with passivity and emotion (see Lloyd, 1984/1993). A woman's social worth—and, thus, what women desired and how they came to shape their selves—was no longer based on social class but, rather, on her embodiment of domestic virtues that balanced nascent capitalism's sordid political economy. Through multiple discourses in fiction, nonfiction, education, science, and medicine, women's economic anxieties were assuaged by inciting their desire through the promise of security paradoxically dependent on a feminine subjectivity dissociated from economic and political reality. Giving up identity as a member of a sociopolitical class, women came to know themselves *as women* by their ignorance of the political economy and by their desire to embody a domesticated goodness.

These historical analyses point to the real concerns that masculine and feminine identities addressed in the early modern era. In a rapidly changing political and social order, the world became divided by gender. For security and the power to influence, then—as now—the feminine subject we recognize was essentially depoliticized and subjected through authority over feeling and over the care of bodies, whereas the masculine subject was the rational public man and the capitalist worker, subjected through distance from nurturance and the family. These new types of people were not simply icons within an emerging popular culture, but the embodied aspirations of real people. Through the dissemination of this knowledge, and in the desire that was created, human minds and bodies became shaped differently than they had been. Human beings recognized themselves as masculine or as feminine, as "normal," based on their approximation to this desirable ideal.

Sensitive Bodies

Furthermore, as Dreyfus and Rabinow explain, a deep assumption within Foucault's work relates to the extraordinary sensitivity of the human psyche, the mind, and the body together. They argue that the only claim a Foucauldian interpretation can make for legitimacy rests in our sensitivity to distress and disorder, our sense of deep well-being or loss of that sense, that is, to "some concrete paradigm of health" (1983, p. 201). These Foucauldian analyses only make sense if we understand that the human mind/body is exquisitely sensitive and yet, even in its sensitivity, resists fragmentation and division through some deep sense of well-being and holistic vitality. Foucault specifically argues that we are such sensitive beings that it isn't the use of force, menacing threats, or overt seduction that coerce us into cultural molds. In fact, that's the least of it. Foucault argues that it is what we know or come to know within the culture surrounding us that irrevocably divides and shapes us. Power functions most effectively not through force but through the creation of knowledge that motivates us to reproduce intrapsychically the hierarchies that divide and classify our social and political world. What, then, does psychology know about the psyche's sensitivity to knowledge that has the power to divide ourselves? Even though psychology itself functions as a discipline of normalization by proposing theories to categorize and hierarchize human behaviors, bodies, and minds as "normal," it also offers ways of understanding the constraints and sensitivities of the material body and mind that can lead to a greater understanding of the forms and means of subjection that result in culturally appropriate forms of subjectivity.

From infancy, the sensitivity of our bodies grounds all subjective experience through direct experience and memories of bodily pleasure and pain. The development of psyche allows us to imagine, extrapolate, and anticipate increasingly abstract forms of pleasure and pain. Research with infants demonstrates that we come into the world open to, and prepared to, integrate and learn from sensory experience and subtle interaction with caretakers (Demos,1991; Stern, 1985). In fact, our first experience of relationship and human connection is sensory, bodily; the ground of relationship is the sensitive, preverbal body. Evidence indicates that the capacity for integration across different modes of experience—an aspect of our earliest knowledge—is both natural to the sentient body and critical for the most basic health of the human being (see Kagan, 1984).

From this integration of experience in mind and body, the development of knowing begins a process of division. Infants' experience of the power of language as a means of communication, their biological predisposition for language, and desire for pathways to connection, motivate them to learn to speak. As Stern explains, this process of learning to speak divides the infant from the world of direct experience in which he or she had lived.

> With [language's] emergence, infants become estranged from direct contact with their own personal experience. Language forces a space between interpersonal experience as lived and as represented. And it is exactly across this space that the

connections and associations that constitute neurotic behavior may form. (1989, p. 182)

While Stern notes that language also offers young children the possibility for new forms of intimacy through sharing aspects of experience
available for representation in language, the development of language—
a child's first incorporation of cultural discourse—begins to disembody
the psyche, leaving the subject divided from aspects of its subjectivity
and more vulnerable to distress.

Freud (1923) theorized that psychic development formed in close relation to neurological responses of the body; however, his model of psychic
development does not assume integration but division between the perception of reality (ego), desire (id) and, later, moral authority (superego).
These basic psychic divisions identified by Freud are an effect of
power/knowledge/desire through symbolic representation and language.
Freud noted that "the ego is first and foremost a bodily ego; it is not merely
a surface entity, but is itself the projection of the surface" (Stern, 1985, p.
16). However, as Stern concludes, the processes of projection are not available to the infant "but are conceivable only after the capacity for symbol-
ization as evidenced by language is emerging, when infancy ends" (p. 11).
In other words, while the subjective self is "first and foremost a bodily ego,"
the projection of that surface is knowledge, a symbolic extension of bodily
pleasures and vulnerabilities. Furthermore, Freud's (1923, 1924) observation of the development of the superego—a split-off aspect of the ego
that assumes the role of paternal authority—suggests that a primary function of the ego is basically defensive and divisive, adapting to *perceived*
dangers in social reality (see Gray, 1994).

The divisions within the psyche identified by Freud follow a pattern of psychic splitting evident in literature on trauma. "Traumatic
events," Judith Herman, "overwhelm the ordinary systems of care that
give people a sense of control, connection, and meaning" (1992, p. 33).
The effect of trauma on the body is to disrupt integration of human
response systems, to divide the mind and body. "The ordinary human
response to danger is a complex, integrated system of reactions, encom-
passing both body and mind," as Herman explains,

Traumatic reactions occur when action is of no avail. When neither resistance nor escape is possible, the human system of self-
defense becomes overwhelmed and disorganized. Each component of the ordinary response to danger, having lost its utility,
tends to persist in an altered and exaggerated state long after
the actual danger is over. Traumatic events produce profound
and lasting changes in physiological arousal, emotion, cognition,
and memory. Moreover, traumatic events may sever these normally integrated functions from one another. . . . Traumatic

symptoms have a tendency to become disconnected from their
source and to take on a life of their own. (p. 34)

Trauma is a fundamentally disintegrating and fragmenting experience.
Traumatic effects are a result of *fear* rather than an effect of physical harm
or brutality. Traumatic events often involve violence, brushes with death,
and threats against bodily integrity or life but also include any experience
of overwhelming fear and helplessness. However, threats to "bodily
integrity," because body roots the ego, also pertain to experiences that
threaten emotional connection or one's sense of subjectivity itself. In other
words, the psyche can experience as potentially traumatic persistent dangers to embodied connection or to the ego itself. So, children who witness
domestic violence or have even been in one acutely frightening situation
or live with continual fear of abandonment and disconnection may exhibit
a range of traumatic responses, from learned helplessness to full-blown
posttraumatic stress disorder (see Cole & Putnam, 1992; Putnam 1989;
Terr, 1990; Seligman, 1975). The effect of trauma on the psyche is change,
often permanent change, in mind and body. Knowledge, then, can be trau-
matizing, leading to actual changes in mind and body.

The sensitivities of our bodies—to connection and integration as
well as to threat and disintegration—provide a paradigm of health and
distress that does not define what is essentially masculine or feminine.
Integration and maintenance of integrity and one's integral intrapsy-
chic connections and connections with others, are fundamental to
human life and health. Human beings respond to danger, at this
moment in our history and evolution, through fragmentation and disintegration, and this leaves us vulnerable to distress and disease.
Power/knowledge, as Foucault has observed, divides a subject from herself by legitimating certain forms of subjectivity and subjugating others. These divisions—Freud's compromise formation—happen both
within historical time and during an individual's life course.

Forms of Resistance

Recognizing the profound sensitivity of the mind/body to power
through knowledge, Foucault (1983) also noted our capacity for resistance to the practices that divide us from ourselves. Gender, as was noted
before, is not only something biological but, as importantly, an enormous
body of knowledge and practices through which we come to know and
experience ourselves as different from others and from aspects of ourselves. Dividing practices give the subject ways of understanding herself
through knowledge that creates divisions—or dissociations—within herself and between herself and others (1980). Do children resist knowledge
that divides the social world and creates identity, such as gender? Just
as Foucault identified points in human history when power/knowledge

created discontinuities in human experience of subjectivity, are there similar transitional points in the human life cycle that point to gender difference in development?

A look at the development of psychopathology reveals an asymmetry in distress in children of different gender. Developmental psychopathology attempts to understand what experiences and behaviors of children are linked to serious psychological trouble later in life. "Significant changes in symptomatology of boys and girls occur during adolescence," write Schonert-Reichl and Offer. "That is, prior to the onset of adolescence, girls are mentally healthier than boys, whereas, after adolescence, this state of affairs is reversed" (1992, p. 28). Boys in early childhood more frequently show signs of psychological distress and behavioral problems (Achenbach, 1982; Offord et al., 1987) most obviously in the form of conduct disorders (Baum, 1989; Martin & Hoffman, 1990; Rutter & Garmezy, 1983). Young boys, known generally to lag behind girls in language development, also stutter more (Yairi & Ambrose, 1992). As several researchers have noted, young boys display "greater vulnerability . . . to family stress and discord" than do young girls (p. 824; Earls & Jung, 1987; Elder & Caspi, 1990). In adolescence, however, while boys continue to exhibit more conduct disorders and delinquency than girls do, the pattern of psychological distress reverses as girls begin to exhibit "more internalizing symptoms" such as anxiety and depression (Schonert-Reichl & Offer, 1992; Allgood-Merton, Lewinsohn, & Hops, 1990; Harris, Blum, & Resnick 1991; Petersen, Sarigiani, & Kennedy, 1991; Whitaker et al., 1990). Girls report making more suicide attempts and being under more severe stress than boys (Minnesota Women's Fund, 1990; see also AAUW, 1991; Gore & Colten, 1991). Anorexia nervosa and bulimia, appearing in adolescence, are predominantly a female phenomenon (Rodin, Silberstein, & Striegel-Moore, 1985; Steiner-Adair, 1986).

Similarly gendered differences are apparent in physical health. Boys in early childhood suffer more from asthma and allergies than girls do (Gold et al., 1993; Luyt, Burton & Simpson, 1993; Tse et al., 1993; Tuuponen, Keistinen, & Kivela, 1993). While the leading causes of death for both women and men are cardiovascular disease and cancer, women generally live longer than men (see, e.g., Society for the Advancement of Women's Health Research, 1991). However, for many women, their longer lives are spent in pain and illness (Pinn, 1994). Women suffer from chronic pain and from chronic illnesses and syndromes far more than men do. Women also suffer from more somatic complaints, such as headaches and stomachaches. Autoimmune diseases and syndromes (with the current exception of AIDS), such as lupus, rheumatoid arthritis, thyroid disease, multiple sclerosis, and chronic fatigue syndrome, are far more prevalent in women than in men (ibid.). Many of these diseases and syndromes that particularly affect women have been referred to as "stress" illnesses, suggesting a body-mind interaction between the social context of women's lives and psychophysical distress, harkening back to Freud's work to bring the knowledge of hysterics' bodies to the conscious awareness of their minds. The patterns of difference in mental distress and physical disease both suggest greater vulnerability for young boys and for adolescent girls and women.

Early childhood and early adolescence have been described and rationalized in various ways by psychologists. They have been pointed to as times of transition. Freud (1900, 1912, 1923) observed that early childhood marked a traumatic transition in boys' lives that was essential for a boy to achieve proper manhood. More recently, cognitive psychologists have noted that early childhood is the time when children create and use basic categories for organizing their experience—categories like gender (Huston, 1983). While clinical psychologists have spent less time exploring adolescence than they have early childhood, cognitive developmentalists, beginning with Piaget (1932, 1967), have explored adolescence as a time of remarkable cognitive change. More obviously, adolescence is a time of rapid physiological changes caused by the onset of puberty that leads to the transition from being a child to becoming an adult.

What might these differences in the effect of these transitions have to do with gender? Gilligan (1990, 1991a, 1991b, 1996) has suggested that the differences in psychological distress for boys in early childhood and girls at early adolescence are the sequelae of a failed "resistance" or struggle relating to expectations and experiences of gender. Reframing Freud's work on early childhood, Gilligan presents a working theory in which she argues that early adolescence is a time of crisis in girls' lives that is equivalent to the Oedipal complex in early childhood for boys. Gilligan observes that psychological distress is a sign of loss of connection to one's self, others and one's experience of reality; distress signals a crisis of relationship. Rupture in relationship has an effect on our bodies because the first, and oldest, sense of self is body-in-relationship. In early childhood, Gilligan argues, "young boys come under pressure from without and within to give up close relationship and to cover their vulnerability—to separate their inner world, their self, from the outer world of relationships" (1996, p. 251). Gilligan views this as boys' initiation into patriarchy and, so, as critical for the maintenance of cultural power structures. Girls at early adolescence undergo a similar initiation: girls learn that they have to disconnect from themselves, from what they know and from the world of women to enter the world of patriarchal heterosexuality (see, e.g., Brown & Gilligan, 1992; Debold, Wilson, & Malavé, 1993; Gilligan, 1990, 1991a, 1991b, 1996).

Gilligan argues further that the asymmetrical crises in boys' and girls' lives are preceded by a *healthy resistance* to loss created out of, and in response to, their knowledge of what is socially acceptable for males and females. In other words, to be loved or to be acceptable, children learn to give up the full range of their thoughts, feelings, and experience to conform to societal expectations of "boy" or "girl" behavior. According to Gilligan, for many boys and girls, their healthy resistance to loss is overwhelmed by a social reality that forces children into a compromise between themselves and continued positive relationships with parents and peers. Gilligan observes the psychological effect of the knowledge that brings children into a relationship with cultural norms: failed resistance results in psychological loss. The resultant compromises , she argues, because it is made at great cost, jeopardizes boys' and girls' psychological resiliency and mental health at these particular times in development.

Gilligan (1990) names this unconscious compromise *psychological resistance,* invoking the more traditional definition of resistance as a motivated not knowing or repression of a previously experienced conflict (see, e.g., Freud, 1933). This psychological resistance is a form of dissociation of what has been known and experienced from what feels permissible to know and feel. This dissociated knowledge often "speaks" in the language of psychological distress—antisocial behavior, eating disorders, depression and so forth. Gilligan argues that "psychologists have marked as progress in charting human development" these "disjunctions or disconnections" in childhood and adolescence (1991b, p. 20, emphasis added). In other words, these dissociations and resultant psychological losses have been normalized as "progress."

Gilligan's identification of these two times in development as points of initiation to culture resonates with Freud's theory on the development of masculine and feminine personality, that is, the sanctioned forms of middle-class subjectivity. Freud (1905, 1923, 1924, 1931, 1933) viewed boys' Oedipal initiation as critical to the development of the masculine personality, and, although his understanding of the development of the feminine personality was murkier, he theorized that early childhood and adolescence were critical times for the development of femininity. Yet, what Freud accepted as normative and, therefore, natural, Gilligan calls into question. She observes that children experience loss and suffering as they make these accommodations with cultural gender expectations.

Gilligan's observation of the transformation of a healthy resistance to loss and disconnection into a psychological resistance to knowing what one knew and was resisting exemplifies, in the individual psyche, what Foucault observed in history. These times of resistance are times of distress when the individual struggles to resist being caught in the web of power/knowledge in order to stay psychically whole. The norms for masculinity and femininity present ways for children to divide their selves into gendered identities. The symptoms of distress seen in children are, ironically but not accidentally, an exaggeration of precisely what is culturally identified as appropriate gendered behavior. Boys

with conduct disorders are aggressive, physically active, and often violent—hypermasculine. Girls who exhibit any of the common forms of
"internalizing symptoms" are typically emotional, excessively concerned
with appearances, and withdrawn—the epitome of feminine passivity.

If these two points in human development generally result in our
taking up historically validated forms of gendered subjectivity, then
what power/knowledge are these forms of subjectivity an effect of? What
knowledge do boys and girls have that divides them from themselves
or, as Sawicki suggests, offers "specific kinds of solutions to problems
they face" (1991, p. 85)? How might this knowledge have an effect on
our bodies such that masculinity and femininity are inscribed into our
being, thereby (en)gendering difference? More simply, why do boys and
girls suffer at different times and evidence different symptoms?

Categorical Imperatives

To determine whether boys' distress in early childhood is resistance to incorporating power relations, we have to ask what knowledge
relating to gender is available at this point in development. Empirical
research in the United States on the development of gender identity
points to early childhood as a time when basic categorical knowledge of
gender as a binary category becomes cognitively available to children.
Gender is one of the first social categories that children learn (Kagan,
1984; Kohlberg, 1966; Maccoby, 1988). While there is some evidence that
children may have implicit, experiential knowledge that this aspect of
identity is rooted in their bodies and stays the same throughout life
(Bem, 1989), intellectually they do not have this information (Emmerich,
et.al., 1977; Leinbach & Fagot 1986; Levy & Carter, 1989; McConaghy,
1979; Martin & Halverson, 1983; Miller, 1984; Slaby & Frey, 1975;
Wehren & DeLisi, 1983). Children are labeled *girl* and *boy* from birth,
but what the categorical distinction is based on is not clear to them.
Young children are faced with the problem of finding out what these
labels mean and what it means for them to "do" "boy" or "girl" correctly
(see Kagan, 1984; Kohlberg, 1966). Between the ages of two and three,
as children's linguistic abilities unfold, they are typically able to accurately identify themselves and classify others with the terms *girl* or *boy*
(Carey, 1985; Harter, 1983; Maccoby, 1988). At the same time, children
figure out that the terms *boy* and *girl* are category labels rather than
someone's name (Maccoby, 1988; see also Carey, 1985; Leinbach &
Fagot, 1986; Kohlberg, 1966; Harter, 1983; Huston, 1983).

Children create and incorporate knowledge of gender as one of the
early acts of categorical process. They understand that this knowledge
relates to their identity and so it incites desire to be *girl* or *boy,* thereby
dividing children from aspects of themselves. It solves a problem of identity created by the social world where labeling by gender ("Is it a boy or

a girl?") is so essential. The fact that these terms denote a *category* brings into play the power of the category to shape children's thinking. Understanding that something belongs to a category indicates to young children that there are hidden similarities among category members— the category label has particular demand characteristics (Gelman, Collman, & Maccoby, 1986). Knowing that one is a girl means that one must share girl-ness with others. As these three researchers note, "Preschool children realize that gender categories go beyond outward perceptual appearances and capture deep similarities. Children recognize that gender is a very special predictor, more important than any single attribute (such as playing with trucks)" (p. 403).

The binary character of the gender category and its intimate connection to identity exert power on children by dividing them from themselves. Young children are not analytic and therefore make global judgments about how something relates to themselves. Like the category of gender itself, their discriminations are also binary: "me" or "not me" (see Harter, 1983; Maccoby, 1988). Kagan (1984) asserts that as children create categories, they are predisposed to invent an opposite. It is likely that children infer that "boy" and "girl" are opposites and oppositional. The category of gender becomes a large part of who and what they think they are. As Maccoby notes, "group membership on the basis of the binary coding of gender identity is the most powerful of all" (1988, p. 763). And the categories that they place themselves in hold a moral standard that dictates their behavior (Carey, 1985; Kagan, 1984; Kohlberg, 1966; Huston, 1983). The inference that maintaining one's "girl-ness" or "boy-ness" is, in fact, a moral issue is evidence of the power of the category to shape identity. That the categorical imperative, so to speak, of this imposed moral standard is perceived within young children's binary intellectual processing as both binary *and oppositional* divides children from themselves and from each other.

Could knowledge of the binary category of gender, with its far-reaching associations along the hierarchical dimensions of masculinity and femininity, create resistance and distress in boys? In learning that their identity must be engendered, boys use the binary category of gender to determine the essence of their identity to be *not* female, therefore *not* mother and not nurturant or emotionally close. Boys seem to resist this knowledge at first—maintaining ignorance about physical differences (despite the fact that they are typically intimate with an adult woman caretaker) and playing longer in gender-integrated groups (Bem, 1989; Maccoby, 1988). The power of gender as a binary category creates a split internally in boys between their prior lived experience—their embodied connection with their mother—and the categorical imperative to assume a male identity (as well as an external split in terms of sex-segregated affiliation). The flowering of imagination due to the semiotic function and holistic and binary intellectual processing set the stage for gender differences to be perceived as threatening to their fundamental sense of self as male and, thus, as internally and socially divisive. Through their desire to "do" maleness in the right way, the knowledge of gender as binary exercises power on boys by tying them to an identity that divides them from aspects of their experience.

This power/knowledge—that gender is an oppositional category of identity—affects boys at the level of their bodies: boys respond to the loss of embodied connection to their mothers with distress. Boys' limited cognitive capacities as concrete operational knowers lead them to divide themselves from aspects of themselves that have been connected to mother or the female—thereby cutting off an embodied connection that has been essential to their survival. Boys express their pain and confusion at this traumatic disconnection through the primitive forms of resistance that are available to them at this concrete operational level, that is, primarily through rage and physicality. Boys are compelled, through their understanding of these binary differences as an essential, concrete reality related to their identity, to maintain separation from things feminine on all levels of human experience. In other words, the constraints imposed by boys' early childhood concrete thinking subject them to psychic divisions that define how they think about themselves, relationships, and social reality as separate from mothers, girls, and the feminine symbolic. Their personalities are built on this divided ground (see Levy & Carter, 1989; Hort, Leinbach, & Fagot, 1991).

Freud (1905, 1924, 1931) argued that this transition from mother connection to identification with father was indeed the basis of the heterosexual masculine personality as well as a foundation of morality. Freud's (1924) hypothesized Oedipal fear of castration can be seen as a symbolic enactment of a boy's fear of losing pleasure and connection to his mother. The resolution of the Oedipal complex through the creation of the superego is an internal division created in response to this trauma. The superego psychically incorporates boys' limited understanding that their gender identity, their core subjectivity, is defined as not-girl, not-mother, not-female. The superego, the internalized father, is a split-off aspect of the mind that serves to stand guard within the psyche to protect the boy from crossing the boundary of masculine identity.

What we recognize today as masculinity, a stance of independence, aggression, and autonomy, is the psychological response of young boys to finding their lived experience of intimacy and vulnerability excluded from their core gender identity. Boys, learning that their essence as "boy" places them in opposition to "girl," nurturance and closeness, respond bodily to the experience of loss that comes from effecting a painful inner separation; the way in which boys respond are what the culture names and what boys come to learn as appropriately masculine behavior. Boys are met by a cultural world of superheroes, masculine gun play, and male-defined public spheres. In this resonance of their core dilemmas

(Who am I? What do I do with my feelings of vulnerability and insecurity?) with the larger cultural surround, boys are rewarded for making this inner division. The power relation of active masculinity over passive femininity seen so clearly in the culture mirrors an internal hierarchy in boys' psyches through which they create and maintain socially defined male identities. Masculinity—an early childhood response to loss of embodied connection—grounds both the subtle and blatant forms of domination that are male privilege as well as laying the foundation for forms of knowledge and rationality that were, historically, driven by a flight from the feminine (see Bordo, 1987).

Images of Abstraction

Girls do not need to divide from their experience of nurturant connection when they learn the binary category labels *boy* and *girl* in early childhood because they find themselves in the same category of person as their mothers (see Chodorow, 1978; Gilligan, 1982). The power of the category similarly affects girls' desire to relate in same-sex groups and to imitate and seek out what is appropriately "girl" (Huston, 1983; Maccoby, 1988). From early childhood, girls tend to resolve problems in their social worlds by negotiation through talk rather than aggression or an emphasis on dominance hierarchies (Maccoby, 1988), and this often makes them appear more psychologically insightful about themselves and others than boys. Girls increasingly become responsible for maintaining relationships—and experience power in the effect they can have in this intimate domain. This is not to say that the recognition that there are biologically two genders has no impact on girls but that, in general, this knowledge has less power to effect an internal division between what girls "should" be and their lived experience.

However, girls, particularly middle-class girls, appear to struggle and show distress in adolescence. Adolescent girls' distress is evident in the greater frequency of depression, stress, body image distortion, eating disorders, and suicidality (Harris, Blum, & Resnick, 1991; Minnesota Women's Fund, 1990; Nolen-Hoeksema & Girgus, 1994). Gilligan (1990) identified girls' struggle with relationships and their inability to bring what they know into relationships for fear of disconnection. Brown (1991) found the ghost image of a "Perfect Girl" to which middle-class girls compared themselves and by which they were internally silenced. Others have noted girls' narrowing of perspective to focus on their appearance (AAUW, 1991; Minnesota Women's Fund, 1990) and adoption of cultural ideals of beauty as their internal standards (see Tolman & Debold, 1994). So it makes sense to ask what knowledge relating to gender, to being a girl or woman in this culture, is available to girls in adolescence?

The timing of girls' distress in adolescence coincides with the development of the cognitive capacity for abstraction, for formal operational thinking. While the term *formal operations* and the Piagetian stages have been reconsidered, the basic content of Piaget's observations about the development of abstract thinking are still relevant (Byrnes, 1988; Keating, 1980, 1988; Sternberg & Powell, 1983). In adolescence, children become more capable of systematic thinking both by using more available information and by creating increasingly appropriate solution schemes (ibid.). Through these abstract capabilities, the mind has the power to create and to grasp systems of differentiations that divide and discipline social and intellectual life. The power of abstraction leads adolescents into a new understanding of their culture through a new recognition of ideals, identities and their "selves" (see Damon & Hart, 1982). By adolescence, children are more aware of psychological process and agency and are prone to reflect on the selves they observe themselves becoming (Broughton, 1978; Damon & Hart, 1982; Hatcher et al., 1990). This "self" becomes visible to an "imaginary audience" that is often so present in an adolescent's mind that thoughts of one's own and those imputed to others can be confused (Harter, 1983, p. 315, quoting Elkind, 1967). The future or the past, more than the present, become objects of thought (Inhelder & Piaget, 1958; Keating, 1980). Whereas children in grade school increasingly become aware of social standards, for instance, "goodness," that they measure themselves by—resulting in complex feelings about themselves (Case et al., 1988), formal thought allows adolescents to create a stable construct of self that becomes an object of thought that can then be compared to the ideals and standards that they also abstract from the social surround (Inhelder, & Piaget 1958; Kegan, 1982).

In adolescence, young people begin to understand the interrelationship of those standards in creating a social system, as well as defining ideals and theories of their own. As the fabric of lived experience becomes increasingly open for reflection and abstraction, what was inarticulately known and felt—one's place in the world and one's individuality—become uncertain and this creates new needs "to commune with something larger . . . [to] express . . . his own uniqueness" (Josselson, 1980, p. 205). These intellectual abilities give adolescents the power to "construct theories and make use of the ideologies that surround them" (Inhelder & Piaget, 1958, p. 336). Adolescents wax philosophical: "Topics of identity, society, existence, religion, justice, morality, friendship, and so on, are examined in detail. . . ." (Keating, 1980, p. 215). Yet, the "discovery" of ideals, of identity and even of philosophy happens within a particular cultural context. Ideals, identity, and philosophy all become a reality through the power of formal thinking to act upon experience and knowledge within a particular culture. This new power of mind exerts pressure on adolescents' understandings of themselves and their experience (see Piaget, 1967). As adolescents are able to understand what ideals the culture values, comparing their "self" with the knowledge of what is valued divides them from their lived experience in new ways.

Abstract thinking—with its power to give the mind full range into the future, the hypothetical, the systemic and the ideal—allows girls to apprehend their relation to cultural power relations and this, in turn, has a profound effect on girls' psyches. The persistent and pervasive images of violence against women and sexual objectification of women in the media give girls a wider range of vicarious experience, in addition to home and school, from which they develop abstract concepts of the adult social world (see Gordon & Riger, 1993; Huston, 1983). Girls find themselves living in frightening territory—their developing bodies (Debold, Tolman, & Brown, 1996; Debold, Wilson, & Malavé, 1993; Tolman & Debold, 1994). Moreover, as Gilligan (1990, 1991, 1996) has observed, girls experience a loss of connection with their feelings and relationships at adolescence.

Thus, as increasing experience allows for self-reorganization and formal thinking, "normal" girls come to understand frightening "power/knowledge" about being embodied as young women. Adolescent girls come into a culture that sexualizes girls and women and in which women and girls compete for male attention and protection. Not only are they not safe within their bodies but they aren't safe with other girls and women either. The power of this knowledge is exercised through the effect of this anxiety and fear on girls' psyches through an internal division, a psychic splitting. Jack (1991) (see also Heatherton & Baumeister, 1991) distinguishes between the Freudian superego and a similar split-off function that she has discerned in her work with depressed women. She named this vigilant, protective system of defense the "Over-Eye." The "Over-Eye" watches over a woman for violations of a rigid and implicit code of goodness and self-sacrifice. It sees the woman through a patriarchal male gaze that is more relentless and dominating than any individual man's gaze. Whether such splitting and dissociation become psychologically dangerous would depend on the degree of conflict around sexuality and experiences with male domination in each particular girl's life. Yet, any splitting increases vulnerability to distress and to a lessening of resilience.

Such a psychic structure is comparable to, but different from, the "superego" hypothesized by Freud because the split occurs at a different developmental time. This Over-Eye can take the self as an object for scrutiny that suggests its "birth" to be at adolescence, the time when such cognitive reflection is first possible. Likewise, boys' dichotomizing of gender—and its sequelae of rigid separation from things feminine—are the result of their more limited cognitive capacity in early childhood. In other words, girls' and boys' symptoms of distress are a direct result of their cognitive capacity at the time when their ability to know led them to knowledge that psychologically frightened and overwhelmed them, necessitating an internal division. Girls' observed anxiety, obsession with appearance, distortions in body image, fears of conflict, and passivity make psychological sense without an appeal to biology or "nature."

Girls on the edge of adolescence take in "power/knowledge" of gendered dominance relations and in doing so they realize their vulnerability within their bodies. Just as boys' early childhood response to the trauma of separation *is* what the culture understands as masculine personality, girls' early adolescent response to the trauma of domination often results in a withdrawal from their bodies' power and sexuality as a means of securing protection. This protective withdrawal is what the culture understands and rewards as feminine personality. Middle-class girls typically assume that they are rewarded through protection for being subjected in this way. For girls, knowledge of gendered power relations creates the realization that they inhabit a dangerous space—their female bodies—from which they must effect a complicated internal division.

In a sense, middle-class girls become abstractions, attempting to embody the image of perfect girl femininity (Tolman & Debold, 1994). Looking to the future, girls' aspirations, like their psyches, tend to narrow, which is not surprising given men's greater economic and political power as well as the masculine rules for success in work (AAUW, 1991; Richards & Larson, 1989). The power of abstraction allows girls to fantasize about perfect relationships and, protectively, to ignore the games of dominance that shade gender dynamics (see Inhelder & Piaget, 1958). Realizing the hierarchical duality that grants power to masculine dominance, girls may choose to adopt those values themselves or to withdraw into apparent passivity (and "femininity") to find a male protector. Either way, girls divide from some aspect of themselves—either their complex experience of being in a female body or their agency and autonomy. Girls from educationally privileged environments may logically find themselves in the double bind noted by Bordo (1993) and Steiner-Adair (1986) in their discussion of eating disorders: to be successful, these girls realize that they must effect a division within themselves to create a public, "masculine" self that can compete within male spheres. The power of abstraction allows adolescent girls to abstract themselves from the experiential reality of being female in a culture where women and the "feminine" are subordinated. Girls end up creating identities that subject themselves through an incorporation of the hierarchical divisions of gender.

Conclusion

Sawicki explains that for Foucault "ways of knowing are equated with ways of exercising power over individuals" (1991, p. 22). Questions of knowledge are also questions of subjectivity and subjection: what we can know defines who we are. Questions about who we are—about our nature, our bodies—are also questions of knowledge: the psyche is a palimpsest of culture. The sensitivities of our bodies to the pain of emotional separation and violation creates different masculine and feminine subjects because we are subjected to overwhelming knowledge about ourselves in this culture at different developmental times. Men's and women's shared sensitivity is a profound source of our differences.

If we read the history of the development of modern gendered culture along with the "history" of psychopathology, both the timing and cost of becoming subjected as masculine or feminine subjects differ. Women's passive subjectivity flows from a discontinuity in historical and developmental time upon which the success of middle-class culture rests. For girls, the transition into adolescence, marking the entrance to womanhood, appears to be abruptly problematic for women's embodied minds. The transition into manhood at adolescence and the taking up of patriarchal public roles appears to be less a source of stress and distress for boys than is early childhood. Boys' distress in early childhood—in the lap of mother, family, and home—echoes the history of men's loss of an integrated home and work life that resulted in the historical idealization of women and home life.

Culture is reproduced by and through each of us as we incorporate knowledge that divides us from our experience but brings us into relation with our social world. The effect of this knowledge on the human psyche is an effect of power: we find ourselves divided, subjected, and, ironically, normal. We become cultural subjects. It is no accident that both Keating (1980) and Broughton (1983) observe that adolescents in the United States appear Cartesian. The sharp division between mind and body that led from Descartes's philosophical meditations subjects us even now. The very shape and form that knowledge takes is cultivated. Our cultural compulsion to create knowledge by categorizing and dividing ends up dividing us from each other and from ourselves.

Power, and the effect of power/knowledge, are ubiquitous. We have no choice but to know that which we grow into, even as we may have some range of options in how we respond. Foucault's hope was to explore historical moments of resistance and thus create "an insurrection of subjugated knowledges"—knowledge not in authorized discourse through which we can understand—and resist further—how it is that we have been subjected as "normal" subjects (1980, p. 81). By revealing the effect of power/knowledge on the creation of gendered subjects, my hope similarly is to reveal the myth of unalloyed progress inherent in developmental theory and to create further possibilities for resistance. We needn't confuse the normalized with the natural.

Once we realize that what we have considered to be natural is simply the normalized, we can be freed from the false ways in which gender has been used to separate us from each other—even as gender constitutes a painful internal division of ourselves from ourselves. To recognize the human in each other means to see that the differences between us are the result of our shared humanity. In this, we are simply and deeply exquisitely sensitive human beings, male and female.

References

Achenbach, T. M. (1982). *Developmental psychopathology*. New York: Wiley.

Allgood-Merton, B., Lewinsohn, P., & Hops, H. (1990). Sex differences and adolescent depression. *Journal of Abnormal Psychology, 99*, 55-63.

American Association of University Women (AAUW) (1991). *Short-changing girls, shortchanging America: A nationwide poll to assess self-esteem, educational experiences, interest in math and science, and career aspirations of girls and boys ages 9-15*. Washington, DC: Author.

Armstrong, N. (1987). *Desire and domestic fiction: A political history of the novel*. New York: Oxford University Press.

Baennenger, M., & Newcombe, N. (1989). The role of experience in spatial test performance: A meta-analysis. *Sex Roles, 20*, 327–343.

Bakhtin, M. (1981). The dialogic imagination. M. Holquist (Ed.) (C. Emerson & M. Holquist, Trans.). Austin: University of Texas Press.

Baum, C. (1989). Conduct disorders. In T. H. Ollendick & M. Herses (Eds.), *Handbook of child psychopathology*. New York: Plenum.

Belenky, M., Clinchy, B., Goldberger, N., & Tarule, J. (1986). *Women's ways of knowing*. New York: Basic.

Bem, S. L. (1989). Genital knowledge and gender constancy in pre-school children. *Child Development, 60*, 521–538.

Bordo, S. (1987). *The flight to objectivity*. Albany: State University of New York Press.

Bordo, S. (1993). *Unbearable weight: Feminism, body, and Western culture*. Berkeley: University of California Press.

Broughton, J. (1978). Development of concepts of self, mind, reality, and knowledge. *New Directions for Child Development, 1*, 75-101.

Broughton, J. (1983). The cognitive developmental theory of adolescent self and identity. In B. Lee & G. Noam (Eds.), *Developmental approaches to the self*. New York: Plenum.

Brown, L. (1991). Telling a girl's life: Self-authorization as a form of resistance. *Women & Therapy, 11*(3-4), 71-86.

Brown, L. (1992, June). Voice and ventriloquism: Girls' development in relational context. In L. Brown (chair), *Voicing relationships, knowing connection: Exploring girls' and women's development*.

Symposium conducted at the 22nd Annual meeting of the Jean Piaget Society, Canada.

Brown, L. & Gilligan, C. (1992). *Meeting at the crossroads: Women's psychology and girls' development.* Cambridge: Harvard University Press.

Byrnes, J. P. (1988). Formal operations: A systematic reformulation. *Developmental Review, 8,* 66-87.

Carey, S. (1985). *Conceptual change in childhood.* Cambridge: Massachusetts Institute of Technology/Bradford Press.

Case, R., Hayward, S., Lewis, M., & Hurst, P. (1988). Toward a neo-Piagetian theory of cognitive and emotional development. *Developmental Review, 8,* 1-51.

Chodorow, N. (1978). *The reproduction of mothering.* Berkeley: University of California Press.

Cole, P., & Putnam, F. (1992). Effects of incest on self and social functioning: A developmental psychopathology perspective. *Journal of Consulting and Clinical Psychology, 60(2),* 174-184.

Damon, W., & Hart, D. (1982). The development of self-understanding from infancy through adolescence. *Child Development, 53,* 841-864.

Damon, W., & Hart, D. (1988). *Self-understanding in childhood and adolescence.* New York: Cambridge University Press.

Debold, E. (1994). *Toward an understanding of gender differences in psychological distress: A Foucauldian integration of Freud, Gilligan and cognitive development theory.* Qualifying paper. Harvard Graduate School of Education.

Debold, E., Tolman, D., & Brown, L. M. (1996). Embodying knowledge, knowing desire: Authority and split subjectivities in girls' epistemological development. In N Goldberger, J. Tarule, B. Clinchy, & M. Belenky (Eds.), *Knowledge, difference, and power: Essays inspired by Women's Ways of Knowing.* New York: Basic Books.

Debold, E., Wilson, M., & Malavé, I. (1993). *Mother daughter revolution: From good girls to great women.* New York: Bantam Books.

Demos, E. V. (1991). The early organization of the psyche. In J. W. Barren, M. N. Eagle, & D. L. Wolitsky (Eds.), *Psychoanalysis and psychology.* Washington, DC: APA Centennial.

Dreyfus, H., & Rabinow, P. (1983). *Michel Foucault: Beyond structuralism and hermeneutics.* Chicago: University of Chicago Press (2nd edition).

Earls, L., & Jung, K. (1987). Temperment and home-environment characteristics as causal factors in the early development of childhood psychpathology. *Journal of the American Academy of Child Psychiatry, 26,* 491-498.

Elder, G. & Caspi, A. (1990). Studying lives in a changing society: Sociological and personological explorations. In A. Rabin, R. Zucker, R. Emmons, & S. Frank (Eds.), *Studying persons and lives* (pp. 226-228). New York: Springer.

Elkind, D. (1967). Egocentrism in adolescence. *Child development, 38,* 1025-1034.

Emmerich, W., Goldman, K., Kirsh, B., & Sharabany, R. (1977). Evidence for a transitional phase in the development of gender constancy. *Child Development, 48,* 930-936.

Ehrenreich, B., & English, D. (1978). *For her own good: 150 years of the experts' advice to women.* New York: Anchor/Doubleday.

Fischer, K. (1980). A theory of cognitive development: The control and construction of hierarchies of skills. *Psychological Review, 87,* 477-531.

Foucault, M. (1970/1973). *The order of things: An archaelogy of the human sciences.* New York: Vintage.

Foucault, M. (1979). *Discipline & punish.* (A. Sheridan, Trans.). New York: Vintage.

Foucault, M. (1980). *Power/knowledge: Selected interviews and other writings, 1972-1977.* C. Gordon (Ed.). New York: Pantheon.

Foucault, M. (1983). Afterword: The subject and power. In H. Dreyfus & P. Rabinow, *Michel Foucault: Beyond structuralism and hermeneutics* (pp. 208-226). Chicago. University of Chicago Press (2nd edition).

Foucault, M. (1986). *The care of the self. Vol. 3* of The history of sexuality. (R. Hurley, Trans.). New York: Vintage.

Freud, S. (1900). *The interpretation of dreams.* (J. Strachey, Trans.). New York: Avon.

Freud, S. (1905). *Three essays on the theory of sexuality.* (J. Strachey, Trans.). New York: Basic.

Freud, S. (1912). *Totem and taboo.* (A. A. Brill, Trans.). New York: Vintage.

Freud, S. (1923). The ego and the id. (J. Strachey (Ed.) (J. Riviere, Trans.). New York: Norton.

Freud, S. (1924). The passing of the Oedipus-complex. In S. Freud, *Sexuality and the psychology of love* (pp. 176-182). (J. Riviere, Trans.). New York: Collier.

Freud, S. (1925). Some psychological consequences of the anatomical distinction between the sexes. In S. Freud, *Sexuality and the psychology of love* (pp. 183-193). (J. Riviere, Trans.). New York: Collier.

Freud, S. (1931). Female sexuality. In S. Freud, *Sexuality and the psychology of love* (pp. 194-211). (J. Riviere, Trans.). New York: Collier.

Freud, S. (1933). Femininity. In *New introductory lectures on psycho-analysis* (pp. 139-167). (J. Strachey, Trans.). New York: Norton.

Gelman, S., Collman, P., & Maccoby, E. (1986). Inferring properties from categories versus inferring categories from properties: The case of gender. *Child Development, 57,* 396-404.

Gilligan, C. (1982). *In a different voice: Psychological theory and women's development.* Cambridge: Harvard University Press.

Gilligan, C. (1990). Joining the resistance: Psychology, politics, girls and women. *Michigan Quarterly Review, 29* (4), 501-536.

Gilligan, C. (1991a). Women's psychological development: Implications for psychotherapy. *Women & Therapy, 11* (3-4), 5-31.

Gilligan, C. (1991b, Aug.). Revision. Invited address presented to the American Psychological Association Annual Conference, San Francisco.

Gilligan, C. (1996). The centrality of relationship in human development: A puzzle, some evidence, and a theory. In G. Noam, & K. Fischer (Eds.), *Development and vulnerability in close relationships.* Mahwah, NJ: Erlbaum.

Gilligan, C., Lyons, N., & Hamner, T. (Eds.). (1988). *Making connections: The relational worlds of adolescent girls at the Emma-Willard School.* Cambridge: Harvard University Press.

Gold, D., Rotnitsky, A., Damokosh, A., Ware, J., Speizer F., Ferris B. G. Jr., & Dockery. D. (1993). Race and gender differences in respiratory illness prevalence and their relationship to environmental exposures in children 7 to 14 years of age. *American Review of Respiratory Disease, 148,* 10-18.

Golombok, S. & Fivush R. (1994). *Gender development.* New York: Cambridge University Press.

Gordon, M., & Riger, S. (1989). *The female fear: The social cost of rape.* Urbana: University of Illinois Press.

Gore, S., & Colten, M. E. (1991). Gender, stress, and distress: Social-relational issues. In J. Eckenrode (Ed.), *The social context of coping.* New York: Plenum.

Gray, P. (1994). *The ego and analysis of defense*. Northvale, NJ: Aronson.

Grieco, S. F. M. (1993). The body, appearance, and sexuality. In G. Duby & M. Perrot (General eds.), N. Zemon & A. Farge (Eds.), *A history of women in the West. Vol. 3, Renaissance and Enlightenment paradoxes* (pp. 46-84). Cambridge: The Belknap of Harvard University Press.

Harris, L., Blum, R., & Resnick, M. (1991). Teen females in Minnesota: A portrait of quiet disturbance. *Women & Therapy, 11*(3-4), 119-135.

Harter, S. (1983). Developmental perspectives on the self-system. In P. Mussen & E. M. Hetherington (eds.), *Handbook of child psychology: Vol. 4. Socialization, personality, and social development (4th ed.)*. New York: Wiley.

Hatcher, R., Hatcher, S., Berlin, M., Okla, K., & Richards, J. (1990). Psychological mindedness and abstract reasoning in late childhood and adolescence: An exploration using new instruments. *Journal of Youth and Adolescence, 19*(4), 307-326.

Heatherton, T., & Baumeister, R. (1991). Binge eating as escape from self-awareness. *Psychological Bulletin, 110*(1), 86-108.

Herman, J. (1992). *Trauma and recovery*. New York: Basic.

Holland, J., Ramazanoglu, C., Sharpe, S., & Thomson, R. (1994). Power and desire: The embodiment of female sexuality. *Feminist Review, 46,* Spring, 21-38.

Hort, B., Leinbach M., & Fagot, B. (1991). Is there coherence among the cognitive components of gender acquisition? *Sex Roles, 24*(3/4), 195-207.

Huston, A. (1983). Sex-typing. In P. Mussen (Ed.), *Handbook of child psychology* (4th edition). *Vol. 4. Socialization, personality and social development* (pp. 387–467), (E. M. Hetherington, Ed.). New York: Wiley.

Hyde, J., & Linn, M. (1988). Gender differences in verbal ability: A meta-analysis. *Psychological Bulletin, 104,* 53-69.

Inhelder, B., & Piaget, J. (1958). *The growth of logical thinking from childhood to adolescence*. New York: Basic.

Jack, D. (1991). *Silencing the self: Women and depression*. Cambridge: Harvard University Press.

Josselson, R. (1980). Ego development in adolescence. In J. Adelson (Ed.), *Handbook of adolescent psychology*. New York: Wiley.

Kagan, J. (1984). *The nature of the child*. New York: Basic.

Keating, D. P. (1980). Thinking processes in adolescence. In J. Adelson (Ed.), *Handbook of adolescent psychology* (pp. 211-246). New York: Wiley.

Keating, D. P. (1988). Byrnes' reformulation of Piaget's formal operations: Is what's left what's right? *Developmental Review, 8,* 376-384.

Kegan, R. (1982). *The evolving self*. Cambridge: Harvard University Press.

Kohlberg, L. (1966). A cognitive-developmental analysis of children's sex-role concepts and attitudes. In E. E. Maccoby (Ed.), *The development of sex differences* (pp. 82-173). Stanford, CA: Stanford University Press.

Laqueur, T. (1990). *Making sex: Body and gender from the Greeks to Freud*. Cambridge: Harvard University Press.

Leinbach, M., & Fagot, B. (1986). Acquistion of gender labels: A test for toddlers. *Sex Roles, 15*(11/12), 655-666.

Levy, G., & Carter, D. B. (1989). Gender schema, gender constancy, and gender-role knowledge: The roles of cognitive factors in preschoolers' gender-role stereotype attributions. *Developmental Psychology, 25*(3), 444-449.

Lloyd, G. (1984/1993). *Man of reason: Male and female in Western philosophy*. Minneapolis: University of Minnesota Press.

Luyt, D., Burton, P., & Simpson, H. (1993). Epidemiological study of wheeze, doctor diagnosed asthma, and cough in preschool children in Leicestershire. *British Medical Journal, 306* (6889), May 22, 1386-1390.

Lytton, H., & Romney, D. (1991). Parents' differential socialization of boys and girls: A meta-analysis. *Psychological Bulletin, 109,* 267-296.

McConaghy, M. (1979). Gender permanace and the genital basis of gender: Stages in the development of constancy of gender identity. *Child Development, 50,* 1223-1226.

Maccoby, E. (1988). Gender as a social category. *Developmental Psychology, 24,* 755-765.

Maccoby, E. (1990). Gender and relationships. *American Psychologist, 45,* 513-520.

Maccoby, E., & Jacklin, C. (1974). *The psychology of sex differences*. Stanford, CA: Stanford University Press.

Martin, C., & Halverson, C. (1983). Gender constancy: A metholological and theoretical analysis. *Sex Roles, 9*(7), 775-790.

Martin, B., & Hoffman, J. (1990). Conduct disorders. In M. Lewis & S. M. Miller (Eds.), *Handbook of developmental psychopathology*. New York: Plenum.

Miedzian, M. (1991). *Boys will be boys: Breaking the link between masculinity and violence*. New York: Anchor Books.

Miller, J. (1976). *Toward a new psychology of women*. Boston: Beacon Press.

Miller, A. (1984). A transitional phase in gender constancy and its relationship to cognitive level and sex identification. *Child Study Journal, 13*(4), 259-275.

Minnesota Women's Fund (1990). Reflections of risk: Growing up female in Minnesota, a report on the health and well-being of adolescent girls in Minnesota. Minneapolis: Author.

Nolen-Hoeksema, S., & Girgus, J. (1994). The emergence of gender differences in depression during adolescence. *Psychological Bulletin, 115*(3), 424-443.

Offord, D., Boyle, M., Szatmari, P., Rae-Grant, N., Links, P., Cadman, D., Byles, J., Crawford, J., Munroe Blum, H., Byrne, L., Thomas, H., & Woodward, C. (1987). Ontario Child Health Study: Six month prevalence of disorder and rates of service utilization. *Archives of General Psychiatry, 44,* 832-836.

Petersen, A., Sarigiani, P., & Kennedy, R. (1991). Adolescent Depression: Why more girls? *Journal of Youth and Adolescence, 20*(2), 247-271.

Piaget, J. (1932). *The moral judgment of the child*. London: Kegan Paul.

Piaget, J. (1967). *Six psychological studies*. (A. Tenzer, Trans.). New York: Vintage.

Pinn, V. (1994, Mar.). Presentation to the Ms. Foundation's Healthy Girls/Healthy Women Research Roundtable. Washington, DC.

Putnam, F. (1989). *Diagnosis and treatment of multiple personality disorders*. New York: Guilford.

Rabinow, P. (1984). Introduction. In P. Rabinow (Ed.), *The Foucault reader* (pp.3–29) New York: Pantheon.

Rich, A. (1979). When we dead awaken: Writing as re-vision. In *On lies, secrets, and silence* (pp. 33-49). New York: Norton.

Richards, M., & Larson, R. (1989). The changing life space of early adolescence. *Journal of Youth and Adolescence,* 18(6), 617-626.

Rodin, J., Silberstein, L., & Striegel-Moore, R. (1985). Women and weight: A normative discontent. In T. Sonderegger (Ed.), *Nebraska symposium on motivation, 1984: Psychology and gender* (pp. 267-307). Lincoln: University of Nebraska Press.

Rorty, R. (1979). *Philosophy and the mirror of nature*. Princeton: Princeton University Press.

Russett, C. E. (1989). *Sexual science*. Cambridge: Harvard University Press.

Rutter, M., & Garmezy, N. (1983). Developmental psychopathology. In P. Mussen (Ed.), *Handbook of child psychology* (4th edition). *Vol. 3. Socialization, personality and social development* (pp. 775-911), (E. M. Hetherington, Ed.). New York: Wiley.

Sawicki, J. (1991). *Disciplining Foucault: Feminism, power and the body*. New York: Routledge.

Sayers, D. (1971). *Are women human?*. Grand Rapids, MI: Wm. b. Eerdmans Publishing Co.

Schonert-Reichl, K., & Offer, D. (1992). Gender differences in adolescent symptoms. In B. Lahey & A. Kazdin (Eds.), *Advances in clinical child psychology, 14,* 27-60.

Seligman, M. (1975). *Helplessness: On depression, development, and death*. San Francisco: Freeman.

Slaby, R., & K. Frey (1975). Development of gender constancy and selective attention to same-sex models. *Child Development, 46,* 849-856.

Snow, M., Jacklin, C., & Maccoby, E., (1983). Sex-of-child differences in father-child interaction at one year of age. *Child Development, 49,* 227-232.

The Society for the Advancement of Women's Health Research. (1991). Towards a women's health research agenda: Findings of the scientific advisory meeting. Washington, DC: Author.

Steiner-Adair, C. (1986). The body politic: Normal female adolescent development and the development of eating disorders. *Journal of The American Academy of Psychoanalysis, 14*(1), 95-114.

Stern, D. (1985). *The interpersonal world of the infant: A view from psychoanalysis and developmental psychology*. New York: Basic.

Sternberg, R., & Powell, J. (1983). The development of intelligence. In P. Mussen (Ed.), *The handbook of child psychology* (4th edition). *Vol. 3. Cognitive development* (pp. 341-419). (J. Flavell & E. Markman, Eds.). New York: Wiley.

Suleiman, S. (Ed.). (1986). *The female body in Western culture: Contemporary perspectives*. Cambridge: Harvard University Press.

Taylor, J., Gilligan, C., & Sullivan, A. (1995). *Between voice and silence*. Cambridge: Harvard University Press.

Terr, L. (1990). *Too scared to cry*. New York: Harper.

Tolman, D., & Debold, E. (1994). Conflicts of body and image: Female adolescents, desire, and the no-body body. In P. Fallon, M. Katzman, & S. Wooley (Eds.), *Feminist perspectives on eating disorders* (pp. 301–317). New York: Guilford.

Tse, M., Cooper, C., Brigdes-Webb, C., & Bauman, A. (1993). Asthma in general practice. *Australian Family Physician, 22*(5), 736-741.

Tuuponen, T., Keistinin, T., & Kivela, S. (1993). Trends in hospitalization among asthmatic children in Finland from 1972-1986. *European Journal of Pediatrics, 152*(12), 1042-1044.

Wehren, A., & De Lisi, R. (1983). The development of gender understanding: Judgments and explanations. *Child Development, 54,* 1568-1578.

Whitaker, A., Johnson, J., Shaffer, D., Rappoport, J., Kalikow, K., Walsh, B., Davies, M., Braiman, S., & Dolinsky, A. (1990). Uncommon troubles in young people: Prevalence estimates of selected psychiatric disorders in a non-referred adolescent population. *Archives of General Psychiatry, 47,* 487-496.

Yairi, E., & Ambrose, N. (1992). Onset of stuttering in preschool children: Selected factors. *Journal of Speech and Hearing Research, 35*(4), Aug. 782-788.

III. CULTURE AS THE CIRCULATION OF SEMIOTIC FORMS

CHAPTER 7

Exploring the Felt Pathways of the Self:
From Experience to Meaning-Making
in Children, K–5

Linda J. Rogers

The debate on nature versus nurture or nature and nurture has been highlighted by recent publications on the human genome project. Articles on the project have appeared in the public press and new controversies have emerged focusing on the biological self. Nevertheless, the more we know about the biology of human life and genetic influences on human behavior (Plomin, 1989), the more we are also aware of the profound influence of culture or nurture in the shaping of an individual's life. The same data that provides the best evidence of the importance of genetic influences on individual behavior is also the data that provides the best evidence for the importance of an individual's environment.

This chapter is an exploration of the dynamics of young children's "cultural taking" from their environments, the semiosis of what I have come to perceive as the "white noise" of childhood. As a data base, approximately one hundred interviews of children, grades K–5, were analyzed and for the purposes of this chapter I will directly focus on a representative sample of those transcripts. What I found when dealing with generalizing the findings of these interviews to existing research was that I needed "new" as in different metaphors and language to describe the dialectical operation of learning between the stated agenda of the children's environment and the signs and role availability that the children read and used in their meaning-making.

The original study began in the early 1990s, in response to the work of Gilligan and her colleagues, who found that there was a dominant "Care" perspective in girl's decisions and that males were more likely to use a "Justice" perspective (see Brown & Gilligan, 1992; Gilligan & Attanucci, 1988; Gilligan, Ward, & Taylor, 1988). A research team consisting of three woman and one male (Rogers & McDonald, 1994; Tillman & McDonald, 1994) conducted interviews at two sites: Grove and Armidale. These are two independent college preparatory schools located in midwestern cities. The majority of the student population represented traditional white Anglo-Saxon, upper middle-class values, although both schools had mission statements with explicitly stated multicultural agendas. The participants of the study were 67 boys, grades K–4, and 37 girls, grades K–5.

What emerged from the data was that the children's decisions were bound by the context in which they occurred and needed to be perceived as representative of that context rather than reflecting a generalized gender orientation (Tillman & McDonald, 1994) or even a generalized developmental perspective. It was the knowledge gained from the child's access and experience to particular information that more cogently characterized their available "schemata of information" rather than a consideration of "raw" or "native" intelligence. As an exapmple, one aspect of the study was to read the children the fable, *The porcupine and the mole* (Johnston, 1988). Most of the children's responses could not be categorized as coming from either a developmental perspective or gender orientation in this sample of statements:

> Tony: (7-grade 1) Porcupines live in trees—the moles should dig down and make two rooms with the tunnel connecting. They should be nice and cooperative with no bad sportsmanship.

> Louise: (6-grade 1) The moles should move out, or, they could use sticks to divide the rooms—the moles should dig a big cave.

> Joel: (9-grade 4) Put the blanket over the porcupine and everyone is happy.

> Brett: (9-grade 4) Maybe he'd move—you shouldn't be rude to guests. The moles should explain what he did wrong and the moles could burrow and the porcupine could have the cave.

> Melody: (10-grade 5) Talk it over; the porcupine agrees—she could be more careful. If not, she'll have to move.

> Hillary: (11-grade 5) Make the porcupine want to leave—outsmart him. I saw that on T.V.

It was interesting that the younger children, Tony and Louise, had the most "scientific" or practical responses. Also, it was the youngest child who knew that porcupines live in trees and one of the older boys who had the least "scientific" of the solutions, to wrap the porcupine in a blanket, and one of the oldest girls who anthropomorphizes. In Melody's solution the moles and porcupine were interchangeable with human actors. "Talk it over; the porcupine agrees—she could be more careful.

If not, she'll have to move." Although I had assumed that most of the children would conceptualize the porcupine as a male, they did not, as can be seen in Hillary's response. Instead, the children used an interesting schemata of an inclusion/accommodation model. The children either attempted to include the porcupine in the cave as in: "Put the blanket over the porcupine and everyone is happy," or, as illustrated by Melody's response, all of the inhabitants of the cave needed to be considered. Melody was not uncaring of the porcupine; she wanted the porcupine to be caring of the other inhabitants as well. We quickly discovered that attempting to reduce the activities and decisions of the children to fit a representation of moral, justice, and care, whether male or female, was inappropriate.

Ten categories (Tillman & McDonald, 1994) emerged from the analysis of that data that articulated a world inhabited by the perspective of children, a world that they moved in, recognized, wondered about, or were present to observe—intentionally and unintentionally (see Appendix). The examples of knowledge, experience, and activities the children provided to many of the questions they were asked also demonstrated that the children knew the socially approved responses that were expected of them, such as, never hit, or pick fair teams. However, the unidimensional representation of "fairness" as taught in their values classes through such activities as, "Word of the Week" or "Project Charlie"—and can be seen in Tony's response of "cooperative" and "no bad sportsmanship"—obscured the density of everyday reality known by these children. Fairness for the children in this group comprised a complexity of issues or multidimensionality (i.e., fairness for whom and to what? Does the child exercise fairness for his or her friend, to the team, or to an abstract utopian ideal?). Instead, we found a more complex dimension of learning; How do children learn to differentiate the concept "fairness" as presented in the ideal taught by adults with the practice of fairness as lived by those same adults?

The children related narratives of life at home and at school, filled with children's dilemmas, and for some of these they had evolved effective and efficient strategies based upon experience gained in their individual situations.

> Hillary: (11-grade 5) I'm nice. I scream when my brother hurts me and it gets my mom to come.

> Jeff: (5-Kindergarten) I can't see the whole room in the dark . . . and when the garage door goes up, it sounds like a dragon. So, I just shut my eyes and hold my pillow close to me.

However, despite being taught utopian ideals about fairness, these ideals were not necessarily practiced by adults at home or at school. The utopian ideal was required to be known and to be given as a verbal response, but in everyday life, such as on the playing field during games, another reality was required. Children, trying to act "fairly," often resorted to obtaining the help of teachers when an "unfair" situation developed. Many of the students reported learning about the reality of games and play at school. This is from a second-grade boy:

> Brett: I don't want to play because they've got like all the stinkiest kids.

> Linda: So, it's not fair. What do you do in that situation?

> Brett: Well, I just walk away. I just say I'm not going to play cause these aren't fair and they don't change them. I come back later during recess and they, and most of them, there's only about five kids playing when there was about twenty kids playing and . . . when I came back there was only about five kids playing cause mostly everyone quit because they had the unfair team. All the kids that had the fair team were still playing.

> Linda: What could be done in that situation to make it fair?

> Brett: Well, you get a teacher and she says she doesn't know whose the best and she gives us numbers like, 1 or 2 and all the 1s go over there and all the 2s go over there, but mostly that doesn't work because after she leaves everyone starts fighting.

We began to examine the structure or arena for decisions that was provided for these children, and the different kinds of knowledge the children used in making decisions, as well as the context in which these decisions were applied, (i.e., fairness at home may or may not operate the same way fairness operates in school). We began to perceive decision making as a reciprocal activity between specifically taught cultural information and the complex everyday world of intended explicit consequences and the unexplained consequences of behavior. For example, children were frequently taught at home and in school not to hit or bully others; however, when a few of the boys in this study attempted to avoid a bully and report him to teachers and parents, the boys were surprised to be confronted with conflicting negative reductionist labels: *sissy* and *tattletale*. Therefore, the children had to learn when, for whom, and in what circumstances fairness operated. For these boys, it was almost always wrong to hit a girl even if she was an older sister who bullied and taunted.

It became increasingly difficult to apply traditional psychological theories of development that defined growth in terms of separation, individuation, and autonomy (Freud, 1905; Piaget, 1965; Erikson, 1950). Development in most models was characterized as unidimensional and universal. The self as separate from others was central to these theories and these theoretical premises influenced theorists focused on moral development (Piaget, 1965; Kohlberg, 1969, 1984).

Nevertheless, the children we interviewed did not recognize a self that was separate and unique, nor could their development be seen in unidimensional segments. Many of the children's responses resembled this from a first-grade boy:

> Linda: What do you think I should know about you in order to know you better?
>
> Brett:You should know that in my room I have two dinosaur beds and um, dinosaur wallpaper.
>
> Linda: Okay, what kind of inside thing should I know about you? Like are you a happy person?
>
> Brett: Um, I have bones.

Primary source of information about the children was received from their families.

> Brett: My family is Italian and we like to on outings and picnics with relatives. My parents make me feel better. Mom taught me my ABCs, how to count to one hundred, and everything. My dad is honest and he laughs and he is a lawyer and I work with him on activities—and he taught me things I've never learned—like how to talk and how to walk. I have a four-year-old sister.
>
> Tony: I read. I am active. I know I'm active because Mom said I should stay in kindergarten for two years and have fun. I like writing and math, I especially like plusing, minusing, times tables, and experimenting with the number ten.

Tony, seven when we interviewed him, knew the importance of people whom he never met and felt their influence on his life. "People before I was born died. . . . I used to have two grampas and two grandmas . . . and my mom's mother and my mom's dad and my dad's dad died." Tony carries in him the identity of family; he exists not only as himself but as the child-sign of family continuance. He also is taught the importance of these people and himself as a developing self—he will grow into the family identity that is being shaped for him, either proactively or reactively. Brett knows and identifies himself as Italian even although at best he is third-generation Italian. His "I-for-himself" (Bakhtin, 1987), the self-identity he has constructed from his interactions in the family, also identifies learning activities with his father before Brett had a self capable of learning. "He taught me things I've never learned—like how to talk and how to walk. I have a four-year-old sister." All the children located themselves in a family construct that provided them with a framework of activities that taught them about themselves and other people.

> Hillary: Mom is an original mom—she cooks and cleans. My brother is fourteen, mean to me and he's embarrassed by me. Dad gets upset about stuff—animals are probably the best because they don't talk back.

> Melody: My brother will be in college next year. I go shopping and play games with Mom—my mom doesn't understand me. I go shopping and play games with my dad—he isn't very good at them.

The children "learned" in their primary environment, the family. They functioned like little blotters absorbing words, incidents, attitudes, and "the social world" or as Vico (Bergin & Fisch, 1968) would call it "the world of the civil society." The world in which they participated was constructed by the agent-actors with whom they were continually in contact and those with whom they were deliberately brought contact: the immediate family, the extended family, the school, and select social events, such as allowing time for friendship formation. The children learned through the deliberately taught lessons as well as the unintended ones and built their perceptive schemata, (i.e., self and gender) to fit in with what they learned.

> Girl: In class the girls think better than the boys.

> Linda: Why do you think the girls think better than the boys?

> Girl: Because the girls don't get overly active that much.

> Linda: Oh, so, because the girls don't get overly active, they can think better?

> Girl: Mmmm, mmm.

> Linda: And what does the teacher say when the boys get overly active?

> Girl: She says, "Calm down; this isn't a zoo."

In this example, a first-grade girl offers the teacher's construct "overly-active" as a reason why girls think better than boys and as the major difference between boys and girls. At this school, one of the boys' and girls' favorite games was to "capture the flag," which they both played at recess and lunch. Nevertheless, it is the boys who are characterized by the teacher as "overly active" and girls are the ones who are expected to do their work promptly and quietly; it is implied that the girls are not by nature "overly active" even though their activities are the same as the boys. The child uses this construct despite her own play experience and her own observational experience. The differences between the boys and girls enters the young girl's imaginative experience as an actual difference and she perceives her own behavior as "girl" behavior—unlike "boy" behavior. She "knows" that she is different than the boys when they are inside the classroom. In this case, the gender role is a construct of the teacher's that the child imitates. "Children excel in imitation; we observe that they generally amuse themselves by imitating whatever they are able to apprehend" (Vico, 1968, p.75). The imitation in this case is the cognitive construction of the teacher's perception "girl" and "boy" behavior, which leads to the girls acting out the behavior in the classroom, and becoming "girls."

In this culturally constructed case of gender differences, I wish to point out that the teacher often sees the children playing the same games on the school ground. The bustling children entering the room are nevertheless perceived differently by her; the myth or metaphor of gender, boy-girl, produces signs of behavior which, for the teacher, produces different categorizes or constructs of the noises and movements of the children into "zoo-behavior" boys and "getting-to-work behavior" girls. The child's perception of her experience is shaped by the teacher's directing how that experience is registered, monitored, and categorized. The actual bodily actions and activities that the children engage in disappear in the cultural creation of the metaphors for female and male behavior.

This captured instant of a classroom day is an example of the connectiveness of human thought processes, a very humanly constructed and known world—Cunningham's model (1995) of a rhizome. Cunningham's discussion, inspired by Eco (1976), includes the following points. The rhizome, an underground root crop, is a system of tangled roots and tubers where

1. Every point can and must be connected to every other point, raising the possibility of infinite juxtaposition,

2. There are no fixed points or positions, only connections (relationships),

3. The structure is dynamic, constantly changing. . . .

4. There is no hierarchy or genealogy. . . .

5. The rhizome whole has no outside or inside, but is rather an open network which can be connected with something else in all of its dimensions. (Cunningham, 1995, p. 2)

Cunningham perceives thinking in that model as "always dialogic, connected to another; either directly as in some communicative action or indirectly via some form of semiotic mediation (Ibid.). I am suggesting that the child's and the teacher's thinking have become connected in a socially appropriated pattern of transforming what is seen and heard into "natural" or physical representations of gender behavior even though there are hardly any physical reasons or signs for those notions. Nevertheless, the child will carry forward into other activities what I perceive as a "white noise" a representation that she is different "as a girl." She will hold that difference as a lens for future activities and future categories. The children in this study held "echoes" of cultural and familial knowledge that guided how they knew themselves and how they interpreted the behavior of others. It is also interesting to note that although there are many excellent examples of the strength of Bandura's (1977) social learning theory, these children often became the representation of a cognitive perception of the teacher and/or parent.

The children in this study remembered complex culturally significant information when it challenged or troubled their conception of self. Information they gleaned from their interactional world did not necessarily "drop out" or disappear if it presented what many adults would consider too great a case of cognitive dissonance as in Piagetian or neo-Piagetian theories (Piaget, 1965; Selman, 1980; Rogoff, 1990). The following extract is the response of a first-grade girl to the question, Has anything happened to you that you thought was unfair?

Claire: Yeah.

Linda: Could you tell me about that?

Claire: I thought it was really unfair, . . . what's the last president we had?

Linda: Bush.

Claire: Yeah, Bush said, "Hey, I think only parents are dumb," and I felt really bad about that because I have only one parent.

Linda: I see, yes, so what do you think you could have done about that?

Claire: Well, I tried to ignore it, but I couldn't really ignore [it] because it hurt my feelings so much.

Linda: Did you do anything? Did you say anything about it?

Claire: I told my mom how I felt.

Linda: That was good. What did she say?

Claire: Well, she said, "I agree with you."

Linda: That's good. Did you wish you'd written a letter to the President and told him that?

Claire: Nah, I would think of embarrassment if he wrote me back saying I was wrong.

Linda: But you wouldn't have agreed that you were wrong, would you?

Claire: Nah.

This interview took place late April 1993. The Republican convention, which the child had sat up watching with her babysitter, was held seven months previously on April 20, 1992, and began at 9:20 P.M. at the Houston Astrodome (personal communication, Walter Finch, April 10, 1995). My informant at the Bush Materials Project did not know if that was central standard time or eastern standard time; however, many adults would not accept the fact that a five-year-old child could or would listen to a formal address late in the evening; it could have been as late as 10:20 P.M. for this child. The girl relates that she "tried to ignore it, but I couldn't really ignore [it] because it hurt my feelings so much." She explained that she and her mother were a "single-parent" family, and she could not understand why the president—an important person— would object to her family structure. She did, in the traditional developmental description of the egocentric thinking of the child, believe that the then president spoke about her family unit. She related other aspects about her mother, her job, her hobbies, and their activities together. The girl compared those to other children's families in the school—and related that she was not quite like the other girls. She was aware of her "not connectedness," of herself; of herself being "other" than many of the children. That echo of the president's speech to his adult political party members remained a resonating white noise within her that perhaps she continually tests, as in watching my reactions when she told me. Although the mother responded to this incident, the emotional marking remained with the child.

This first-grade girl was able to approach her mother and ask for help in trying to understand what perplexed her. The child recorded the information, which she perceived to be about herself, at both a cognitive and emotional level of knowing. Although many adults had intellectually explained their understanding of the president's message, tried to assure her that Mr. Bush was not directly referring her, and the young girl appeared "to know" what was explained—she was certainly not emotionally or intellectual satisfied.

Many of the children spent a great deal of time trying to read the conflicting signs and symbols of their lives. They constructed family texts and/or fables that provided them not only with coping strategies, but with behavioral patterns to fit a metaphoric self they tried to grow into. A second-grade boy, Brill, had an urgent consistent theme that appeared early in his transcript of "keeping Daddy happy—it's very important to keep Daddy happy." He was concerned because there was a bully in the second grade who had been taunting quite a few of the boys. They all related how they were told not to fight but when they appealed to the teaching faculty they were given another message of, "Learn how to fix it yourself." Brill asked his mother what to do; her message echoed the school's; don't fight. But his father's did not. His father did not want him to be a "marshmallow."

> Brill: "You shouldn't be such a softy, you should do for your rights. Don't let people walk all over your face." And I am doing that.
>
> Linda: So what would you do?
>
> Brill: He said, I'm allowed to punch JF when it is really reasonable. And I haven't done that yet, but I can tell, I can smell it; soon he's gonna do something mean.

Brill was tense with anticipation as recess was coming. He also did not want to let go of the opportunity to discuss the topic. He was literally moving between the two metaphoric constructions of self: "softy"/"marshmallow" and "tough cookie." Not hitting belonged to the utopian ideal taught by the school and articulated by his mother, but it was not an ideal that kept him safe, nor, in his opinion, did it bring the positive attention of his father.

> Brill: Because I can be a really tough cookie when I feel like it.
>
> Linda: What does it mean to be a tough cookie?
>
> Brill: It's like, when you're really tough and you want to do something there's just so much aggravating that you have to do it, and it's really tough to brave that thing. . . .
>
> Linda: And why do you like to play with tough kids?
>
> Brill: It makes me feel like I am tough except I'm not really tough; I'm really really soft to people.

The theme of "softness" was difficult for him; he very much wanted his father's approval. Although he doesn't say his feelings were hurt, the confusion as to why his sister can be "soft" with the father and he could not was clear. Brill certainly responded emotionally to these incidents, not intellectually. He did not claim this distinction as a gender issue.

Brill: One night, I was like very, like, how can I put it, like confused because my sister had, took a catnap, and she got to stay up all night with my father, and we hardly ever, ever get to see my father, so that was a great privilege, and I had to stay in my bedroom.

Linda: How old is your sister?

Brill: She's four.

Linda: What did you do; did you say anything?

Brill: No, I, I just did what my father told me, and went to sleep. Because when he gets angry, he can really be angry.

For Brill "keeping Daddy happy" also included doing well in school, especially spelling. Spelling was important, but not because he was learning new words, their meanings, and adding to the way he could describe his life in verbal or written narratives. The gold star on his spelling paper was one strategy that would help him obtain his father's positive attention.

Brill: I would like to impress my father because he only likes what my sisters do. He says, "Oh, that's great." I show him my test with the star on it, and he says, "OK, I like it."

Brill uses the indexes of success in school as a hope of gaining the positive attention of his father, which his sister so mysteriously seems to be able to have bestowed upon her. These markers of his successful learning do contribute to his life, but not in the same personal way that they contribute to Tony's life. Schoolwork, for Brill, is another forum where he can prove himself to his father. This is the academic component of the the social set of behaviors that Brill tries "to become" in order to please his father. Brill does know what to do, and is able to read the signs and discern the rules of the family unit that the father sets in motion. He utilizes his common sense to gain safety and he applies that same common sense to his own "becoming" in the sense of a self. He has gained this common sense from all of his years of "being" in the family: he utilizes his life experiences, his obsevations of his mother's life experience, and perceptions of his sister's life experience (Vico, 1968).

The two selves Brill was contemplating in terms of "becoming," the tough cookie or the marshmallow are metaphoric selves. They have little to do with the physical being of Brill—the blood and bone of his existential being. Instead, he is trying to co-opt a set of behaviors; these behaviors serve as indexical markers of the "tough cookie" for the father. The father, therefore, is not perceiving Brill, the trembling boy who lives in fear and longing, but the boy Brill will represent by demonstrating the required behavior.

I see Brill's dilemma as crucial to our understanding of the crafting of a self. Not an individual self that grows uniquely to fruition through a series of hierarchical, invariant, sequential progressive stages, but a self that is crafted from available cultural roles and shifts, in an often uneasy balance between the expectations of the family unit and expectations in the social order the child is situated within. For these children the biological parameters of their corporal existence or "self" had little to do with the behaviors that were set for them to act out or the definitions that were waiting for them to grow into. Brett's "Italian" definition makes him a part of a particular ongoing social communal life, a life that had little to do with the language or geography of Italy other than as metaphor. It would make him, for himself and others, different and in fact, more Italian than the children who lived next door and with whom he attended school.

These acts of attention to being Italian and "keeping Daddy happy" were signs of the children's astute readings of the symbolic and iconic reality in which they lived. It was not simply cognitive attending—concentrating on cognitively structured information that "explained" what the children needed to know. The children learned the artifacts of their lives out of a combined cognitive and social/emotional awareness. Tony's delight at knowing himself as skilled at "plusing" and "minusing" was not just the thrill of a gold star. Tony gained knowledge that made him a self he enjoyed being—a self that had an accepted place, which could star as well as have a star. Langer's (1967) discussion of aesthetic knowing recognizes that a person has a dual experience when an art form is appreciated. That experience combines, at the same time, the cognitive recognition and understanding of the "event" or artifact and emotional reciprocity.

All of the children in this study were aware of the structuring of their environments, cognitively and emotionally. They also recognized the limits the environments placed upon them: the child-sign of the academy is expected to stand straight and not droop in public when tired; a child-sign who is also a son-sign may be required to be a softy with his sisters but a tough cookie in the school grounds. A child must not correct a teacher. A child-sign must articulate the utopian ideal of fairness but practice a "reality" of everyday living. It is interesting that most of the models or strategies that teachers and researchers use to "measure" or "monitor" what children know actually limits the public acknowledgment or attention to what children know. Most tests of children's learning are focused on very limited cognitive aspects of what these children spent most of their time learning. The white noise in the life of a child may work to have the girl, or boy, sit down and do their homework as it is not acceptable to do otherwise. Or, the white noise may keep the child too focused upon creating the accepted artifact. Brill carried within him constantly playing echoes of home. Although it did not "fit" the question the interviewer asked, Brill managed to incorporate what he had "on his mind" into the interview.

Brill: There's one more thing, um, there was so many things around, and my sisters aren't very careful; they're not very responsible, and my sister had broke a picture that had fallen off, and it was lying on the floor, except it wasn't broken; she was walking like this; she was dancing like a ballerina; she was pretending, she went "chub" and my father heard it. For ten years he had that picture. He got that for my mother as a birthday present.

Linda: What did he do when he got angry like that?

Brill: He, he, he, like got really mad and tossed her in her room, and bounced her head forward on her bed and then she started crying, and then he shut the door and left. And she was there for an hour.

Linda: What did your mom say?

Brill: Um, Mom doesn't like to go into this stuff, because then my dad gets mad at her.

Linda: And what happens if your mom and dad, if your dad gets angry with your mom, does that happen much?

Brill: No. Not anymore, but when I was four and my sisters weren't born yet, they used to always have fights. I felt very sad for my mom and my dad. My mom would always cry.

Linda: What did you do when your mom cried like that?

Brill: I just went into my room because I didn't want to be involved in it, because then I would be in trouble. They [sisters] take my Game Boy which was very expensive, and they say, "Come and get me." And that, it's like a balloon on a balloon, and there's so much pressure against it it has to pop. So I usually get really mad. After that I have really hot breath. And, my sisters, I don't hit them or anything; sometimes I just use my words and hands like this, and things like this. [clenches his fists and hits the chair.]

Linda: You mean you clench your fists and kind of hit the chair?

Brill: Yeah, like that, but I don't hit them or anything. I just scare them because then on family night my mom reports that to my dad.

This study supported a Vygotskian (Vygotsky in Davydow, 1995) construction of the learning of children—learning as socially constructed between actor/agents. Cunningham's (1995) discussion of the rhizome, which was not meant to be used to look at individual lives, can be seen

as a metaphor for understanding the social constructedness and con-
nectivity of all of the acts of learning that take place in and between the
various context rich environments of the children. These children used
the intentional as well as unintended experiences and examples in their
contextual frameworks to make meaning in their lives. But these experiences were dependent upon the adults who constructed the parameters of their world as well as the metaphor "child" that came with available behaviors and roles that the children could use. The children
learned the information available to them as intellectual and emotional
components at the same time, so that "knowing" needed to be seen as
an intellectual, social, and psychological artifactual "becoming" of a self
(Langer, 1967). Information that was discordant or that provided dissonance for the children, in more traditional Piagetian and neo-Piagetian terms, was often maintained in the form of echoes, or white noise
that produced varying resonances in the children's lives.

Appendix

The following ten categories are the findings that emerged from the
research team's (Tillman & McDonald, 1994) two years of interviews
and data analysis:

1. *Friends:* All of the children have very strong and sophisticated understandings of friendship. The capacity to be expressive about the role and
value of friends increased with age, but the concept of the role of a friend
was stable from kindergarten through early childhood.

2. *Family:* The family is the context in which the participants unavoid-
ably dwell, their first and primary frame of reference. Home was most
often referred to as a "place of safety, security, and personal comfort"
despite their descriptions of waiting almost continually for parents,
being teased by siblings, and being in tense situations.

3. *Self-description:* Participants' description of self rarely contained references to cognitive or affective characteristics, but consisted of physical properties such as height, weight, coloring, or age. If pressed, participants occasionally described themselves in terms of their behaviors
(i.e., "I'm nice, or I try to be nice").

4. *Absence of Academic Subjects:* This refers to a lack of any reference
to course work (school or otherwise) involving academic content or char-
acterization of themselves as being seen as having academic competencies. One of the very few responses in the boys' interviews indicates

that "sometimes math is pretty good" and history is "awesome"; however, what is on his time line of personal importance is where he is in his family's history and what he wants to be, in this case a baseball player. The girls were asked direct questions concerning their academic subjects and they almost always referred to classroom activities or social interactions rather than discussing their academic ability.

5. *Care-Justice:* Considerations of care, caring for others and being cared for were primary in the lives of all of the children interviewed. They expressed a Care voice about all aspects of their life, parents being cared for and caring for them, teachers caring for them, their caring for friends, and others taking care of them. Justice appeared in the boys' and girls' interviews as considerations of fairness, or fair play. Care and Justice were presented as being interrelated, degrees of balance, rather than as opposites or as separate considerations. The examples that the children provided of Care and Justice could have been given by either a girl or a boy—it would be impossible to give a typical "gendered" vignette.

6. *Fear:* This was an interesting category as fear was not necessarily the same experience among these boys and girls. The state of fear was the most commonly expressed emotion of all the children in this study. It often resulted from their inability to control a given situation (i.e., for girls this was usually discussed in terms of physical fear as in their older siblings or other schoolchildren hurting them). They also discussed being "hurt" or fearful of having their feelings hurt. Boys designated more situations of encounter (i.e., archetypal fears of the dark or when being confronted with change).

7. *Empowerment:* These children, when quite young, often perceived themselves as powerless to act or to take a self-determining role during events. For them the world was full of waiting: they waited for their parents, teachers, siblings, and their own friends. They also often appealed to adults for help during times of conflict. The girls expected to be heard and to be assisted by the adult to whom they appealed. However, the boys in this data set learned, over time, not to expect much help from adults. As the boys developed (matured) they became more capable of perceiving themselves as being able to exert control or agency (Perry, 1970). Some learned to internalize an authoritative construct and were able to take effective action due to this emerging sense of control. They practiced strategies of management and control among their cohorts to resolve conflicts between themselves. This was not typical for the girls; the strategies that the girls used as young children still worked; they turned to adults who in turn changed the situation for them. The girls felt secure in that mode of operation. Conversely, in viewing strategies

of empowerment, one could also see how powerless, often fearful, and dependent these children often felt.

8. *Conflict and / or Resolution:* The children related a great deal of conflict in their world. The most common method or strategy they employed in dealing with conflict was to walk away or avoid any painful, psychological, or physical outcome. Avoidance did not solve the conflict, but a temporary space was created that enabled the child to "forget" the event and began again as if nothing happened. It was in typical games or sports that the boys and girls most frequently had to deal with conflict at school. In order to equalize teams or bring order to an activity they would appeal to an outside authority (parent or teacher). The boys often gave examples depicting what happened after the authority figure left; the imposed resolution was discarded and chaos returned.

9. *Games:* Games made up much of these children's lives. There were games organized by the school as formal sport, and games the children organized during recess and lunch. Playing games (i.e., Nintendo, basketball, four square, and swimming) were also what friends did together. A few times boys felt that games had the power to be viewed as future employment. "I want to play baseball for one of the big teams." Games were also an area of fear as, "Well that's sorta the whole thing of the game, if I didn't want to get hurt, I shouldn't be playing the game". Games were a large part of their social interaction, with their friends and family, especially fathers. "Linda: What do you do with your dad? B: Play catch or things like that".

It was within the context of games that they had the greatest opportunity to practice decision making, to demonstrate the characteristics of friendship, to find out how they coped with fear and pain, and came up against situations of fairness and unfairness. The girls emphasized playing games as often as the boys and played the same games. Games also had the capacity to extend their imagination and to provide role-play opportunities.

10. *Social / Political Astuteness:* The children demonstrated the ability to recognize and gauge their psychological, social, and/or physical environments and the reciprocity of these responses to their behavior.

As this category emerged from the data we became aware of the children as carefully constructing their place in the world that they were given and slowly building a definition of themselves and their abilities in response to their understanding of their world. They were acutely aware, and sensitive to, individuals who had influence in their lives. They knew that there were expectations of behavior and obligation that the adult world had and that they needed to learn, often by inference, that is, Who will help me? What can a person like me do? What is a good (safe) thing for a person like me to do?

References

Bakhtin, M. M. (1987). *Speech genres and other late essays*. (V. McGee, Trans.) (C. Emerson & M. Holquist, Eds.). Austin: University of Texas Press.

Bandura, A. (1977). *Social learning theory*. Englewood Cliffs, NJ: Prentice-Hall.

Bergin, T. G., & Fisch, M. H. (1968). *The new science of Giambattista Vico*. Ithaca, NY: Cornell University Press.

Brown, L., & Gilligan, C. (1992). *Meeting at the crossroads: The psychology of women and the development of girls*. Cambridge: Harvard University Press.

Burke, P. (1985). *Vico*. New York: Oxford University Press.

Cunningham. D. J. (1995). Timeless ideas. Paper presented at Central States Anthropological Society, Indianapolis, IN.

Danesi, M., & Santeramo, D. (1992). *Introducing semiotics: An anthology of readings*. Toronto: Canadian Scholar Press.

Davydov, V. V. (1995). The influence of L.S. Vygotsky on educational theory, research and practice. (S.T. Kerr, Trans.). *Educational Researcher, 24,* 12-21.

Eco, U. (1976). *A theory of semiotics*. Bloomington, IN: Indiana University Press.

Erikson, E. (1950). *Childhood and society*. New York: Norton.

Erikson, E. (1968). *Identity: Youth and crisis*. New York: Norton.

Freud, S. (1905). Three essays on the theory of sexuality. *Vol. 7. The Standard Edition*. London: Hogarth Press.

Gilligan, C., & Attanucci, J. (1988). Two moral orientations: Gender differences and similarities. *Merrill- Palmer Quarterly, 34,* 223-237.

Gilligan, C., Ward, J., & Taylor, J. (Eds.). (1988). *Mapping the moral domain*. Cambridge: Harvard University Press.

Johnston, D. K. (1988), Adolescents' solutions to dilemmas in fables: Two moral orientations—two problem solving strategies. In C. Gilligan, J. Ward, & J. Taylor (Eds.), *Mapping the moral domain*. Cambridge: Harvard University Press.

Kohlberg, L. (1969). Stage and sequence: The cognitive-developmental approach to socialization. In D. A. Gosling (Ed.), *Handbook of socialization theory and research*. Chicago: Rand McNally.

Kohlberg, L. (1984). *The psychology of moral development. (Vol 2)*. San Francisco: Harper.

Langer, S. K. (1967) *Mind: An essay on human feeling*. Baltimore: John Hopkins University Press.

Perry, W. G. (1970). *Forms of intellectual and ethical development in the college years: A scheme*. New York: Holt, Rinehart, & Winston.

Piaget, J. (1965). *The moral judgement of the child*. New York: Free Press.

Plomin, R. (1989). Environment and genes: Determinants of behavior. *American Psychologist, 44*(2), 105-111.

Rogers, L. J., & McDonald, L. L. (1994, June). *Time bytes: The self in construction*. Paper presented at the annual meeting of the Semiotic Society of America, Philadephia.

Rogoff, B. (1990). *Apprenticeship in thinking: Cognitive development in social context*. New York: Oxford University Press.

Tillman, L. R. and McDonald, L. L. (1994) Decision making perspectives in young children (K-5): Choices in the world of young boys and girls. In F. Erickson (Ed.), *Fifteenth annual ethnography in education forum*. Philadelphia, PA: Ethnography in Education Association.

Selman, R. L. (1980). *The growth of interpersonal understanding*. New York: Academic.

Vico, G. (1968). *The new science of Giambattista Vico*. (T.G. Bergin, & M. H. Fisch, Trans.) Ithaca, NY: Cornell University Press.

CHAPTER 8

Adolescent Girls, Class, and the Cultures of Femininity

Lyn Mikel Brown

Introduction

The psychological struggles and losses adolescent girls sustain as they confront cultural pressures and messages to be traditionally feminine—that is, to be nice and kind, silent, passive, and accommodating—have been well documented by recent research in psychology and education (AAUW, 1991, 1992; Bernardez, 1988; Brown & Gilligan, 1992; Orenstein, 1994; Pipher, 1995). Unfortunately, because very little attention has been given to girls who are not white and middle-class, researchers rarely interrogate the very notions of culture and femininity on which their work rests.

In this chapter, I explore the ways in which sixth-, seventh-, and eighth-grade white girls from working-class and working poor families in rural Maine understand, express, and react to conventional definitions of femininity (see Brown, 1998). Using data gathered over the course of a year from videotaped focus groups and individual interviews, I underscore the contradictory nature of what constitutes appropriately feminine behavior for these girls—behavior radically different from the dominant white middle-class cultural ideal; offering these girls a wide range of physical and verbal expression not usually considered under the rubric of conventional femininity. I suggest, moreover, that while such behavior may signal a rejection of white middle-class propriety and, in this sense, a resistance to the dominant ideologies of femaleness as passive, accommodating and helpless, it may also work to cement the girls' lower-caste status.[1]

This research builds on a feminist research program that is grounded in a notion of voice as a relational, discursive phenomenon—linguistically constituted, socially constructed, physically embodied and, thus, by definition, polyphonic, layered, infinitely varied, often contradictory, fragmented, and rich with intentions (Brown et al., 1988, 1989, 1991; Brown & Gilligan, 1991, 1992; Rogers, Brown, & Tappan, 1994; Gilligan, 1990). Adopting such a perspective, I thus assume subjectivity is constructed, often unconsciously, within ongoing power relations and acknowledge power as historically, socially, and personally contingent.

And yet, while I assume "the plurality of language and the impossibility of fixing meaning once and for all," and question "the sovereignty of subjectivity as the guarantee of meaning," hallmarks, if you will, of feminist poststructuralism (Weedon, 1987, pp. 85–86), my research carries the tension between such a view and an appreciation of the *experience* of an authentic self to which the girls I listen subscribe. In other words, while I acknowledge subjectivity as a process, I also acknowledge the agentic power of the felt experience or phenomenology of an integrated, conscious, more or less continuous, permanent subjectivity. Because I am concerned not only with understanding and describing what girls from different social and material locations know and say in particular contexts, but also the way in which they resist or comply with normalizing views of femininity, such appreciation and documentation of this tension is necessary: It has been my experience that girls who express confidence about what they know to be true from their experiences, who feel they are genuine or true to their thoughts and feelings in particular times and places, are more like to critique and resist norms or conventions of what it is to be a "proper" woman.

Authenticity, in this research program, is thus not meant to connote essentialism, but to convey girls' experiences of feeling genuine and to document those places where girls feel safe, at home with themselves and in the world. From such a subjectively powerful reference point, I follow girls to those places where they feel foreign, false, and out of relationship, insecure and unsafe. I can then move with them and hear their various culturally grounded understandings of femininity, note their strategies for resistance, and witness their performances. Such a way of listening reveals new possibilities, identifies contradictions, and challenges the legitimized fictions of idealized femininity (Walkerdine, 1990).

Class Accents

"In recent years, while gender and race have become common currency," the British psychologist Walkerdine notes, "it has become almost impossible to speak about class" (1990, p. 157). Certainly, the psychological literature on class in the United States is sparse, on white girls and class it is nearly nonexistent. Perhaps this is so because, as Walkerdine suggests, there is little that can be said about the subject in general terms, so culturally varied, complicated, and full of contradictions are class experiences and struggles.[2]

Stevenson and Ellsworth argue that, unlike either the working-class "lads" Willis (1977) described in northern England or working-class and poor African American and Latino students in the United States (Fine, 1988, 1992; Fordham, 1993), white working-class youths in the United States are unlikely to develop what the anthropologist Ogbu terms an "oppositional culture": a "cultural frame of reference [that] gives them a sense of collective or social identity and a sense of self-worth" in opposition to white middle-class society (1989). White working-class culture, Stevenson and Ellsworth explain, "has been described as 'fractured': historically along regional, racial and ethnic lines, and more recently by the displacement of industrial workers and the erosion of the labor union as a social and political collectivity." Therefore, they argue, "the working class has lost any form of collective consciousness that is distinct from the dominant culture" (1993, p. 269). White working-class youth in the United States do not have a shared cultural history or social narrative from which to draw or with which to identify.

In the introduction to her memoir, Steedman notes that what *has* been written about class attributes a superficial, uncomplicated "psychological sameness to the figures in the working-class landscape." This is partly because, she explains, "delineation of emotional and psychological selfhood has been made by and through the testimony of people in a central relationship to the dominant culture, that is to say by and through people who are not working class" (1987, p. 14). Psychological studies that include class as a variable, with notable exceptions (Fine, 1988; Fine & Macpherson, 1992; Pastor, McCormick & Fine, 1996; Way, 1995), give little sustained attention to the effects of social and material location on girls' emerging subjectivities. Indeed, amid growing attention to the psychological struggles and losses middle-class white girls sustain as they confront dominant cultural notions of femininity— that is, as they are pressed at early adolescence to become more passive, silent, accommodating, and nice (see Bernardez, 1988; Brown & Gilligan, 1992; Gilligan, 1990)—very little attention has been given to poor and working-class white girls.

Given that, as Fordham argues, "in a socially, culturally, and racially stratified society like the United States, culturally specific routes to womanhood are inevitable" (1993, p. 8), it becomes important to appreciate the ways in which differences in social location, and the political ramifications of such differences, are taken in and made sense of. How do those of us who stand in different relationship to the dominant—that is, white, middle-class, and still, with respect to economic and political power, male—culture come to understand ourselves, our relationships with each other; how do we negotiate the connections between the wider society and the values and norms of our local communities? Such questions and

explorations about the impact of social and material location on individual subjectivities and interpersonal relationships require in-depth
qualitative analysis of the language and forms of discourse of different
groups of people in different contexts.

The Girls

The thirteen girls in this study live their daily lives in Mansfield,
a small town in a rural area of central Maine. Mansfield's population of
about nine hundred, spread over a wide expanse of farm and woodland,
also includes a nucleus of houses, a few combination grocery store-gas
stations, an old hotel, a bait and tackle shop, two small wood mills, a
post office and a K-8 elementary school. More than half of the girls live
on farms or "in the woods," their homes located down miles of dirt roads
and up long driveways. All but three houses are very small or are trail-
ers; the others are old New England farmhouses, long and rambling.

Mansfield, like many small Maine towns, boasts residents with
deep family roots. Indeed generational claims, rather than financial or
material wealth, are often the real measure of one's social position. People who lack such claims are considered to be "from away" whether they
have newly moved to the area or have lived there for the past ten or
twenty years. Although there are a few people in town who "have
money," most feel lucky to scratch out a living and support their families with low-paying or part-time jobs. This puts everyone more or less
on equal footing. Some of the girls' fathers work in the woods cutting
trees; others drive trucks or haul gravel; one is a self-employed
mechanic; another is unemployed because of a physical disability. More
than half of the girls' mothers work part-time; one as a Licensed Practical Nurse, another at a wood mill, and others in local stores or as wait-
resses in town. Nine of the girls live with both parents, three live in single-parent homes, and one lives with a stepparent.

I was introduced to the Mansfield girls by Diane Starr, an educational technician at the Mansfield school. Diane worked intensively with
a multi-age classroom of about 20 girls, ages 11 to 14. These girls had a
personal closeness with Diane well before the project began in any official capacity. They would seek her out for counsel and support during
tough times; they considered her trustworthy and loyal, someone who
would speak to them straight but who would not sell them out. While I
was introduced to the girls and they knew that I would be viewing their
tapes and interviewing them individually at the end of the year, it was
very clear that Diane should facilitate this group.

The Mansfield girls usually began their videotaped sessions jockeying for position, some grabbing chairs, others sitting on desks or on the
floor in a relaxed, haphazard manner.[3] Videos of their interactions reveal
a lively, physical, often boisterous, outspoken group, vying for the

attention of the camera, shouting, often pushing each other before settling into more concentrated conversation.[4] Each group session brought a fresh intensity. The girls seemed to rely on the camera to be a recorder of their insistence, their sincerity, and their humor, capable of objectively rendering and fairly judging the truth of their experiences and observations about each other and the world around them. The camera became at times a supportive witness to their aggressive play, to their impertinence, and to their audacity. Meetings often ended with girls crowding the camera, laughing and pushing—individual faces peer into the lens, the camera jostles, hands appear, a peace sign becomes a middle finger, laughter, then the white noise on the tape until the next session begins.

The range and depth of the Mansfield girls' experiences interrupt any simple or innocent or conventional rendering of their early adolescence. Of the thirteen, six have experienced physical and/or sexual abuse in their families either from fathers, cousins, or older brothers. At least one girl is intimately familiar with the court and child welfare systems, having testified against an abusive father; two others, sisters, understand the dire consequences of being uninsured, having experienced homelessness after fire destroyed their trailer; still others know the poverty that lies just on the other side of their parents' unstable jobs and meager benefits. A number of the girls in the group are sexually active; two are on the pill. Some speak fondly and with excited anticipation of their sexual and emotional relationships with the migrant workers from Honduras and Mexico who come through the Mansfield area during the summer months. At least three of the girls smoke and some drink.

Performing Femininities

During a seemingly ordinary gathering one autumn afternoon, four of these white working-class girls illustrate the regulatory fictions of idealized femininity and also the failure of such fictions to define or contain them. "How would you describe the ideal girl?" Diane begins. The room is animated and the discussion moves at rapid-fire pace. Amber, a small, tough twelve-year-old, is the first to answer. "OK. The ideal girl is very pretty. . . ." Stacey, also twelve, slim, and herself conventionally pretty, immediately points to herself and interjects, "Me."

Amber: Talented—

Stacey: (Smiling, with a look of false modesty) Me again.

Amber: Smart, everybody likes her, everybody. . . . (Stacey shrugs her shoulders, throws up her hands, as if to say "me, again.") That's about it.

Diane: What do you mean by pretty?

Amber: Pretty, beautiful, good-looking. Long hair. I don't know. Pretty eyes. Nice figure. (Donna and Amber look at Stacey accusingly.)

Stacey: My idea of a perfect girl is somebody who's tall and pretty, and they have, like, perfect hair and perfect skin. They get good grades. Not afraid to make mistakes and stuff.

Diane: Does anyone know anyone like these perfect people? You guys know anybody like this?

At this question the girls look at one another. "No." "No." "No," they say in low voices. Diane continues, "Have you ever seen anybody like this?" The girls shake their heads; they have not. "Does this person exist?" Amber is certain she does "somewhere in the world"; maybe she is "not perfect, but close to perfect," she determines. The others, however, are not so sure, although they think they might like to become someone like this. "I already am," Stacey interjects again, "Just kidding."

Perhaps in response to this last comment, Amber continues

Amber: I know someone who's really pretty, but her attitude is blown way out of proportion . . . is right out of it. . . . Yeah, major attitude problem.

Stacey: Snobby.

Patti: Yeah, people who have attitudes. . . .Nosy.

Diane: What do you mean, like stuck up?

Stacey: Yeah, two-faced.

Donna: They don't keep secrets. . .

Amber: She's accusing. . .

Donna: (Says aloud to everyone, but looks at Patti pointedly) You can tell them anything and they give you good advice. You can trust them . . . I don't know.

Diane: So now we're getting a different picture of the perfect girl. Not so much looks.

Amber: Personality plays a big part of it.

Donna: You have to be able to trust them. . . a person who doesn't take over . . . in a group.

Stacey: Oh, yeah. They're trying to be the center of attention.

At this point Patti, at age eleven one of the youngest in the group, interrupts, "No one's actually perfect," she says in a loud voice. "I'd wanna be different than everybody else." But her comment is lost in a hum of debate, not about whether the girls want to be different from others, but about how they wish they could be different from who they are. Stacey begins in earnest, "I wish I was skinnier. A lot! I wish I could lose at least ten pounds." Amber concurs, "At least 12 or 15 pounds!" To this Donna, tall and very thin, laments, "I only weigh 102." As the conversation turns inward and the girls murmur in low voices to one another about the ideal weight, Patti, the only one of the girls who is not small or thin, looks down. Sitting away from the other girls, she visibly pulls herself out of the conversation.

Diane: So what would be the ideal weight?

Donna: Eighty.

Stacey (in a definitive tone): The ideal weight is 110.

Amber: One hundred and ten is not the ideal weight! I weigh 110! I should weigh at least 85.

Diane: Who says you should weigh 85?

Amber: I do! Look how short I am! I should weigh 85!

Stacey: I want to weigh between 105 and 110.

Donna: I would like to weigh 122.

Stacey: I think everyone wants to lose weight no matter what. Everybody wants to be better and lose weight.

Diane: No matter what your weight?

Stacey: Yeah. No matter what your weight.

Amber. Well, I'm always trying to be better. Taller. Skinnier.

Stacey: Well, I don't know, I could be . . . I could be happier.

Amber: If I was taller and skinnier.

Diane: You think being taller and skinnier would make you happier?

Amber: Oh, definitely.

As the girls continue to argue about how much they should weigh and how tall they should be, Donna pulls her right foot up on her chair seat to tie her shoe. This ordinary act has the unlikely effect of shifting both the tone and the substance of the conversation. It is as though Donna's movement signals something humorous or farcical in the exchange that has just taken place. What began as sincere and serious suddenly turns to a sort of theater of the absurd. "I want bigger feet," Amber says a bit too emphatically. "I want smaller feet!" Stacey exclaims. The girls laugh; Patti's face lights up as she rejoins the group. Diane decides to continue the new mood.

Diane: I want straight hair.

Stacey: I want curly hair.

Patti: I wish I had smaller feet.

Diane: Unfortunately, I gain a shoe size every time I get pregnant.

Stacey: Then I'm never going to get pregnant!

As the conversation turns to who has "big clown feet" and "shoes that look like hot dogs," the girls break from their orderly row of chairs. Amber jumps up and moves toward the camera. "I want to get closer. I want to get closer!" she exclaims, symbolizing, I suggest, her desire to shatter the distance between her and the image she has projected. At this the entire group jumps in front of the camera, first putting their faces up close, then hopping on one foot, holding onto one another in order to keep their balance as they raise their feet toward the camera lens in a kind of clumsy chorus line.

Stacey: See my feet? They're all my feet!

Diane: Are they clown feet?

Stacey: Yes, these are my clown feet. Smell!

The girls shout to the camera, "These are mine! These are mine!" In the background Donna and Amber hug. In an exaggerated manner the girls then compare their heights. Standing back-to-back, they laugh and shout, "Who's taller?" "Am I taller? I hope not!" Amber pushes in front of everyone and says directly to the camera: "Ain't I short!? I'm only 4'11." The girls, laughing, compare themselves to one another and then with Diane, who has joined them in front of the camera. "What about me! What about me?" they shout, laughing uncontrollably. As the drama ends, Patti, who has taken Diane's place behind the camera, announces, "You are watching *Channel Five News*!"

Four different voices converge initially to re-create an image of the "perfect girl" recognizable to anyone who opens the pages of a teen fashion magazine: beautiful, tall, long hair, perfect skin, pretty eyes, nice figure. This girl must also be talented and get good grades; she is humble,

modest, and liked by everybody, with a personality to match her looks. That
these girls do not know or have not actually seen anyone like this does not
dissuade them from expressing their desire to be like her. She is the standard against which others, quite literally, are measured, or so it would first
appear—accusatory looks say that either you have come too close or you
have swayed too far from her likeness. That dissonant voices are lost in
the group construction of this image—Patti's wish to be different from the
ideal, for example, and Donna's desire to weigh more rather than less—
speaks to its potential to control their collective imagination.

And yet even as they speak, the limits and even the absurdity of this
ideal are communicated among the girls through their body movements
and facial expressions. As they talk with great seriousness about trust and
loyalty, about always being nice, about having a good attitude and not
demanding attention, envy, competition, irritability, and signs of mistrust
and betrayal seep into the spaces between them. Their bodies convey what
is not directly addressed or acknowledged: the "psychic excess" that falls
outside the narrow confines of such an ideal (Butler, 1991, p. 24).

Thus while the dialogue among Donna, Patti, Stacey, and Amber
is ostensibly about their desire and struggle to imitate narrow conventions of white middle-class femininity, they simultaneously signify their
inevitable failure and persistent refusal to do so. What falls outside the
ideal, that which is and can never be fully expressed inside its boundaries, erupts within the intervals of the girls' gestures and interactions
(Butler, 1991, p. 24). At the height of intense debate, an unremarkable,
barely discernible act threatens to reveal what had seemed so true and
possible and intensely important to be an illusion—indeed to be farcical and ridiculous.[5]

The girls' consistent failure to approximate the ideal thus provides
an opening that threatens to reveal the perfect girl for who she is, a
"phantasmic ideal" of feminine identity (Butler, 1991, p. 21). The potential of this threat to be disruptive or subversive, depends on the girls'
relationships—on their attention and responsiveness to one another in
this key moment. Indeed, the association between Donna's tying her
shoe and the girls' heightened mood ignites a dramatic shift in relationship. As the girls' concerns about beauty elevate to the level of parody, their collective voices gather momentum and their expressions
toward one another change. Gone are the accusatory looks and the argu-
mentative voices. Their wariness and defensive postures vanish as they
jump from their seats, and wrap their arms around each other, and move
close together. They are at once raucous, active, funny, loud, and loving—they are not, as it were, a "pretty" sight. Now the camera, rather
than other girls, becomes the audience and witness to their performance; they are, in a sense, in this together, undivided, and from this
group display comes their power to redirect and redefine the terms of
the situation.

The significance of this collective, relational act cannot be over-stated, since by definition the ideal girl is isolated in her perfection. By comparison, all other girls are deficient, and so she elicits the envy, com-petition, and disloyalty commonly associated with girls' and women's relationships. In their initial construction of this ideal, the girls too are separate: they are bodies in a row facing the camera, each concerned with comparing herself with the image. The fiction of the feminine ideal, in this sense, serves to divide girls psychically and socially, to discon-nect them from themselves and from one another. Only when this fic-tion is disrupted and made ridiculous do the girls move close together.

According to Butler, the ideal of white middle-class heterosexual femininity, constitutive of a compulsory sex/gender system, "is always in the process of imitating and approximating its own idealization of itself—and failing." Such "repetition," Butler argues, "is the way in which power works to construct the illusion of a seamless . . . identity." And yet, "it is this constant need for repetition that points to the very instability of the ideal, reveals it to be an imitation, an illusion, always at risk of coming undone—for what if it fails to repeat, or if the very exercise of repetition is redeployed for a very different performative purpose?" (p. 24).

In one scene after another these working-class girls disrupt the repetition, and thus the controlling power, of the dominant cultural fem-inine ideal. By elevating it to the level of parody or farce, or by dra-matically shifting from identity to identity, they allude to the instabil-ity of the ideal itself. In this way they reveal its constructed, performative nature, contest its claim to coherence or truth, illuminate its seemingly unrehearsed, "essential" qualities, and thus attenuate its power to regulate or contain them.

Speaking in and through Patriarchy

There is a common belief, expressed repeatedly, among the work-ing-class girls that "other" girls are, by nature, indirect and deceitful, that they talk behind people's backs and have a propensity for break-ing confidences or telling secrets. Such girls are "two-faced" and untrust-worthy, and make private conversations public out of revenge or to seek attention. Often, the Mansfield girls complain in voices full of anger and disgust; these are the same girls who are "stuck on themselves," "who think they're the best," who want to be "the center of attention," and who "strut around" all "stuck-up," with "an attitude problem." Such girls will do anything for attention—lie and steal other girls' boyfriends—and are therefore deceitful and traitorous, perhaps two of the oldest character flaws associated with femininity.

Such associations and opinions instigate perhaps the most clear and striking examples of ventriloquation of patriarchal voices: the ways in which the Mansfield girls appropriate sexist, misogynistic, and homophobic language to tease or poke fun at each other and, more pointedly, to denigrate those girls, mothers, grandmothers, aunts, and women teachers who they feel have betrayed or hurt them in some way. "She was a bitch," Stacey says of a teacher who treated her badly the day before. Later in the same session she exclaims, "My mother's a cheap ho!"[6] "I called Dawn a ho," Rachel admits, explaining why she was in trouble with one of her teachers. She and her friend can't "be together" with another girl, Susan laughingly explains, "Not unless she's a lezzie." Like a Greek chorus, the girls shout derogatory comments about other girls and women. Terms like "hos," "bitches," and "lezzies," accompanied by "Maybe it's PMS" or "She's such a cow," and "What a bag," assault those others the girls feel have let them down or betrayed them.

Such misogynistic terms and phrases seem funny to the girls; on the surface they are playful in a threatening sort of way; a linguistic sign of their insider status with the group, sometimes a verbal test of toughness. When asked why they say these things, they deny that such words mean anything significant. "That's just joking around," Amber protests when Diane asks her if girls' feelings are hurt when they are called "hos." The other girls interrupt each other in their eagerness to dismiss the significance of the word. "Ho?" they shout in practiced voices. "It's a garden tool!" "It doesn't hurt me," Angela insists. "Everybody does that! We just fool around."

The Mansfield girls' denigration and put-downs of other girls and women signal their momentary alignment with conventional views of women and understandings of femininity. That is, they speak about girls and women in a language drenched in a patriarchal history of women's oppression. In this sense, their language or forms of expression forge an unexamined truce with the prevailing social order that polices the borders of appropriately gendered expression and activity and ultimately situates girls and women, to the degree that they express such "feminine" qualities, in subordinate positions relative to boys and men.

Forswearing their connections to other girls and aligning or bonding with male views of femininity requires that these girls, if they are to be strong and willful and direct, distance themselves from anything explicitly feminine. This means both vulnerability and bitchiness, but also homosexuality. By using terms like *fag* and *lezzie* to put down others, as they do often, the girls participate in a conventional sex/gender system that normalizes oppressive structures and categories.

Acting tough, talking trash, giving the camera the finger, pushing and pinching each other, shouts of "Shut the hell up!" or "He's a jerk-off!" "She's a bitch!" invite Bakhtin's questions: "Who precisely is speaking, and under what concrete circumstances?" (1981) Such actions and discourse distance the girls from the traditionally feminine and align them with the observed behavior and discourse of boys and men they know. Talking about "really cool," "really funny" guys at a party, for example, the girls are quick to put down another girl who was, as Stacey says, "playing hard to get. The bitch." When the boys begin to bet on whether this girl "would do it" with the boy she was with, some of the girls try to join in.

> Stacey: Yeah, he goes . . . he said . . . he told her to "Come on, I've got five bucks riding on this!". . . He said that to her. Cause him and Charles had a bet.

> Rachel: Yeah, they did. And I did too, but I didn't have enough money, so they wouldn't let me bet.

> Stacey: Yeah, me neither. I only had eleven cents.

> Diane: Well, who was betting who?

> Stacey: Charles and Jon. Charles won.

> Rachel: He's so nice. He's really cool.

In this instance the girls fully accept the boys' reading of the reluctant girl's refusal to have sex at the party—she is "a tease" and "a bitch"—and identify with their behavior by trying to join in on the joke. They further align themselves with these "cool" boys who were "sitting there swearing in the car," bragging about who "could kick the piss out of" who, by insisting they too, as Rachel says, "swear all the time."

In other instances, as they talk about sexual and physical abuse they have experienced or witnessed, the girls struggle with how to understand such experiences, seesawing between the evidence of their own senses and identifying with the perspectives of the abusers. Donna, who has been physically assaulted by her father, talks in one session about how she learned that "no one deserves to be hit," and in another session rejects her father's girlfriends' accusations of rape. "He wouldn't do that. He don't rape. He doesn't do that," she insists—even as she ventriloquates her father's justification for assault.

> Anyway, he said that . . . when she asks dad something and dad doesn't answer back—he's mad or something—he like walks away and she runs after him and wants an answer from him. And dad, when he gets mad he just walks off, and he wants to deal with it on his own, and she runs after him and tries to get answers and so he got mad and hit her. . . . She had a bruise right here [pointing to the side of her face], and a bruise on her forehead and he threw her . . . and she hit the top of the door thing and broke it, broke the door.

While the working-class girls distance themselves from other girls and women on the basis of relational treachery and vulnerability read by them as signs of feminine weakness, middle-class girls struggle with rigid categorical divisions long mapped onto white middle-class conventions of femininity, predominantly opposing good girls with bad. Good girls, nice girls, with whom they identify, are kind, considerate, and selfless; they always care, listen, do not hurt others, do not get in trouble, and do not express anger directly or publicly; they don't cause scenes, are well behaved, do not feel or at least express sexual desire, and are not sexually active. Nice girls try to meet others' expectations, do well in school, are involved in various activities, and don't brag or call attention to themselves.

Renegade Voices

The Mansfield girls' ideological struggles reveal the complex relationships between discourse and power, and language and domination. They also reveal, what hooks calls the possibility of "outlawed tongues, renegade speech."

> Like desire, language disrupts, refuses to be contained within boundaries. It speaks itself against our will, in words and thoughts that intrude, even violate the most private spaces of mind and body, . . . Words impose themselves, take root in our memory against our will. (1994, p. 167)

The Mansfield girls find strength in the renegade voices and outlawed tongues of those who refuse to be narrowly contained in or made invisible by the language and categories and expectations of conventional white middle-class femininity. These working-class girls convey their parents' mistrust of, and irreverence for authority derived solely from material wealth or status, and reiterate their parents' stubborn refusal to be dismissed and their predilection for expressing strong opinions openly. Her courage to speak out and criticize the way the school is run and the values it espouses, Susan says, for example, "comes from my parents. They always taught me if I had something to say, just say it."

Echoing their parents and other adults in their community, the Mansfield girls resist the white middle-class notions of femininity espoused at their school. Speaking through their fathers and mothers, many of whom work more than one part-time job, the girls talk of the practical necessity of hard work and their willingness to do menial jobs and endure long hours of physical labor to achieve their dreams of having enough. Qualities fostered at home such as toughness, boldness, and straightforward expressions of thought and feeling that often label them as *difficult* and *disruptive at school,* connect them with each other, their families, and their community. Such qualities and behaviors hold different meanings and intentions. Reprimands from teachers and administrators for such behavior, in turn, invite open critique and anger from their parents. Dana's mother is notorious at the Mansfield school for her support of her children's right to physically protect themselves or to fight for a just cause, for example, and has been to the school a number of times in Dana's defense. Dana and the other girls openly admire her for such physical and psychological toughness, qualities Dana, in particular, imitates.

In fact, Dana's pride in, and love for, her mother become apparent as she ventriloquates her mother's belief in self-protection and the defense of those weaker or less powerful, and enacts her devotion to her family, their sense of humor, and their beliefs about what it means to be a woman. For the Mansfield girls, other women too—aunts, cousins, and friends—embody and give voice to the possibility for an economically successful, healthy, self-propelled, contented life against the dire predictions they read in many of their teachers' faces and reactions.

So too, over the course of the year, does a woman teacher, Diane Starr, provide a language and course of action for the girls to effectively resist unfair school practices they encounter. The girls take in Diane's bold commitment to them, a commitment that interrupts the prevailing discourse in the school about themselves as difficult, "stupid," with "dim" futures, and also complicates the girls' too simplistic descriptions of all teachers and all administrators as uncaring, unpredictable, and unjust. Channeling the girls' strong feelings and opinions into constructive avenues, Diane facilitates what becomes a formidable group of resisters over the course of the year.

Renegade voices from diverse sources thus enter and take root in the Mansfield girls' minds and bodies. Their over-size T-shirts and baggy shorts, their slang—references to each other as "hos" and "bitches"—read negatively in one light, also loosely identify them with the sexuality, boldness, resistance, and the marginalization of Black rappers they listen to and watch on MTV, particularly their favorites, Salt n' Pepa. Within strictly heterosexual parameters these white girls play on and reappropriate the particular sexualized audacity of Salt n' Pepa, as well as more general stereotypes of Black women as sexy and dangerous. Taken in and taken on by these white working-class girls, such voices, gestures, and ways of dressing become highly contradictory, heightening their resistance to white upper middle-class feminine ideals of niceness and sexual purity, as well as their tension with the relentless expressions of material abundance relayed through television—particularly the MTV shows the girls watch, such as *The Real World, House of Style* and the popular but short-lived *My*

So-Called Life.[7] Such tensions and contradictions among voices and viewpoints open the Mansfield girls to an indeterminacy of meaning; to creative possibilities, alternative values, feelings, and thoughts; and also gives voice to longings and desires that contrast sharply with their material realities.

The Mansfield girls occupy that liminal space between childhood and adulthood where intentions are questioned, meanings are indeterminate. In their struggles for personal truth and self-definition, in their desires to make the different voices they hear and take in coherent and understandable, to make them their own, they ferret out, expose, and wrestle with the contradictions, the limitations, the hypocrisies, and the pretense around them. In their anger, expressed throughout their interviews and group sessions, they react stubbornly to the constraints white middle-class femininity, indeed, the traditional categories "girl" or "woman," place on their personhoods, and to the frustrations they experience as they search for words to describe their difference, to speak what they know and who they might become.

Girls on the Verge of a Political Breakthrough

The Mansfield girls seem to be acutely aware of the expectations to perform idealized notions of white middle-class femininity even as they experience the complexity of their lives—a complexity that assures themselves and others that they are, as it were, a bad fit within such a narrow context. This has particular implications for their experience in school, where their persistent failure to fit in with this fictional identity places them in tension with their teachers, many of whom operate as though the ideal were real and thus possible and preferable. At times these girls directly and openly express their frustration and anger to their teachers, but also know well the consequences of their outspoken protest—a quality which, itself, places them off the map of acceptability and thus out of relationship. "What can you do?" twelve-year-old Susan asks. "If you do something, if you say anything, then you get sent down to the office." As a result the girls learn to shift identities, develop acceptable personae and perform idealized femininity as a way to traverse the chasm between home and school.

And yet the Mansfield girls also insist on bringing their loud, direct, relational selves to school. In doing so, they engage in a daily public struggle with their teachers over the interpretation of reality and the contours of legitimate knowledge. Their refusal to be contained, to be ordered, disciplined, their resistance to splitting feeling and thought, private and public, their desire to be heard in their own terms reveals, as it does in Luttrell's study of white working-class women, an implicit critique of schooling that ignores "the exigencies of poor and working-class families" by rewarding "'good girl' behavior and traditional middle-class femininity" and denying "the reality and legitimacy of working-class femininity, an image of women as hardworking, responsible caregivers" (1993, pp. 524, 525). Having a propensity to "just say it," they unwittingly disrupt tacit boundaries between public and private speech; their laughter, playfulness, and anger disturb the "bourgeois class biases" that determine proper behavior and that shape and inform "pedagogical process (as well as social etiquette) in the classroom" (hooks, 1994, p. 178). And too, their toughness and active, physical aggressiveness contest the well-mannered "good girl" most teachers imagine and perhaps hope to meet each day in school.

The contradictions the Mansfield girls live and breathe during early adolescence bring to the surface the multiple voices and visions that vie for their allegiance. Their range of feeling and behavior, their complex understandings of, and expressions of, femininity, put them at odds with the expectations of their teachers and thus underscore their displacement in school and white middle-class society. Cast against white middle-class feminine ideals, their strong voices sound off-key, become unrecognizable, and difficult to hear; their bold, self-protective actions become signs of failure or distress. Ironically, therefore, the very behavior that frees them from idealized stereotypic gender conventions may also label them, according to the dominant notions of femininity, as *psychologically troubled, socially inferior,* or *marginal.*

"Where the notion of 'proper' operates, it is always and only improperly installed as the effect of a compulsory system," Butler stresses (1991, p. 21). And yet, as Walkerdine states, the proper is inevitably undone because "we never quite fit the 'positions' provided for us in these regulatory practices. . . . That failure is . . . both the point of pain and the point of struggle. It shows repeatedly that the imposition of fictional identities—or socialization—does not work" (1990, p. 198). As I listen to the Mansfield girls describe themselves as "stupid" and their personal and academic futures as "dim" and "black" I hear their expressed failure to fit the positions provided for them; I hear them ventriloquate their teachers' predictions of the dire consequences of their failure or refusal to meet the demands of idealized femininity—a femininity that would endorse silence over outspokenness, passivity over active resistance, a pleasing ignorance over knowledge of the complexity and difficulty of lived experience and relationships, weakness over physical strength and aggressiveness. With the pain and struggle, however, is also the possibility. Among and between the girls renegade and resistant voices, and gestures, interactions disrupt the regulatory fictions of idealized femininity, revisioning both who they are and who they might become.

The Mansfield girls bring into focus the limited and limiting discourse of conventional femininity—how it serves to blur, cover over, and make incomprehensible the complex and contradictory realities of young women's present-day experiences—but also how such limits trigger an outrage that intersects with race, culture, and girls' different concrete material lives to create openings, new possibilities, and sites for successful struggle. These young women, within the boundaries of very different social and structural constraints, use the subversive power of body, sexuality, and language to challenge conventional meanings and expectations of femininity and to disrupt the regulatory practices that keep such meanings in place. The edge of adolescence may thus constitute a key developmental and political moment in girls' lives, a critical period if you will, for possibility and potential. Girls' struggles with the push and pull of often contradictory, fragmented voices telling them who, as young women, they are or should be, provide an opening, a juncture in the life cycle where the incongruity between the personal or experiential and the "externally authoritative" (Bakhtin, 1981) comes into focus and where the processes of ideological becoming are salient and pronounced. In their struggle with varying conceptions of what it means to be female, adolescent girls destabilize the categories of girl and woman, revealing them to be what Butler calls "structures of impersonation," exposing the fact that gender is performative, a construct, "a kind of imitation for which there is no original," a phantasmal idealization of what a woman is supposed to be in a given culture (1991, p. 21). In their resistance to increased attempts to regulate or train their voices and actions, girls at this developmental juncture call attention in different ways to this idealization, and to the demands and costs of female impersonation. Their strong feelings and their questions are disruptive of the way things "naturally" go and anxiety-provoking for those who like such things the way they are.

Notes

1. Willis (1977) makes a similar point in his study of British working-class boys in *Learning to labor*.

2. The U.S. literature on class tends to focus more on sociological rather than psychological processes; even the best-known psychological studies on class, written in the 1970s—Rubin's *Worlds of Pain* and Sennett & Cobb's *Hidden Injuries of Class* originate in sociology. Most of the more recent literature on girls and class is out of Britain, and much of this literature, such as the work of McRobbie (1991), focuses on girls and popular culture.

3. Most often the girls met together in an upstairs school classroom after lunch, during their recess period. The group was voluntary—initially each and every girl in the sixth, seventh, and eighth grades who wished to participate and who obtained parental permission was welcome. Although the number of girls varied on any given day, the group

formed a fairly solid core of two eleven-year-olds, six twelve-year-olds, two thirteen-year-olds, and three fourteen-year-olds.

4. On camera and in individual interviews the Mansfield girls' voices carry the language and culture of the Maine woods and its working-class roots: its attention to self-protection and survival, its respect for personal and family privacy, and its suspicion of authority and disdain for government intervention or outside regulation of community or family life.

5. It is perhaps significant that it is a gesture around the feet that generates the girls' reactions and that changes the course of the conversation. The girls' reaction seems to imply that regulating feminine perfection down to the feet reveals how absurd the whole enterprise is.

6. *Ho* is an idiomatic reference to "whore" that the working-class girls have appropriated from popular black rap music they listen to. It is a term that has its own popular cultural manifestations within this music genre— a genre still considered, like the working-class girls, somewhat marginal and problematic within dominant white middle-class culture. The term is polyvalent to the girls, and their use of it depends on the person they are talking about, the situation and the audience. While their use of *ho* is not fully disconnected from its popular cultural meanings, it has its own power and significance within their group and community. The girls appropriate its misogynistic overtones when they use the term as a form of threat or to denigrate other girls and women they dislike. (In other words, the girls use *ho* much the way Lees [1993] describes boys' use of the term *slag*. Thus, in these moments, they speak through or ventriloquate male voices.) The term is also used playfully, however, and can serve as a linguistic marker of intimacy; that is, a word whose layers of meaning are understood by only the initiated (hence their response to Diane Starr, the adult group facilitator, when she queries them about the term: "Ho? It doesn't mean anything. It's just a garden tool.") *Ho* can also be used to threaten those who have been disloyal to the group or may indicate the girls' rejection of someone who has, in some way, challenged their understanding of what is appropriate treatment of those in the group or of appropriate behavior for girls like them. Hence the term is drenched in intentions, some parodic and some subversive.

7. This show is a favorite of the girls. Because MTV in the United States continuously reruns the episodes, the girls know each episode nearly by heart.

References

American Association of University Women (AAUW). (1991). *Short-changing girls, shortchanging America*. Washington, DC: AAUW Educational Foundation.

American Association of University Women (AAUW). (1992). *How schools shortchange girls*: Washington, DC: AAUW Educational Foundation.

Bakhtin, M. (1981). *The dialogic imagination*. (M. Holquist, Ed.) (C. Emerson & M. Holquist, Trans.). Austin: University of Texas Press.

Bernardez, T. (1988). Women and anger—Cultural prohibitions and the feminine ideal. Working Paper, No. 31. Wellesley, MA: Center for Research on Women.

Brown, L. M. (1998). *Raising their voices: The politics of girls' anger*. Cambridge: Harvard University Press.

Brown, L. M., Argyris, D., Attanucci, J., Bardige, B., Gilligan, C., Johnston, K., Miller, B., Osborne, R., Tappan, M., Ward, J., Wiggins, G., & Wilcox, D. (1988). *A guide to reading narratives of conflict and choice for self and relational voice*. (Monograph No. 1). Cambridge: Project on the Psychology of Women and the Development of Girls, Harvard Graduate School of Education.

Brown, L. M., Debold, E., Tappan, M., & Gilligan, C. (1991). Reading narratives of conflict and choice for self and moral voice: A relational method. In W. Kurtines & J. Gewirtz (Eds.), *Handbook of moral behavior and development: Theory, research, and application* (pp. 25-61). Hillsdale, NJ: Lawrence Erlbaum.

Brown, L. M., & Gilligan, C. (1991). Listening for voice in narratives of relationship. In M. Tappan & M. Packer (Eds.), *Narrative and storytelling: Implications for understanding moral development* (pp. 43-62). (New Directions for Child Development, No. 54). San Francisco: Jossey-Bass.

Brown, L. M., & Gilligan, C. (1992). Meeting at the crossroads: Women's psychology and girls' development. Cambridge: Harvard University Press.

Brown, L. M., Tappan, M., Gilligan, C., Miller, B., & Argyris, D. (1989). Reading for self and moral voice: A method for interpreting narratives of real-life moral conflict and choice. In M. Packer & R. Addison (Eds.), *Entering the circle: Hermeneutic investigation in psychology* (pp. 141-164). Albany: State University of New York Press.

Butler, J. (1991). Imitation and gender insubordination. In D. Fuss (Ed.), *Inside / out: Lesbian theories, gay theories*. New York: Routledge.

Fine, M. (1988). Sexuality, schooling, and adolescent females: The missing discourse of desire. *Harvard Educational Review, 58,* 29-53.

Fine, M. (1992). Disruptive voices. Albany: State University of New York Press.

Fine, M., & Macpherson, P. (1992). Over dinner: Feminism and adolescent female bodies. In M. Fine, *Disruptive voices* (pp. 175-203). Albany: State University of New York Press.

Fordham, S. (1993). "Those loud black girls": (Black) women, silence and gender "passing" in the academy. *Anthropology and Education Quarterly, 24,* 3-32.

Gilligan, C. (1990). Joining the resistance: Psychology, politics, girls, and women. *Michigan Quarterly Review, 29,* 501–536.

hooks, b. (1994). *Teaching to transgress*. New York: Routledge.

Lees, S. (1993). *Sugar and spice: Sexuality and adolescent girls*. London: Penquin.

Luttrelll, W. (1993). "The teachers all had their pets": Concepts of gender, knowledge, and power. *Signs, 18 (3),* 505–546.

McRobbie, A. (1991). *Feminism and youth culture*. Boston: Unwin Hyman.

Ogbu, J. (1989). The individual in collective adaptation: A framework for focusing on academic underperformance and dropping out among involuntary minorities. In L. Weis, E. Farrar, & H. G. Petrie (Eds.), *Dropouts from school: Issues, dilemmas, and solutions*. Albany: State University of New York Press.

Orenstein, P. (1994). S*choolgirls: Young women, self-esteem and the confidence gap*. New York: Doubleday.

Pastor, J., McCormick, J., & Fine, M. (1996). Makin homes: An urban girl thing. In B. Leadbeater & N. Way (Eds.), *Urban girls* (pp. 15-34). New York: New York University Press.

Pipher, M. (1995). *Reviving Ophelia*. New York: Ballantine.

Rogers, A., Brown, L., & Tappan, M. (1994). Interpreting loss in ego development in girls: Regression or resistance? In R. Josselson & A. Lieblich (Eds.), *Vol. 2. The narrative study of lives* (pp. 1-36). Newbury Park, CA: Sage.

Rubin, L. (1976). *Worlds of pain*. New York: Basic.

Sennett, R., & Cobb, J. (1972). *The hidden injuries of class*. New York: Vintage.

Steedman, C. K. (1987). *Landscape for a good woman*. New Brunswick, NJ: Rutgers University Press.

Stevenson, R., & Ellsworth, J. (1993). Dropouts and the silencing of critical voices. In L. Weis & M. Fine (Eds.), *Beyond silenced voices: Class, race, and gender in United States schools* (pp. 259-271). Albany: State University of New York Press.

Walkerdine, V. (1990). *Schoolgirl fictions*. London: Verso.

Way, N. (1995). "Can't you see the courage, the strength that I have?" Listening to urban adolescent girls speak about their relationships. *Psychology of Women Quarterly, 19,* 107-128.

Weedon, C. (1987). *Feminist practice and poststructuralist theory*. Oxford: Basil Blackwell

Willis, P. (1977). *Learning to labor*. New York: Columbia University Press.

CHAPTER 9

The Cultural Reproduction of Masculinity: A Critical Perspective on Boys' Development

Mark B. Tappan

Introduction

"If you woke up tomorrow as a girl instead of a boy, how would your life be different?" We posed this question to a group of first-grade boys (all European-American) living in a small town in rural Maine.[1] Here is how two of those seven-year-olds answered:

Ned: Not too good!

Mark: How so? Why wouldn't it be good?

Ned: My mother wouldn't like it. She'd probably kick me out of the house.

Mark: You'd be kicked out of the house if you were a girl, huh?

Ned: Yeah. She wouldn't like it too much.

Mark: And how would you feel about it?

Ned: Not too good.

Mark: Not too good.

Ned: I'd try to go find myself again.

Adam: I would ask my dad if he could build a machine to turn me back into a boy.

Mark: [Laughter] That's a good idea! So you really like being a boy, huh? How else would your life be different? Say it took your father two days to build that machine; how would those two days be different?

Adam: Um, then I would change myself into a boy with my finger.

Mark: With your finger? Well, what if you couldn't do it with your finger and had to wait for your father to build the machine?

Adam: Then I would rip him to pieces.

Mark: You would what?

Adam: I would rip my dad into pieces.

Mark: But then you'd never get turned back because you wouldn't get the machine built.

Adam: Then I would build it myself.

Mark: So you would build it, ok. Meanwhile, what would it be like to be a girl?

Adam: Mmm, stupid.

Mark: Why?

Adam: Because it would be; it would be too much different, I don't know.

Within the intersection of psychology, sociology, anthropology, history, and cultural studies that define the contemporary field of "gender studies" there is widespread interest in masculinity and in the male gender role (Bly, 1990; Brod, 1987; Connell, 1987; Keen, 1991; Kimmel, 1996; Kimmel & Messner, 1989; Miedzian, 1991; Pleck, 1981; Rotundo, 1993; Stoltenberg, 1989, 1993). Explorations of masculinity in the United States have examined the influence of male gender role across a variety of dimensions, including male-female relationships, male-male relationships, sexuality, parenting, and "problem behaviors" (e.g., substance abuse, violence, delinquency, dropout, and other school-related difficulties). Inspired by pioneering work in feminist studies, there is increasing recognition that gender is a primary feature of social life for both men and women, so much so that "gender has now taken its place alongside race and class as the three central mechanisms by which power and resources are distributed in our society, and the three central themes out of which we fashion the meanings of our lives" (Kimmel & Messner, 1989, p. 2).

Yet in spite of this growing interest in understanding the experience of men *as men*, until very recently (see Garbarino, 1999; Pollack, 1998) little attention has been paid to *boys,* like Ned and Adam, particularly as they experience the developmental processes that give rise to their understanding of their own masculinity and male gender identity. There has, of course, been a great deal of developmental research conducted on boys over the past century or so—in fact, as Gilligan (1982) has noted, much of the critical theory-building research of such luminaries as Piaget, Kohlberg, and Erikson was based primarily on interviews with, and observations of, boys and young men. But it was not the experience of boys as boys that was of interest to these investigators. Rather, they assumed that studying boys and men was a perfectly acceptable way to study *human development,* since gender was, for them, a difference that made no difference in their quest to understand and explain human experience.

Things have changed, however, in recent years. Following Gilligan's (1982) recognition that the experience of women *as women* had largely been ignored in developmental research, there have been a host of studies focusing exclusively on the developmental processes at work in girls' and women's lives (see, e.g., Belenky, et al., 1986; Brown, 1991; Brown & Gilligan, 1992; Gilligan, Lyons, & Hanmer, 1990; Gilligan, Ward, & Taylor, 1988; Jordan, et al., 1991; Rogers, 1993; Taylor, Gilligan, & Sullivan, 1995; Walkerdine, 1990). Most centrally, this work has highlighted both the importance of relationships in the formation and reformation of girls' identity and morality, and the powerful effect that cultural expectations and prescriptions have on girls' understanding of themselves and their relationships. As such, Brown and Gilligan (1992) identify early adolescence as a time when girls encounter and struggle with cultural conventions, when they begin to feel pressure, that is, to capitulate to traditional notions of femininity and feminine behavior and dominant images of beauty and attractiveness. Some girls resist these pressures and the losses they engender, but others become tentative and unsure of themselves, experience a loss of voice, a narrowing of desires and expectations, and seem to move from genuine and authentic relationships to idealized notions of friendship and love.

While this groundbreaking research on girls has shed important new light on the developmental processes at work in the lives of half the population, it also raises the possibility of a new and deeper understanding of boys' development (see Pollack, 1998). That is to say, it is clearly time to turn the tables, and to view the experience of boys through lenses crafted, at least initially, by those studying girls. This is not to repeat the mistakes of the past (i.e., to study the development of one gender and to assume that the findings apply to the other gender as well). But it is to acknowledge that the recent theoretical and empirical work on girls' development can provide a useful starting point for a similar exploration of boys' development—focusing particularly on the ways in which boys' gender identity development is shaped and influenced by cultural processes.

Such attention to the "cultural reproduction of masculinity" is enabled, moreover, by recent advances in the field of sociocultural psychology (see Cole, 1996; Martin, Nelson, & Tobach, 1995; Wertsch, 1985, 1991, 1998; Wertsch, del Rio, & Alvarez, 1995). Influenced and inspired by the work of Lev Vygotsky (1934/1987, 1978), sociocultural scholars have focused sustained attention on the ways in which "mediational means" (i.e., tools and language), appropriated from the social world, shape human mental functioning (see Wertsch, 1985, 1991, 1998). As such, the sociocultural perspective seeks to offer an alternative to the explicitly individualistic perspective that has dominated our thinking about human development for the past century or more, by exploring and explicating the relationship between human mental functioning (understood as "mediated action") and the social, cultural, and historical situations in which such functioning occurs (Wertsch, 1995, 1998).

My aim in this chapter, therefore, is to sketch the outlines of a sociocultural perspective on boys' development that considers how boys' masculine gender identity is forged in their relationship to, and encounter with, the culture in which they live. For heuristic purposes I will present this perspective as an alternative to the psychodynamic approach to gender identity development—the most widely known and well-accepted approach to these issues. I begin, therefore, with a consideration of the psychodynamic perspective on boys' development, derived primarily from the work of Chodorow (1974, 1978). I then turn to the task of outlining a sociocultural perspective on boys' development, based largely on the recent effort of Penuel and Wertsch (1995) to formulate a sociocultural approach to identity formation. Next I consider a sociocultural interpretation of a gender-related incident that occurred among a group of boys and girls the same age as Ned and Adam. I conclude, finally, with a brief consideration of the methodological and educational implications of this new perspective on boys' development.

The Psychodynamic Perspective on Boys' Development

Based on Freudian and neo-Freudian/object-relations accounts of the effect of early childhood experience on personality development, the psychodynamic perspective assumes that the boy's relationship with his mother profoundly influences his masculine gender identity development. This influence begins early, during the pre-Oedipal period (birth to age three). During the first year of life, Chodorow argues, the young boy (like the young girl) develops a strong attachment and a sense of "primary identification" with his mother—he can not and does not differentiate himself from his mother, but instead "experiences a sense of oneness with her" (1974, p. 46). This attachment and primary identification represents, at least in part, a continuation of the child's prenatal experience of being physically part of his mother's body. It is also encouraged in most societies by the fact that mothers lactate; thus mothers tend to assume the role of primary caretaker for their infants and young children (both boys and girls).

During the next several years the primary task facing both boys and girls is to begin the process of separation and individuation—that is, "breaking or attenuating the primary identification with the mother and beginning to develop an individuated sense of self, and mitigating the totally dependent oral attitude and attachment to the mother" (ibid.). Here, Chodorow suggests, the pre-Oedipal experience begins to differ for boys and for girls. Mothers of daughters, it seems, often experience a sense of "double identification": "a woman identifies with her own mother and, through identification with her child, she (re)experiences herself as a cared for child" (p. 47). This double identification (whereby the mother identifies with her daughter just as her daughter identifies with her) does not occur in a mother's relationship to her son, and thus the processes of separation and individuation become organizing principles for boys' self-understanding from a very early age. A mother tends to treat her son as different and distinct from herself, even at a young age, "usually by emphasizing his masculinity in opposition to herself and by pushing him to assume, or acquiescing in his assumption of, a sexually toned male-role in relation to her" (p. 48). Thus, argues Chodorow, mothers identify less with their sons than with their daughters, pushing sons, in the process, toward differentiation and separation, and toward the formation of clear and distinct ego boundaries.

This process continues during the Oedipal period (ages three to five)—a period wherein two important developments occur as the boy's emerging sense of masculine gender identity begins to replace his early primary identification with his mother.[2] The first is that his father (and men in general) begin to become important in the boy's relational world, as a person (or persons) with whom to identify and to emulate. The second is that the boy begins to explicitly denigrate and devalue feminine aspects of his own and others' experience. Let me explore each of these developments in turn.

A boy's developing masculine gender identity is typically based on an identification with his father or with other important adult males in his life (grandfather, uncles, older brothers, etc.). Because, however, traditional social and cultural arrangements typically take the father away from the family for a large amount of time each day, much of a boy's masculine identification typically becomes an identification with an "invisible father," or with a fantasized masculine role, rather than with his father as a real person with whom he is involved in a genuine relationship. As a result, Chodorow argues, "a boy's male gender identification often become a 'positional' identification, with aspects of his father's clearly or not-so-clearly defined male role, rather than a more generalized 'personal' identification—a diffuse identification with his father's personality, values, and behavioral traits—that could grow out of a real relationship to his father" (p. 49).

As the boy begins to identify more strongly with his father, or at least with an idealized image of his father's role, he also strives to further weaken his identification with his mother by denigrating and devaluing her as a woman.

> A boy, in his attempt to gain an elusive masculine identification, often comes to this masculinity largely in negative terms, as that which is not feminine or involved with women. There is an internal and external aspect to this. Internally, the boy tries to reject his mother and deny his attachment to her and the strong dependence on her that he still feels. He also tries to deny the deep personal identification with her that has developed during the early years. He does this by repressing whatever he takes to be feminine inside himself, and, importantly, by denigrating and devaluing whatever he considers to be feminine in the outside world. (p. 50)

These two elements—the identification with his father and the subsequent rejection of the feminine—characterize Freud's vision of the "typical" resolution of the Oedipal crisis for the young boy. Moreover, from the psychodynamic perspective, a successful resolution of the Oedipal crisis gives rise to the superego—the seat of conscience and morality.

> As his early attachment to his mother takes on phallic-sexual overtones, and his father enters the picture as an obvious rival (who, in the son's fantasy, has apparent power to kill or castrate his son), the boy must radically deny and repress his attachment to his mother and replace it with an identification with his loved and admired, but also potentially punitive, therefore feared, father. He internalizes a superego. (pp. 50–51)

More importantly from the psychodynamic perspective, however, the attainment of masculine gender identity for boys, at its core, "involves denial of attachment or relationship, particularly of what the boy takes to be dependence or need for another" (p. 51).

While this perspective can be used to interpret Ned's and Adam's interview excerpts, in which both strongly reject—even to the point of violence—the possibility that their gender identity might somehow become that of a girl instead of a boy, a number of questions are nevertheless raised by this approach. The most important concerns how such a complex and complicated process as gender identity formation can occur completely unconsciously and intrapsychically, in the inner reaches of the mind. The psychodynamic perspective assumes, in other words, that boys develop their masculine gender identity completely out of relationships with others (parents, siblings, teachers, and friends), as one internal "object" is replaced by another. But what about the role that social, cultural, and historical factors and forces play in gender identity formation? Perhaps, in short, there is another way to look at some of these issues.

A Sociocultural Perspective on Boys' Development

A sociocultural perspective on boys' gender identity development begins with three basic themes that form the core of Vygotsky's approach to the study of human mental functioning: (1) "the use of genetic or developmental analysis to study individual functioning"; (2) "the claim that individual mental functioning has sociocultural origins"; and (3) "the claim that human action is mediated by tools and signs" (Penuel & Wertsch, 1995, p. 85; see also Wertsch, 1985). These three themes, taken together, highlight the primary emphasis Vygotsky places on the role that social, cultural, and historical forces play in shaping and influencing the process of development. For Vygotsky, therefore, development is a process whereby mental functioning is transformed, as forms of social practice/"intermental" functioning are internalized to become forms of mediated action/"intramental" functioning (see Wertsch, 1985, 1991, 1995).

In extending these general Vygotskian principles to the domain of identity development, Penuel and Wertsch have sought common ground between the work of Vygotsky and Erikson. While Erikson, who defined identity as "a subjective sense of invigorating sameness and continuity" (1968, p. 19), tended to emphasize individual functioning in his analysis of identity formation, and Vygotsky tended to emphasize sociocultural processes in his analysis of developmental phenomena, it is possible, Penuel and Wertsch argue, to "integrate individual functioning and sociocultural processes into a kind of mediated-action approach to identity formation" (1995, p. 88). That is, by seeking to maintain the dynamic tension that necessarily exists, as both Vygotsky and Erikson recognized, between the individual, on the one hand, and society, on the other, an understanding of the role that social, cultural, and historical processes play in the formation and transformation of individual identities is not only possible, but quite desirable.

Penuel and Wertsch's "mediated-action approach" to identity formation, grounded in Vygotsky's insights about developmental analysis, sociocultural processes, and mediation, and taking human action as its starting point, gives rise to three central claims:

1. "Mediated action," rather than an inner sense of identity, provides a basic unit of analysis;

2. Cultural and historical resources for identity formation are integral as empowering and constraining tools for identity formation;

3. The use of a genetic method calls attention to the importance of studying identity in settings where forming identities are at stake in the course of the activity. (p. 90)[3]

Let me briefly explore each of these claims in turn, before considering
their implications for understanding boys' gender identity development.

With respect to the appropriate unit of analysis to be used in a
sociocultural approach to identity formation, Penuel and Wertsch
argue that we must move beyond Erikson's notion of an "inner sense"
of coherence and stability as characteristic of identity, toward a focus
on the forms of "mediated action" in which an individual is typically
engaged. Mediated action entails two central elements: an "agent,"
the person who is doing the acting, on the one hand, and "cultural
tools" or "mediational means," the tools, means, or "instruments" used
by the agent to accomplish a given action, on the other. Following
Burke (1969), understanding and analyzing any action as mediated
action therefore involves focusing on both *agent* and *agency,* on both
"what person or kind of person performed the act" ("who did it"), and
"what means or instruments [she] used" ("how [she] did it") (Wertsch,
1998, p. 12).

Such a focus on agents and the cultural tools that mediate their
action (and interaction), moreover, entails acknowledging the fundamental and irreducible tension that necessarily exists between these
two elements (Wertsch, 1998). That is, in examining the dialectic
between agents and cultural tools at work in any given (inter)action, it
is always tempting to reduce the action in question to a function of one
or the other element. Such a temptation must be resisted, however, or
we run the risk of destroying the phenomenon under observation. Consequently, this means focusing less on what persons *say* about their own
sense of self-understanding, and more on what they *do* in specific situations and circumstances.

Taking mediated action as the unit of analysis . . . allows us to
ask a different set of questions about the way individuals use
cultural tools to form an identity, without having to sacrifice
Erikson's concern for coherence. In this approach, what we are
attempting to interpret, explain, or analyze is meaningful
human action, rather than either inner states of individuals or
sociocultural processes, considered in isolation. . . . [T]he sociocultural framework asks us to focus on specific questions about
the mediational means or cultural tools that people employ to
construct their identities in the course of different activities and
how they are put to use in particular actions. When identity is
seen in this framework as shaped by mediational means or cultural tools, questions arise as to the nature of cultural tools and

why one, as opposed to another, is employed in carrying out a particular form of action. (Penuel & Wertsch, 1995, p. 91)

Turning to the fundamental role that cultural and historical resources play in individual functioning, Penuel and Wertsch focus on the *ideologies* that are available in a particular social-cultural-historical context—ideologies that shape and mediate identity in critical ways. Such ideologies, moreover, can have both empowering and constraining effects on the development of identity.

> On the one hand, cultural tools in the form of ideologies provide individuals with a coherent world view, something that, in [Erikson's] view, youth desperately need to fashion an identity. In that way, these ideologies are empowering, providing youth with a compass in a contradictory and complex world. At the same time, these resources are, according to Erikson, constraining, in that individuals are limited in who they can become by the array of choices of ideology, career, and self-expression. (p. 90)

Penuel and Wertsch also argue that the meaning of cultural resources and tools is not fixed and immutable, but is rather quite fluid and flexible, determined, in large measure, by how such tools are used in a particular situation.

> The cultural and historical resources for identity formation do not constitute a single, undifferentiated whole, but represent a diversity of mediational means. In that way, identity may be conceived as formed when individuals choose on particular occasions to use one or more resources from a cultural "tool kit" to accomplish some action (see Bruner, 1990; Wertsch, 1991). Ideologies are embedded in a multitude of tools and signs; in this respect, identity researchers must be open to the variety of settings and signs in which an individual's identity is being constructed or expressed. (p. 90)

Finally, Penuel and Wertsch argue that "identity research must examine contexts in which identity is contested or under[going] transforming shifts" (ibid.). As such, they highlight not only the role that social processes play in the formation and transformation of identity, but also the degree to which identity is always as much a distributed or collective phenomenon as it is an individual phenomenon. They suggest studying identity in social-movement organization meetings, community support groups, and psychotherapy sessions, for example, to "provide insight into the way that individuals and groups can struggle against dominant discourses of their identity to co-construct a different way of speaking about themselves and develop new forms of action" (ibid.). It is important to undertake such studies in such settings, more-over, because "they are concerned . . . with the multitude of ways in which women and men struggle to come to terms with their member-ship in societies and with their own sense of who they are in the midst of a vast but structured field of signs, symbols, and voices from the cul-ture(s) in which they live" (ibid.).

These three claims about the domain of identity development can be easily extended, I would argue, to the subdomain of boys' gen-der identity development: (a) mediated action provides a basic unit of analysis in the study of boys' gender identity formation; (b) cul-tural and historical resources for boys' gender identity formation serve as both empowering and constraining tools for the development of masculine identity; and (c) boys' gender identity development must be studied in settings where forming masculine gender identities is at stake in the course of the activity. In other words, boys' gender iden-tity development is not simply the result of internal psychological processes that occur largely unconsciously, as early object relations are reconfigured and identification shifts from mother to father—as the psychodynamic account would have it. Rather, the development of boys' masculine identity is profoundly shaped by social and cul-tural forces, as boys form their understanding of themselves as boys in the course of mediated action and interaction that occurs in social settings in which identity is at stake, mediated by cultural tools and symbols—specifically, ideologies about what it means to be a male in this culture at this time in history.

Such a sociocultural perspective on masculine gender identity for-mation resonates with recent work on "masculinity ideology" (see Pleck, 1981; Pleck, Sonenstein, & Ku, 1993a, 1993b). On this view "masculin-ity ideology" (a sociocultural construction) is distinguished from "mas-culine gender-related personality traits" (the degree to which a person actually possesses or demonstrates psychologically or biologically based characteristics traditionally expected in men). Thus "males act the way they do not because of their male role identity, or their level of mascu-line traits, but because of the conception of masculinity [i.e., the mas-culinity ideology] they internalize from their culture" (Pleck, Sonenstein, & Ku, 1993b, pp. 14–15).

The "traditional" or "conventional" masculinity ideology—the social construction of masculinity most prevalent in the contemporary United States—consists of an interrelated set of attitudes regarding how a "real man" should act in relation to self and others (Pleck, 1981). Writing from an explicitly critical perspective, Connell calls this constellation of atti-tudes "hegemonic masculinity."

In the concept of hegemonic masculinity, "hegemony" means . . . a social ascendancy achieved in a play of social forces that extends beyond contests of brute power into the organization of private life and cultural processes. Ascendancy of one group of men over another achieved at the point of a gun, or by the threat of unemployment, is not hegemony. Ascendancy which is embedded in religious doctrine and practice, mass media content, wage structures, the design of housing, welfare/taxation policies and so forth, is. (1987, p. 184)

Traditional or hegemonic masculinity thus include attitudes about "status" ("A man always deserves the respect of his wife and children"), "toughness" ("A young man should be physically tough, even if he's not big"), and "antifemininity" ("It bothers me when a guy acts like a girl") (Pleck, Sonenstein, & Ku, 1993a).[4]

A variety of symbolic structures and cultural practices serve to perpetuate traditional/hegemonic conceptions of masculinity, ranging from those that operate on the social and cultural levels, to those that operate on the interpersonal level. Across the board, however, the common feature is that these structures and practices both privilege and perpetuate "men's dominance over women."

Hegemonic masculinity must embody a successful collective strategy in relation to women. Given the complexity of gender relations no simple or uniform strategy is possible: a "mix" is necessary. So hegemonic masculinity can contain at the same time, quite consistently, openings towards domesticity and openings towards violence, towards misogyny and towards heterosexual attraction. (Connell, 1987, pp. 185–186)

Male bonding is the term Stoltenberg has coined to describe one of the most common and widespread of these cultural practices. The male bond, he says (quite sardonically), is fundamentally a "sudden and spontaneous" drama in four acts.

Act I occurs when another player—someone who wishes to make you believe he is a real man—issues a challenge to your ranking on the vertical scale of manhood. To make you believe his own ranking [he] insinuates, for instance, that you are weak, not strong ... vulnerable, not tough ... powerless, not powerful. ...

Act II occurs when you accept the challenge and you sign the loyalty oath, swearing your allegiance to manhood. You do this not by attacking your attacker back [but] by forswearing your connection to some other human life. You sell out or put down or deride or dismiss some other human life such that in your challenger's eyes, and in your own, that human life is nobody to you. ...

Act III occurs when you have successfully met the challenge—and your challenger accepts your personal signature on
the loyalty oath. Your challenger has been persuaded that you
feel more loyalty to the bond between you as make-believe men
than you feel to some other connection you may have once felt
to another human life. . . . Your challenger and you can now
bond, in the blissful relief that you both truly love manhood. . .

Act IV occurs when you encounter—in the flesh, face to
face—the human you recently disavowed or betrayed or put
down or mocked in order to qualify as a real man during the
challenge of the male bond. If you handled your emotions correctly during the drama of that bond, the memory of your recent
gender success ought to still be fresh in your body and your
brain. Hence you should have no difficulty conducting your
affairs in Act IV, when you now must deal with this particular
human as if they are indeed nobody to you. Treating such an
actual human as a nobody is much the preferable course of
action . . . [because] it is so much simpler than trying to resus-
citate in your frame of mind either their humanity or yours.
(1993, pp. 266–268)

Male bonding is thus a form of mediated action by which men internalize, and thus reproduce, in the context of their interactions with other
men, a conception of male gender identity that necessarily links masculinity, power, and violence.[5]

A sociocultural perspective on boys' gender identity development
offers a way to understand how masculinity is shaped and mediated by
social, cultural, historical, and institutional processes—processes, that is,
that give rise to and support the ideologies of traditional or hegemonic
masculinity that so often shape boys' and men's (mediated) action and
interaction. But these processes still remain quite abstract, and it is difficult, without a concrete example in hand, to understand fully the way
in which masculine identity-as-mediated-action is forged. Let me turn,
therefore, to a brief exploration of an event in the lives of Ned and Adam's
peers that will shed additional light, I think, on these important issues.

"I'm Gonna NAIL it on 'til the Blood Comes Out!"

Several years ago, a group of first-graders attending a primary
school in a predominantly poor and working-class community in rural
Maine were involved in the following incident, as described to us by the
principal of the school:[6]

We had these girls go to a teacher after lunch time and they
were upset, visibly upset. And they said the boys were saying

some words to them that were scaring them and they didn't like it . . . . The boys started to say, "Well, you're my girlfriend. And I'm gonna marry you and . . . we're gonna have sex." And . . . the little girl . . . said, "Oh, I know you. You just want to tie us up and have sex with us." And the little boy went on and on and pretty soon two other boys joined in, until there were . . . four boys . . . and it got pretty aggressive and real loud and pretty soon there were lots of things coming out from all the boys: "Yeah, we're gonna have sex with you," and "Yeah, we're gonna rape you; we're gonna kill you." And "Yeah, 'cause you're our girl-friend." And then one boy said, "I'm gonna put an engagement ring on you 'cause that's what you do when you love someone, but I'm gonna NAIL it on 'til the blood comes out!" And another boy said, uh, "Well, I'm gonna . . . put an ax in your head 'til blood comes out your eyes!"

Talking with the children after this incident, the principal became convinced that they did not fully understand what they were saying (the boys said that they did not know, for example, what the word *rape* meant), but were repeating things they had heard elsewhere. The one little girl who spoke back to the boys said she had overheard junior high students reading the opening scenes from Stephen King's most recent novel, *Gerald's Game,* on the school bus. The novel begins with a man tying his wife to their bed, enacting his sexual fantasy. The boys also spoke of repeating comments they had heard on TV magazine shows like *Hard Copy* and *A Current Affair.*

Although this incident perpetuated by a group of young boys against a group of young girls does not explicitly contain all of the elements Stoltenberg (1993) attributes to the classic model of male bonding, it nevertheless does represent, I would argue, an early and largely implicit form of a social practice that will likely, and sadly, play a ongoing role in the lives of the boys involved. In other words, this incident clearly contains elements of the kind of ritual and discursive reproduction of male gender identity, premised on male domination and female subordination, which perpetuates the ideology of traditional or hegemonic masculinity in this culture at this time in history. Let me briefly highlight some of these elements.

While there is no indication that the boys were responding to an explicit "challenge" to their masculinity, thrown down by one of their peers (Act I), there is an escalation in the incident as more boys joined in, and as things got more aggressive and louder, that clearly can be read as a kind of a "who can top who" competition among the boys involved. Moreover, the boys clearly insulted, threatened, and demeaned the girls, and while they professed not to know what "rape" means, they clearly knew that the words they were saying had the power to hurt

(Act II). Similarly, while there is no explicit sense that the bond between the group of boys was made stronger because of their "successful" participation in the harassment of the girls (Act III), again, the fact that the group of boys expanded as the incident progressed can be read, I think, as at least an implicit indication that it was a "successful" male-bonding experience.[7]

Here, then, from a sociocultural perspective, is an example of how boys' masculinity is forged in a setting where gender identity is at stake (the boys clearly egged each other on), of how boys' masculinity is shaped by cultural resources and tools (words—like *rape*—and images—like the engagement ring—and ideologies—like the understanding of the relationship between sexual attraction and violence that is so pervasive in our contemporary culture), and of how boys' masculinity is manifest as mediated action (the threatening behavior directed toward the girls, using words and images as weapons). Consequently, even in its early and not-yet-full-formed-state, this example of male bonding among first-grade boys illustrates Penuel and Wertsch's claim about the rhetorical character of identity-as-mediated-action.

> We suggest that identity be conceived as a form of action that is first and foremost rhetorical, concerned with persuading others (and oneself) about who one is and what one values to meet different purposes. . . . It is always addressed to someone, who is situated culturally and historically and who has a particular meaning for individuals. (1985, p. 91)

It is an example, in other words, that clearly illustrates how boys' masculine gender identity formation is shaped and influenced by the sociocultural context in which the actions that constitute that identity occur. Masculine gender identity is not an internal trait or a characteristic of boys or men so much as it is a form of mediated action—rhetorical action—that has as its aim to persuade others (and oneself) that one is a "real man."

Conclusion

In this chapter I have argued that the emerging sociocultural approach to the study of human development provides a richer and ultimately more useful perspective on the development of boys' masculine gender identity than does the more well-known and well-established psychodynamic paradigm. As such, conceptualizing masculine gender identity as a form of "mediated action"—that is, a form of action or activity shaped by cultural tools and resources—rather than an individual psychological trait, attribute, or characteristic, leads to an understanding of boys' gender identity development as fundamentally a process of cultural reproduction. On this view, therefore, prevailing ideologies of masculinity are used as tools to shape actions and interactions (both male-male and male-female, as the "male bonding" example illustrates), and boys' gender identity, in the end, is as much about rhetorical and performative attempts to convince others (boys and girls) of one's masculinity as it is about actually "being" a boy.[8]

To conclude, let me briefly consider some of the methodological and educational implications of the kind of sociocultural perspective on boys' development I have sketched in this chapter. Methodologically, it is critical that both ethnographic and interview methods be used to document the cultural and symbolic practices in which boys engage, the cultural resources employed in those practices, and the forms of masculine-identity-as-mediated-action to which such practices and resources give rise. Most importantly, as Penuel and Wertsch suggest, these methods must provide access to the settings in which these practices occur—settings (e.g., the "male-bonding" incident just described) in which forming identities are at stake in the course of the activity, and struggles with conventional expectations, and critiques of dominant discourses of masculinity, are possible. Needless to say, these methodologies must be largely qualitative—not to "generate hypotheses" or to "explore new areas of research," but to focus sustained and rigorous attention on the discursive and semiotic dimensions that are part and parcel of social, cultural, and historical processes.

Educationally, a sociocultural perspective on boys' gender identity development, in contrast to a psychodynamic perspective, suggests that the formation of masculinity is not an immutable internal process necessarily tied to the unconscious dynamics of the family romance. Rather, it is an external cultural process mediated and shaped by discursive and symbolic resources which, while quite powerful in their own right, can be altered. This resonates, moreover, with the view that cultural conceptions of masculinity do change over time (see Kimmel, 1996; Rotundo, 1993); hence what it means to be a boy or a man in one day and age does not necessarily correspond to what it means to be a boy or a man in another.[9]

Masculine gender identity, in other words, is malleable, and what it means to be a boy/man can be contested and negotiated. But this process must begin early, as boys struggle to hold onto and express their experiences of vulnerability in relationships—particularly their feelings of sadness, pain, and abandonment in the face of the conventional discourse about what it means to be a "big boy" or a "real man" that pressures boys/men to "be tough" (see also Pollack, 1998).

All of this is to say that there is a critical role for parents and educators to play in the lives of young boys—to interrupt the cultural reproduction of hegemonic masculinity, by providing boys with a different set of cultural resources and ideologies, and by encouraging them to participate in a different set of practices, than those currently available to boys as their gender identity is being formed. "Changing the script," so to speak, will not be easy, but it is possible, and if it means that the kind of negative, hurtful, and even violent behavior in which boys so often engage in order to "prove" their masculinity to others and to themselves can be avoided, it is definitely worth the effort.

Thus, to return to the example of male bonding I have presented, because the process of male bonding is not fully fleshed-out among this group of first-graders, because the boys involved are questioning and looking to adults in their lives for guidance and understanding, there is hope, I think, for a critical intervention, to interrupt the process and to plant the seeds of resistance. To do so would require adult men, primarily, to find ways to encourage young boys to resist pressures to engage in male bonding, and, instead, to develop relations with both boys and girls characterized by genuine mutuality, respect, and responsiveness— to help boys learn, as Stoltenberg (1989) says, "to refuse" conventional conceptions of manhood and hegemonic masculinity. To do so, moreover, would also undoubtedly disrupt the lives of the men involved, for forging authentic connections between men and boys in this culture and this time in history is as radical and risky as forging authentic connections between women and girls (see Brown & Gilligan, 1992).

In the end, though, however difficult it may be, interrupting the cultural reproduction of masculinity, as it currently occurs in the contemporary United States, may be our only hope for a more just, more compassionate, more caring, less violent world.

> Manhood is the *paradigm* of injustice. *Refusing to believe* in manhood is the personal and ethical stance of resistance to all injustice done in its name. And refusing to accept the manhood imperative—the lie that there *must* be a "male sex" to "belong" to—is a personal and political principle of revolutionary liberation. (Stoltenberg, 1993, p. 304)

Notes

1. This study has been conducted in collaboration with Peggy Stubbs, Lyn Mikel Brown, Devon Waugh, Nick Waugh, and Chris Mathews.

2. Note also Chodorow's (1974) statement that "All theoretical and empirical accounts agree that after about age three (the beginning of the "oedipal" period, which focuses on the attainment of a stable gender identity) male and female development becomes radically different" (p. 49).

3. A fourth claim, that "variation in the use of cultural resources for identity formation must be viewed in terms of commitments in Erikson's domains of identity—fidelity, ideology, and work" (p. 90), is not central to my aim in this paper.

4. It is important to note that this formulation has not been analyzed from the standpoint of race or class or sexual orientation. Thus is

must be assumed that the conventional masculinity ideology to which Pleck and his colleagues refer is most typically associated with White, heterosexual, middle-class men.

5. William Pollack's (1998) recent discussion of what he calls the "boy code", which he defines as "a set of behaviors, rules of conduct, cultural shibboleths, and even a lexicon, that is inculcated into boys by our society—from the very beginning of a boy's life" (p. xxv), represents another example of the process by which masculine gender identity is mediated by cultural tools.

6. This is work done in collaboration with Lyn Mikel Brown, who has also written about this episode, primarily from the girls' point of view (see Brown, 1998).

7. It is also important to note, I would argue, the degree to which this incident reflects Connell's (1987) analysis of the strategies used to perpetuate the ideology of hegemonic masculinity. As such, it mixes messages about domesticity and heterosexual attraction ("I'm gonna put an engagement ring on you 'cause that's what you do when you love someone . . ."), with messages about violence and misogyny (". . . but I'm gonna NAIL it on 'til the blood comes out!").

8. See also Lyn Mikel Brown's (1998) analysis of the performative dimensions of girls' encounter with cultural conventions of femininity.

9. Thus a *sociocultural* perspective on boys' development necessarily goes hand-in-hand with a *critical* perspective on boys' development.

References

Belenky, M. Clinchy, B., Goldberger, N., & Tarule, J. (1986). *Women's ways of knowing*. New York: Basic.

Bly, R. (1990). I*ron John: A book about men*. Reading, MA: Addison-Wesley.

Brod, H. (Ed.). (1987). *The making of masculinities*. Boston: Allen and Urwin.

Brown, L. (1991). A problem of vision: The development of voice and relational knowledge in girls ages 7 to 16. *Women's Studies Quarterly, 19*, 52-71.

Brown, L. (1998). *Raising their voices: The politics of girls' anger*. Cambridge: Harvard University Press.

Brown, L., & Gilligan, C. (1992). *Meeting at the crossroads: Women's psychology and girls' development*. Cambridge: Harvard University Press.

Bruner, J. (1990). *Acts of meaning*. Cambridge: Harvard University Press.

Burke, K. (1969). *A grammar of motives*. Berkeley: University of California Press.

Chodorow, N. (1974). Family structure and feminine personality. In M. Rosaldo & L. Lamphere (Eds.), *Woman, culture, and society*. Stanford: Stanford University Press.

Chodorow, N. (1978). *The reproduction of mothering: Psychoanalysis and the sociology of gender*. Berkeley: University of California Press.

Connell, R. W. (1987). *Gender and power: Society, the person and sexual politics*. Stanford, CA: Stanford University Press.

Cole, M. (1996). *Cultural psychology: A once and future discipline*. Cambridge: Harvard University Press.

Erikson, E. (1968). *Identity: Youth and crisis*. New York: Norton.

Garbarino, J. (1999). *Lost boys: Why our sons turn violents and how we can save them*. New York: Free Press.

Gilligan, C. (1982). *In a different voice: Psychological theory and women's development*. Cambridge: Harvard University Press.

Gilligan, C., Lyons, N., & Hanmer, T. (Eds.). (1990). *Making connections: The relational world of adolescent girls at the Emma Willard School*. Cambridge: Harvard University Press.

Gilligan, C., Ward, J., & Taylor, J. (Eds.). (1988). *Mapping the moral domain*. Cambridge: Harvard University Press.

Jordan, J., Kaplan, A., Miller, J., Stiver, I., & Surrey, J. (1991). *Women's growth in connection: Writings from the Stone Center*. New York: Guilford.

Keen, S. (1991). *Fire in the belly: On being a man*. New York: Bantam Books.

Kimmel, M. (1996). *Manhood in America: A cultural history*. New York: Free Press.

Kimmel, M., & Messner, M. (Eds.). (1989). *Men's lives*. New York: Macmillan.

Lees, S. (1993). *Sugar and spice: Sexuality and adolescent girls*. London: Penguin.

Martin, L., Nelson, K., & Tobach, E. (Eds.). (1995). *Sociocultural psychology: Theory and practice of doing and knowing*. New York: Cambridge University Press.

Miedzian, M. (1991). *Boys will be boys: Breaking the link between masculinity and violence*. New York: Anchor Books.

Penuel, W., & Wertsch, J. (1995). Vygotsky and identity formation: A sociocultural approach. *Educational Psychologist, 30,* 83-92.

Pleck, J. (1981). *The myth of masculinity.* Cambridge: Massachusetts Institute of Technology Press.

Pleck, J., Sonenstein, F., & Ku, L. (1993a). Masculinity ideology and its correlates. In S. Oskamp & M. Costanzo (Eds.), *Gender issues in contemporary society* (pp. 85-110). Newbury Park, CA: Sage.

Pleck, J., Sonenstein, F., & Ku, L. (1993b). Masculinity ideology: Its impact on adolescent males' heterosexual relationships. *Journal of Social Issues, 49,* 11-29.

Pollack, W. (1998). *Real boys: Rescuing our sons from the myths of boyhood.* New York: Henry Holt and Co.

Rogers, A. (1993). Voice, play, and the practice of ordinary courage in girls' and women's lives. *Harvard Educational Review, 60,* 265-295.

Rotundo, E. A. (1993). *American manhood: Transformations in masculinity from the Revolution to the modern era.* New York: Basic.

Stoltenberg, J. (1989). *Refusing to be a man: Essays on sex and justice.* New York: Meridian.

Stoltenberg, J. (1993). *The end of manhood.* New York: Dutton.

Taylor, J., Gilligan, C., & Sullivan, A. (1995). *Between voice and silence: Women and girls, race and relationship.* Cambridge: Harvard University Press.

Vygotsky, L. (1978). *Mind in society: The development of higher psychological processes* (M. Cole, V. John-Steiner, S. Scribner, & E. Souberman, Eds.). Cambridge: Harvard University Press.

Vygotsky, L. (1987). Thinking and speech. In L. S. Vygotsky, *The collected works of L.S. Vygotsky. Vol. 1. Problems of general psychology.* (R. Rieber & A. Carton, Eds.) (N. Minick, Trans.). (pp. 37-285). New York: Plenum. (Original work published 1934.)

Walkerdine, V. (1990). *Schoolgirl fictions.* London: Verso.

Wertsch, J. (1985). *Vygotsky and the social formation of mind.* Cambridge: Harvard University Press.

Wertsch, J. (1991). *Voices of the mind: A sociocultural approach to mediated action.* Cambridge: Harvard University Press.

Wertsch, J. (1995). The need for action in sociocultural research. In J. Wertsch, P. del Rio, & A. Alvarez (Eds.), *Sociocultural studies of mind.* New York: Cambridge University Press.

Wertsch, J. (1998). *Mind as action*. New York: Oxford University Press.

Wertsch, J., del Rio, P., & Alvarez, A. (1995). Sociocultural studies: History, action, and mediation. In J. Wertsch, P. del Rio & A. Alvarez (Eds.), *Sociocultural studies of mind*. New York: Cambridge University Press.

CHAPTER 10

"Dead Poets Society": Deconstructing Surveillance Pedagogy

Peter McLaren
Zeus Leonardo

In a metacommentary, we don't theorize postmodernism so much as we map the necessary conditions for the standard thought on postmodernism: why has it become so necessary to talk about a postmodern condition, what needs does that talking fulfill? The question then is not so much about the referents of postmodern discourse—what the postmodern condition is, and whether the discourse has described that condition correctly—but about what that discourse enables, and how it functions.
—Stam, "Mikhail Bakhtin and Left Cultural Critique"

The human body was entering a machinery of power that explores it, breaks it down and rearranges it. A "political anatomy", which was also a "mechanics of power", was being born; it defined how one may have a hold over others' bodies, not only so that they may do what one wishes, but so that they may operate as one wishes, with the techniques, the speed and the efficiency that one determines. Thus discipline produces subjected and practised bodies, "docile" bodies.
—Foucault, *Discipline and Punish*

I went into the woods because I wanted to live deliberately.
I wanted to live deep and suck out all the marrow of life!
To put to rout all that was not life
And not, when I came to die, discover that I had not lived.
—Neil Perry, quoting Thoreau, in *Dead Poets Society*

Introduction

The current postmodern condition strongly suggests that reculturation is an important focus for educational reform. In particular, critical theories enable educators to question for the "first time" the differential incorporation of high and popular culture in schools. Critical theories encourage us to identify the repressed margins of unofficial cultures, to name the struggles within the lifeworld of subaltern groups, and to legitimate the silenced culture of the popular in the attempt to subvert the prevailing structures of power and authority associated with high academic culture. However, if we are to observe course offerings in schools of education—especially in teacher preparation programs—not much about popular culture is taken seriously in schools. Studying it in classrooms is considered an illegitimate and ill-conceived use of pedagogical means by many educators. Popular cultural "texts" are often deemed nonacademic and unworthy of scholarly pursuit, and people too closely associated with them are quickly dismissed as being undiscriminating and common. There are stratifications within popular culture as well. For example, films are usually considered inferior to books. There is a valorization of the written, as opposed to the spoken, word. As a result, when films are used in schools, they are often utilized as academic fillers, brain candy, or as an electronic coping strategy when substitute teachers entertain students for a few days. Films are seen as effective pedagogical instruments to "take up time," as simple diversions, or as "special schedule" activities. Rarely do they receive extensive critique by students or are they legitimated as evidence to support historical arguments (Cohen, 1996).

For these reasons and for many more, popular culture, and in particular film, becomes even more important for critical educators since how students live "the popular" receives such little attention in schools of education. As a result, students are denied the opportunity to learn how their identities have been constituted and shaped by quotidian forces and relations both ideological and material. Without the pedagogical space for critical dialogue about the semiotics of the everyday and what Foucault refers to as the "political anatomy" (1977) of film, educators rob students of potentially transformative ways in which they can understand their everyday lives and work strategically toward interrogating them for hegemonic relations as well as for emancipatory spaces. Through our critical analysis of the film *Dead Poets Society* (Haft, Witt, Thomas, & Weir, 1989) we argue that understanding popular culture must become an integral part of any critical education if students are expected to understand both their location within the global economy and their situatedness within local vectors of power and privilege.

Some Definitions

At this juncture, some definitions are warranted. For clarification, we adopt Giroux and Simon's statement about the status of popular culture in schools. "The dominant discourse still defines popular culture as

whatever remains when high culture is subtracted from the overall totality of cultural practices. It is seen as the trivial and the insignificant of
everyday life, and usually it is a form of popular taste deemed unworthy
of either academic legitimation or high social affirmation." (1994, p. 238).
Because educators privilege high culture at the expense of popular culture
and thus dismiss the popular in one sweeping stroke, students and educators forego the benefit of critically analyzing larger systems of social relations and entrenched interests that inform popular culture. Ironically,
these are the systems of meaning many students take with them to classrooms and through which they act. Furthermore, research failing to attend
to the social semiotics of the quotidian shows a bias against the "popular"
and its low-brow mischief as well as a lack of engagement with "culture"
in its specific articulations as opposed to culture in its totalizing sense. We
want to make clear that our interest in popular culture is not to exercise
the fashionable apostasy of deconstructive analysis costumed in the academic salons of Paris but rather to analyze the ways in which education
is not only embedded in its own institutional and pedagogical practices
but secures its very condition of existence by requiring people to be located
within the social division of labor, and now within the current practices of
superexploitation linked to the globalization of capital.

Storey (1993) locates the term *popular* in those cultural practices
that have a strong presence in commercial culture. Gramsci and Freire sit-
uate "culture" as a historical site of struggle over the production of meaning (San Juan Jr., 1992; McLaren, 1994). Considered together, the work of
Storey, Gramsci, and Freire draws attention to an important political project: theorizing popular culture. For us, such a project must involve a search
for a radical theory that neither treats the mass as Adornian dupes of popular spectacles nor celebrates the popular as "authentic" folk culture created in a revolutionary mix from below (Giroux & Simon, 1989). In addition, a critical theory of everyday life must avoid a purely rational analysis
of subject positions within the circuits of semiotic economies of images, as
if audience response is a purely reasoned activity involving informed consent. Moreover, Giroux and Simon, following Grossberg, remind us that
critical educators must work at deconstructing the way in which students
affectively invest in popular practices and texts. In an era characterized
by the waning of affect it becomes even more imperative to construct a critical theory of popular culture that works against the totalizing and eclips-
ing force of reason in its monolithic sense.

The Body Portrayed in Film

For us, a specific point of theoretical importance in analyzing the
popular is the way the body is portrayed in popular films. Films often
oppose the ephemeral images of the carceral body with rationality's ethe-
real themes, favoring the latter. The body represents the site of desire,

sexuality, and pleasures. In mainstream culture, somatic experimenta-
tions such as body piercing and painting become deviant symptoms of a
mind gone awry. Current developments in technology, media, and marketing slogans abound on the importance of using the mind. For what
exact purpose beyond exercising the mind, we are rarely told. For the capitalist class, it seems enough to announce that the mind should not be
wasted. Educational propaganda about the need to use our minds is perhaps a telling sign of what Baudrillard would likely suggest is an "alibi"
for the general mindlessness in social life. It is not that people lack mind-
ful activity; it is that we have an overabundance of it to the point that it
loses its specificity from that which we consider physical. For example, in
contrast to the conservative assertion that our era is marked by the loss
of meaning, there is evidence to suggest that the social is saturated with
technological information that subjects convert into meaning, or cyber-
signs. To enter the debate around the mind-body split, we must first come
to grips with what we mean by "mental" (Rorty, 1979). More important,
intellectual labor for its own sake is never justifiable without attempting
to grasp the often myriad interests that such labor serves. In our own
classroom teaching we have come to understand that students benefit
from discursive strategies that offer a theory of subjectivity as well as
educational practices that recognize them as subjects. In short, becoming
a student in the Gramscian sense of having a phronetic mind and a revolutionary disposition toward the body is a political project that can potentially transform our notions of what it means to be an active agent of history who enunciates a pledge of emancipation in the face of current forms
of capitalist superexploitation. Furthermore, it points to the struggle for
an altered historical reality where domination would cease to exist.

Appadurai notes that contemporary analyses of the body have
revealed how the emotions and affect are not simply "raw, precultural
materials that constitute a universal, transsocial substrate" but rather
are "culturally constructed and socially situated" (1996, p. 147). Sensory
experience and bodily technique become, in this view, "parts of historically constituted regimes of knowledge and power" (ibid.). The notion of
"embodied experience" or "enfleshment" (McLaren, 1993) has emerged
as a powerful conceptual tool to understand how bodily states and experiences of the popular, and bodily techniques and affective dispositions,
are inscribed upon corporeal rituals of self-control and discipline that
serve through everyday popular practices the material interests of the
nation-state. How are individuals motivated as body subjects through
cultural and political schemata that have imprinted themselves on bodily experience? How are macroconceptions of civility and dignity constructed by interests and ideologies that in turn link language and representations to the world of emotion and affect (Appadurai, 1996)?

Understanding how popular culture has structured our ideas about
the body is one way to theorize our everyday practices. A critical discourse

that engages the concept of corporeality affirms the micropolitics of desire as it is articulated at the level of living in the flesh. Our perspective recognizes that the body must neither be essentialized nor immaterialized. Instead, the body is an effect of ideological and discursive processes, all of which overdetermine its formation at any one time. Thus, combating a social incarceration of the body entails waging discursive battles on many fronts in order to avoid essentializing any one of its fields of articulation. This does not suggest a rejection of essentialist discourses *in toto*. Haraway reminds us of the differences *within* essentialism (in Calhoun, 1994). In particular, she encourages radical theorists to take up the challenge of biological feminists, especially their contribution to understanding the ways in which images of women's bodies have been used in social discourse. However, it should be clear that the body is not simply an effect of discourse, a semantic field or semiotic backdrop of flesh and marrow that reflects back to us our particular (i.e., phallocentric, androcentric, Eurocentric, heterosexist) reading strategies. Bodies are more than signifiers that 'secure' particular readings; they exceed their description as ludic arenas of linguistic performance that delineate and order gender/sexual/racial differences. The body is more than a site of immanent desire but space in which capitalist social relations are 'enfleshed'. That is, a body is a site where social relations of production are metaphorized in the flesh. Bodies, therefore, can be seen as non-discursive products through which ideological relations and concrete social practices are lived. Here we draw attention to the materialization of the body and its irreducibility of labor and its constructive implication in practico-material activity. Capitalist social relations produce bodies in alienation, an alienation linked to their reduction to relations of exchange value (McNally, 2001). Bodies, in other words, become 'capitalized'. Bodies, as such, are crushed under the weight of capitalist extraction and produced within the iron jaws of profit. Bodies - as human capital, and through their labor-power, become transformed into a value relations, a relation of abstract or alienated labor. The body is a commodity that cathects its desirs for other commodities. Critical educators are interested in the body not only to reform our ideas about the body, but to re-form the body itself as a politiccal space of agential power.

Teaching Popular Culture

Pedagogically speaking, teaching popular culture in the classroom is as important as theorizing about it. Teaching popular culture is simultaneously a discourse and a practice. During classroom discussions, educators must recognize the element of student voices. Problematizing student experiences is a way of cultivating student voices by inviting students to problematize the routines and rituals of their daily lives and to thematize the collective and singular events that shape their self-understanding and social dispositions. In doing so, Freire (1993) suggests using problem-posing pedagogical strategies. Problem-posing education is an activity that is conducted *with* students, not *for* them. By working with students, critical educators attempt to cultivate an ethics of collectivity. Building a community of learners opposes the totalizing effect of establishing unity. Community-building is a position guided by an ethics of solidarity that recognizes differences between people. It acknowledges the pressing need to take active steps toward reconstituting the public sphere without imposing a "same page" ethos.

We recognize that popular culture consists of its own bodies of knowledge and systems of intelligibility found on street corners, playgrounds, and other embodied ways of living (McLaren, 1993). In part students invest in popular practices as a result of their oppositional character to academic life and their "wastefulness" in the Baudrillardean sense. Educators who expect full participation from students on the basis that popular culture is *about them* may be thwarted by moments of resistance from the students themselves (Shumway, 1989). By sanctioning popular culture as a legitimate topic of study, educators are confronting one of the important meanings that students derive from participating in traditionally nonacademic practices: their opposition to schooling (McLaren, 1993). Educators risk colonizing student culture if they ignore the element of ownership. Of course essentialist ownership of popular culture must be guarded against as well. Students benefit from becoming more aware of the slippage of cultural autonomy. Popular culture is an amalgamation of hybrid practices, the original source of which escapes us.

The Film Dead Poets Society

The Director Peter Weir's film *Dead Poets Society* is a semiotically pregnant filmic text offering a powerful examination of the ways in which the body is schooled as well as transformed. During a summer course in educational foundations at University of California at Los Angeles where we cotaught a class of approximately thirty-five prospective elementary and secondary school teachers, we were able to use the film for textual analysis in conjunction with theoretical pieces of writing about popular culture. Students were encouraged to assess critically the film's possibility as a critical pedagogical instrument. More important, we asked them to interrogate critically the film's assumptions about the purpose of education as well as to problematize the film's project with regards to the struggle over cultural politics. By and large, the students responded well to the film's inclusion into the course syllabus. And with the benefit of critical readings on popular culture, students gained insight on the multivalenced ways in which subjectivities are constituted within everyday life. Without disparaging the important role that written texts play in teaching and learning, experimenting with traditional formats by including both a film and discussing theoretical expositions of popular culture enabled the class to envision relevant and embodied pedagogies.

The process of schooling reflects Plato's concept of *idiopragein,* which is the process of harmonizing an individual's talents and interests with the needs of the social whole or larger community. Each person is given his or her place in society so that the better the fit the healthier the state. The social purpose of teaching is to bring about *idiopragein* (Blacker, 1996). In order to bring this about, Plato realized that select "guardians" would have to perpetuate the "noble lie" that some people are inherently superior to others. For Plato, this lie meant perpetuating the idea that some people are gold, silver, or bronze. We live in an era of fast, casino style, gangster capitalism in which schools are designed to give people tradable skills that are intellectual or vocational. Schools are also designed to equip people with character traits such as competitiveness and acquisitiveness (Blacker, 1996). The noble lie in this case is that only the "gold" people are destined to rise to the top of the capitalist hierarchy. The students of Welton High School—the school in the film—represent the "gold" stratum of future corporate and professional leaders. The noble lie perpetuated by their teacher, John Keating is that the students live in a meritocratic society and that an unquestioning obedience to authority and a slavish veneration of tradition are the key to success.

Dead Poets Society is a film of great pedagogical interest. In it, a group of wealthy, private-school students learn a lesson about humanistic peak experiences from their new english teacher, John Keating. A former Welton High School graduate himself, Keating returns to his alma mater to inject romantic thinking, liberation pedagogy, and a sense of embodied knowledge into the otherwise rational humanist curriculum at Welton. Keating mobilizes the students' desires and passions, and unleashes their sexual repression through his charismatic teaching and alternative methods. Subsequently, the students (Neil, Charlie, Todd, Knox, Cameron, Pitts, and Meeks) establish a group based on Keating's former society of romantic poets, the "Dead Poets Society." In the process, the boys experience the pleasure of resistance by committing various school transgressions and by experimenting, with their desires. Also in the process, we witness the boys struggle for a discourse that best explains their oppression.

Dead Poets Society makes sincere attempts to fracture the hegemonic discourse of what the school administration in the film values as a pedagogy built on the pillars of "TRADITION, HONOR, DISCIPLINE, and EXCELLENCE." Embodied in Keating's commitment to the search for a transgressive pedagogy and the students' cry for "TRAVESTY, HORROR, DECADENCE, and EXCREMENT," the film's overt message resurrects the avatars of Romanticism by evoking the sign of carpe diem, or "seize the day." In doing so, Keating, played by the actor Robin Williams, encourages, better yet, makes it imperative for the Welton students to pursue education to the ends of self-actualization, existential freedom, and a humanistic quest for peak experiences. For example, in one scene he spiritedly challenges the students to tear out the pages of their poetry anthology, urging them to live the verse of life rather than to simply read about it, albeit from someone else's aesthetic vantage point. Keating's progressive pedagogy is an unequivocal attempt to free students from the shackles of schooling for schooling's sake in order to remind them of the richness in experience, the potential for passion, and the vitality in a life freed from a technicist mode of learning. However, critical interrogation of the film leads one to question the political project suggested by the encounter between Keating and the students. By emphasizing the cultivation of self, Keating's humanistic discourse ultimately falls short of politicizing a collective project toward cultural emancipation. Although there is much in Keating's pedagogy that is liberating, it lacks the politicized and self-reflexive discourse students need in order to combat the school's reabsorption of their fleeting transgressions. Ultimately the school serves as a flat, contiguous, and homogeneous space that works to produce a compliant national citizenry. It is here that students are produced within modes of subjectivity most congenial to the nation-state. Yet while the students resist the normative charter of the school, there is little recognition in the film of the links between this charter and the manner in which schools perpetuate asymmetrical relations of power that in turn are linked to the larger social division of labor within white supremacist capitalist patriarchy.

Our Analysis

Keating's intervention accomplishes its initial objective of stirring up an apparently antiseptic school environment. He appropriates the discourse of carpe diem such that the body becomes a site of struggle. During his first day of teaching, Keating unsettles the scene by having the students follow him out into the hallway, thereby breaking the ostensible bondage between the students' bodies and their seats. Foucault (1977) reminds us of the way in which the body is perfected by the architecture of surveillance. Indeed, Welton students initially hesitate to leave their antiseptic, regimented, and cellularized space, perhaps out of fear of the consequences of leaving their seats. This is autosurveillance at its most invisible. As Keating tempts the students to follow him into the hallway, they look at one another in puzzlement as if they do not own their bodies. The students seem to wait for a bell to signal their next move, as it does so many times to signal the end of a class period. Eventually, the students rise from their seats and gingerly walk behind Keating into the cold hallway.

Foucault has revealed that the contemporary regime of discipline regiments the body's location, temporality, and behavior. In *Dead Poets Society* Welton depotentiates the students' carnal possibilities by compartmentalizing and repeatedly sending them to their chairs, the symbolic chains of schooling. The classroom becomes a mirror of official society where resistance occurs in the cavities that separate the real from the possible. The classroom becomes the prison-house of knowledge, a site of the totalization of regulative functions, yet the site of unmarked possibility. As in the case of so many other schools, the classroom walls at Welton represent the lost horizon of possible worlds and the limit-text of freedom. Similarly, in *Discipline and Punish,* Foucault outlines the prisoners' day from their rising from sleep at 6:00 in the morning, then accounting for approximately twenty-minute intervals and the activities accompanying them, until the inmates return to their cells at 8:30 in the evening to return to sleep (1977, pp. 6-7). Prison life ritualizes the inmates' bodies not only by assigning their stations at given intervals, but also by regulating a period of time for their body to be in certain locations. What results is a microtechnology of power that institutes spatiotemporal oppression.

In *Dead Poets Society* Welton ritualizes the *student body* by beginning the day with a lesson on poetry with the students sitting "properly" in their (apparently) assigned seats. This sets the tone for what the students can expect as normal usage of the body while learning: sitting quietly and speaking when asked to speak. Keating disrupts this arrangement by having the students follow him into the corridor, thereby transforming their potential energy into kinetic movement. Their bodies are made to relate to poetry under new circumstances by gazing at the pictures of former Welton students in the glass casing rather than being forced to engage a canonized classroom textbook. Keating's students set their poetry anthology aside and instead carry on a dialogue. Shumway explains the importance of such disciplinary controls.

> The body for Foucault is not a euphemism for the sexual, and desexualizing is only one aspect of the way the body is constructed in schooling. The body is used by Foucault to indicate the fact that disciplinary controls are not merely memorized and accepted, but actually form the body itself. One could say that they are habits in the sense that they work without the conscious choice of an individual but are ingrained in the very posture and musculature of the body. (1989, p. 227)

Keating unsettles the students' atomistic configuration by huddling them together in the hallway. There is tactile contact between them as their uniforms scratch against one another when they crowd around to stare at the hallway photographs. Keating encourages his students to look into past (and "dead") students' faces and identify themselves in the faces on the wall. The students stare at the Welton graduates only to find their own blank faces staring back at them in the reflections in the glass. At stake here is the moment of misrecognition, in the Lacanian sense, of locating identity in reflections other than ourselves because the students neither identify with the photographs of former students nor with their own reflections in the glass casing.

Contrast student reactivation of body zones in the hallway with their isolation from each other when sitting in their own chairs in the classroom. In the classroom, Welton student bodies are still close to the each other but maintain a critical distance that reinforces their alienation from one another. Such closeness at arm's length in the classroom reflects Fiske's concept of "distantiation."

> Such distance devalues socially and historically specific reading practices in favor of a transcendent appreciation or aesthetic sensibility with claims to universality. . . . This distance from the historical is also a distance from the bodily sensations, for it is our bodies that finally bind us to our historical and social specificities. As the mundanities of our social conditions are set aside, or distanced, by this view of art, so, too, are the so-called sensuous, cheap, and easy pleasures of the body distanced from the more contemplative, aesthetic pleasures of the mind. (1992, p. 154)

Jameson explains postmodern distance this way:

> Distance in general including critical distance in particular has very precisely been abolished in the new space of postmodernism. We are submerged in its henceforth filled and suffused volumes to the point where our now postmodern bodies are bereft of spatial coordinates and practically (let alone theoretically) incapable of distanciation. (Cited in Montag, 1988, p. 94)

Fiske is critical of bourgeois distantiation from the body's materiality. To Fiske, abstract distance is a dangerous gap between the subject and material history (always *with* others). To Jameson, the postmodern condition practically annihilates historical distance through involution and dedifferentiation. The "I" and "Other" are involutionized (as opposed to revolutionized). Yet our bodies betray the interests of bourgeois distantiation. Whereas bourgeois distance emphasizes a certain sacred individualism that escapes the other, the body reminds us of our physical propinquity to the other. It is the point where the self is confounded by the other and (mis)recognizes itself through the other. Due to the students' increased proximity to one another, statements can be felt in people's breath, heard in the slightest whisper. "Carpe diem," Keating haunts as a student feels Keating's moist breath on his neck.

In our current viral society, distance between host, or self, and parasite, or other, is preserved only to the point that self and other fail to connect. "Touch" is approached, but never accomplished. Critical distance has been all but abolished in our tactile universe where McLuhan's dictum "the medium is the message" becomes "the massage" (Baudrillard, 1983, pp. 123–124). Closeness is achieved only asymptotically in order to maintain the enigma of chance.

> In a sacred, ceremonial universe, things do not touch each other, and they never meet. They link up without fail, but without contact. Tact in this matter is precisely avoiding contact. Remark how ceremonial gestures, dress, and bodies roll, intertwine, brush past each other, challenge one another, but without ever touching. . . . The same is true for our bodies in everyday lives. . . . A very powerful force was required to break this magnetic distance where each body moves, as well as to produce this indifferent space where chance is able to put them in contact. (1990, p. 146)

The bodies of Welton students do not occupy any safe space on their own or a safe landscape for the functioning of the autonomous self. Critical distance does not exist at arm's length, as it were. An ecology of critical inter*views* between concrete voices is what remains. In this move from distantiation to implosion, the body represents what Pagano refers to as our "radical nearness" (1995). Pagano turns the body's "attachments to the world" against the "fantasy of unfettered mind" (p. 343). She affirms our libidinal connections that simultaneously "guarantee identity" (p. 349) through differences between bodies. Pagano does not see the choice as merely *either* identity *or* consensus, but a critical hybrid of *both* difference *and* connection through the "specificity of the body" (p. 352).

Keating assists in reposturing the students' bodies in ways against which Welton's establishment has guarded. Whereas they sit robotlike with hands on their desks, with erect posture, and equidistant from one another, Keating's hallway huddles are more informal, disorganized, and flexible. Welton Academy rigidifies the body's demeanor; Keating uncoils it. Compare this with Foucault's description of embodied handwriting exercises in schools:

> A well-disciplined body forms the operationalized context of the slightest gesture. Good handwriting, for example, presupposes a gymnastics—a whole routine whose rigorous code invests the body in its entirety, from the points of the feet to the tip of the index finger. The pupils must always "hold their bodies erect, somewhat turned and free on the left side, slightly inclined, so that, with the elbow placed on the table, the chin can be rested upon the hand, unless this were to interfere with the view; the

left leg must be somewhat more forward under the table than the right. A distance of two fingers must be left between the body and the table. . . ." (1977, p. 152)

At Welton, with class seats arranged in rows that are equidistant from one another and facing the front of the room, a teacher is able more efficiently to supervise student bodies. Such a perfect arrangement of the room improves what Cohen refers to as a teacher's periscopic "'super'-vision" (1996) and her technology of control.

Keating fractures Welton's surveillance pedagogy by holding class sessions in hallways, sport fields, and school quads. And when he conducts discussions in the classroom, on the importance of poetry, for example, he crouches on the ground whereas the students remain standing and looking downward at him, thereby suggesting a disruption of their relationships vis-à-vis the body. As a result, the students are able to use the classroom as a space to experiment with what Goodman calls "ways of worldmaking" (1978). This intensifies in a scene where Keating encourages the students to stand atop the teacher's desk and to take a moment to survey the room in order to see it—in a sense see the world—from a different perspective. In another outdoor scene, Keating asks the students to experiment with their style of walking in order to show "the dangers of conformity." At first the students walk like one another, almost in militia formation. Then prompted by Keating's suggestion, some students begin to strut; some waggle. Charlie sits out this exercise saying that he is, "Exercising the right not to walk." By making the familiar strange, Keating begins the rudiments of a lesson on the unnaturalness of the classroom setting, that is, its hierarchical spatial organization and centralized arrangement.

Body and Language

In light of Bakhtin's insights, we can think of the body as an ideological effect of language. The body becomes a sign in discourse and communicative exchanges. In reference to Bakhtin's notion of "tact," or to the codes of dialogue, Stam writes,

> In the sound film we not only hear the words with their accent and intonation, but witness the facial or corporeal expression which accompanies the words—the posture of arrogance or resignation, the raised eyebrow, the intimidating look, the ironic glance which modifies the ostensible meaning of an utterance. (1988, p. 125)

This analysis blurs the distinctions between what is cognitive and what is bodily. Eyes speak volumes. Postures communicate emotion. Speech and the body conflate. A revolutionary discourse must not only liberate the mind, it must also decolonize the body. Ideologically speaking, the body houses various social grammars and norms, not in their Durkheimian sense as accepted rules for conduct (Durkheim, 1961), but as discursive sites that are struggles over meaning in the Gramscian and Freirean sense.

Keating's somatic pedagogy remolds the students' musculatures into a formation conducive to what Bakhtin refers to as a "dialogic relationship." As such, Keating suggests that the body is social. It only gains recognition and, more important, meaning, when juxtaposed with other bodies. Bodies, as it were, converse on the level of signs. Similarly, Fiske observes,

> The body, its geography and history, are not empiricist facts in a Newtonian nature. Their natural essences are semiotically inert: they become epistemologically interesting only when they enter a social order, for only then do their differences become structured rather than essential; only a social order, therefore, can make differences signify. The concrete practices of everyday life are the insertion of the body into the social order, and, de Certeau would argue, the inscription of the social order upon that body. (1992, p. 163)

In *Dead Poets Society* we understand Todd's unwillingness to inject his body into class interactions and Dead Poets events in relation to more exoticized expressions of the "savage" body—for example, Charlie's. Charlie's "yawping" behavior sets the context for Todd's reluctance to let out a "barbaric Yawp" during Keating's class. A similar situation occurs during one of Keating's field exercises. In an attempt to provide an embodied pedagogy of movement, Keating takes the students out to the grass field, and they take turns kicking a soccer ball as classical music blares in the background. One student in particular is tentative to recite a line from a poem and weakly kicks the soccer ball. A resounding "boo" from Keating results, strategically juxtaposed with Charlie bellowing "To indeed be a god!" and followed by his thundering kick at the next ball. "To indeed be a god!"—a sentiment fostered in Keating's teachings—is certainly one of the repressive myths of empire and Keating leaves such ideological impulses unchecked and free to be cathected to any movement in search of gods to serve the empire or otherwise. Last, Knox's sexual repression in his pursuit of the virginal Kris gains more context when we consider Charlie's overbearing sexual and sexist comments. In one scene, Charlie unfolds a pornographic centerfold; in another, he exposes a lightning bolt on his chest: according to him it is a symbol of his virility. These characters do not, as an essentialist reading might suggest, possess a transparent self independent of their social coconstruction with others. The students' bodies are in constant and *anticipatory dialogue* with one another. Their bodies are not already formed but are always involved in a process of becoming, betwixt and between social contexts.

The issue of the body invokes the materiality of the oppression that the Welton students suffer at the hands of their teaching and administrating counterparts. We use the word *administration* to suggest a formal body of laws developed for purposes of normalization. As a backdrop, Welton's natural surroundings (e.g., the grassy fields, lakes, and wildlife) point to the unnaturalness, the ironic perversion of their schooling. When Knox rides a bike down a grassy hill, a flock of birds flood the sky to avoid getting hit. The trees, ponds, and wildlife that canopy the school grounds mask Welton's manufactured and instrumental education. This juxtaposition reminds us how instrumental reason subjugates nature for technical purposes, rather than for emancipatory interests. The students' objective world sets the context for their learning. They have very little to say about the work that they do in class, on the production of knowledge that is evaluated, and on the creative directions that they would like to pursue.

Welton's official curriculum—which the school principal, Nolan, boasts "is set, proven, and works"—follows a program of inquiry that fetishizes the production of knowledge. It concentrates more on "what works" and disregards the work that goes into knowing. On Keating's first day of class, we learn the "Prichard Scale" Welton uses to determine the "greatness" of a poem. Keating strategically sketches the scale on the chalkboard as a two-coordinate system with the poem's "importance" on one axis and its "perfection" on another. Beauty, or what Prichard calls "artful rendition," is rendered quantifiable. We are reminded here of Kant's compendium on beauty. Consider his words in the following passage:

> *Taste* is the faculty of judging of an object or a method of representing it by an *entirely disinterested* satisfaction or dissatisfaction. The object of such satisfaction is called *beautiful*. . . . Consequently he must believe that he has reason for attributing a similar satisfaction to everyone. He will therefore speak of the beautiful as if beauty were a characteristic of the object and the judgment logical. . . . Consequently the judgment of taste, accompanied with the consciousness of separation from all interest, must claim validity for every man, without this universality depending on objects. That is, there must be bound up with it a title to subjective universality. (1970, p. 381; original emphasis)

For Kant, self-interest taints the ideal representation of beauty. Any purposiveness on the part of the subject renders beauty less than ideal. Any conceptualization of an object (e.g., a rose or, in our case, a poem) with relations outside of itself stains the objectification of beauty. According to Kant, such is the human capacity for reason. Kant critiques the Western obsession with ideal, sublime rationality in his attempt to synthesize the objective with the subjective, and reason with faith. The Prichard Scale reifies the neutral and ahistorical concept of beauty. It fails to note that a critic of poetry cannot divorce her values from the hermeneutics of beauty. *A priori* assumptions are always constitutive of our perceptions which, in turn, provide the necessary elements of our conceptual maps. This has been the staple of sociological wisdom for several generations.

Beauty is a political construct with consequences as well as liberatory possibilities. Beauty is part of a system of relations involving prior commitments to valuation of qualities between things and people, not quantifiable measures of worth. Rather than seeking consensus on the "nature" of beauty, critical educators should look for contradictions in the aesthetic. Keating never extends his critique of schooling to include an interrogation of Western male standards of beauty. Keating ignores the fact that different cultures have different standards of judgment. When the students ask Keating in the courtyard about the original Dead Poets, he recalls his group reading poems from Whitman, and Thoreau; in sum, he says, "The biggies." Keating fails to weave his insights outside of a Western discourse on language and beauty, unabashed by the Western deletion of competing subaltern voices from the margins. Poetic verse is always imbricated with technical standards for beauty that suppress the social production of beauty in exchange for meter, rhyme, and form (e.g., Shakespearean or Italian sonnets). Keating fails to realize that the poetics of beauty never speaks for itself but is refracted by particular interests and produced by ideological imperatives that have been shaped by history.

"Seize the Day!": Agency and Resistance

"Seize the day," Keating advises. In effect, he is asking the students, What is it about yourselves that you no longer want to be? Keating counsels Neil to practice the moral courage required to live his life in the direction he desires. Neil's longing to act in *A Midsummer Night's Dream* represents his desire to will his life in the direction he wants, to produce his life's own dramaturgy, to be autonomous as opposed to being an automaton. Keating's oppositional teaching style unsettles Welton's hegemonic relations of power, especially those that reconfirm parental authority and decision making. Neil resists his father's impositions by circumventing and thwarting his father's control: by lying about dropping out of the play. Furthermore, he lies to Keating about having confronted his father about his desires. Neil "seizes the day" by activating the agency he possesses in order to fulfill his destiny on stage. After his father threatens to send him to military school, Neil commits suicide. Suicide becomes his last opportunity to act, to make an existential choice that joins him with the Dead Poets of the past.

Keating's inspirational, and at times transgressive, pedagogy lacks the critical discourse necessary for liberatory practices. Resistance is primarily confined to the secrecy of the cave meetings where students privatize their dialogues. Thus, it does not threaten Welton's hegemonic hold on the student population. The film fails to consider the fact that ideological hegemony relies upon a certain exercise of resistance. Activities such as cave meetings, tearing pages from assigned books, and reciting self-generated poetry are personalized moments of resistance which, when kept private, reconfirm hegemonic relations. Resistance is reduced to idiosyncratic acts of bourgeois transgression, performative moments of apostasy without the benefit of critical analysis.

Kerkvliet reminds us about the important differences between "everyday resistance" and "unusual resistance" (1990). Everyday resistance is usually composed of individual acts by private individuals lacking formal organization. It includes such acts as pilfering small items from a company one works for in response to low wages. Unusual resistance is characterized by a group of individuals with a chosen leadership and an agreed upon central target of opposition. Though unusual resistance benefits from the added organization, its members are also more visible to their targeted opposition and can be more vulnerable to disciplinary measures than everyday resistors. The students who comprise Dead Poets Society II celebrate resistance without the benefit of calculated actions toward a collective goal. The group also lacks what de Certeau (1984) refers to as "tactics" or those acts that resemble guerrilla warfare and lack predictable sites and centers of activity (Sleeter and McLaren, 1995, p.26). Distinct from "strategies," which belong to a category of surveillance, tactics escape the gaze of official power through indeterminate strikes. Without the benefit of a discourse extending beyond a celebration of transgression and conceptions of self, students lack the political power to produce "bodies without organs" (Deleuze & Guattari, 1983). By bodies without organs, Deleuze and Guattari do not suggest bodies without hearts, lungs, and stomachs. As opposed to "full bodies," bodies free from *organ*izational territories of desire involve the discharge of institutions as excrement from humans as desiring-machines. In the film, this is semiotically accomplished when Todd vomits on the vast whiteness of snow after he learns of Neil's death. Todd's body rejects what his social conditions have made of him, a docile body. After the discharge, Todd runs wildly away, his screams reverberating against the still trees and into the white darkness of the field at dawn, as he finally lets out his barbaric "yawp."

Members of Dead Poets Society II *feel* they are challenging the status quo without actually transforming asymmetrical relations of power. Their actions fail to move beyond the pleasure of resistance for its own sake. Resistance at Welton takes the form of a personal revelation rather than a rebellion and actually serves to reify the alienation of the students through their absorption of the mere facticity and inevitability of defeat into their very conception of themselves. From the perspective of Bakhtinian sociolinguistics, the students participate in a pseudocarnival, a bourgeois excursion on the wild side (Bakhtin, 1981). In Stam's words,

> Carnival in our sense is more than a party or a festival; it is the oppositional culture of the oppressed, the official world as seen from below; not the mere disruption of etiquette but the symbolic, anticipatory overthrow of oppressive social structures. On the positive side, it is ecstatic collectivity, the joyful affirmation of change, a dress rehearsal for utopia. On the negative, critical side, it is a demystifying instrument for everything in the social formation that renders collectivity impossible: class hierarchy, sexual repression, patriarchy, dogmatism and paranoia. (1988, p. 135)

Welton students have an easy time affirming the positive side of carnival. They welcome the liberationist opportunities and controlled *jouissance* that Keating opens up for them: for instance, the tearing out of book pages, the standing atop their desks, and the cave meetings. However, they fail to self-reflect on the challenges to carnival. They fail to understand how the social logic of dominant society is actually inscribed and enfolded in the ambivalent vicissitudes of their daily lives. Keating fails to enact a pedagogy that provides students with a critical vernacular that could distance them from their pleasure in participating in the act of refusing authority. Occupying a privileged linguistic capital, Charlie seduces Gloria and Tina with lines from a sonnet created, according to Keating, to "woo women." The young women's apparent amazement at Charlie's poetic sensibilities, albeit plagiarized from original authors, suggests their uneducated class background. In another scene, Charlie creates a spectacle of sexual repression when he relays a phone message from God to the principal saying "It's God. He says we should have girls at Welton." In other instances, students objectify women as objects of sexual desire or subject them to the male gaze, as in Knox's fixation with Kris during the pep rally. Desiring the beautiful Kris, Knox rides his bike from Welton to attend a school rally where Kris is performing as a cheerleader. When he arrives at the scene, Knox lowers his sunglasses to sneak a peek at Kris dancing and cheering for her team. Subsequently, after having been discovered to be a Dead Poets Society II member, Cameron advises the rest of the group to cooperate with the administrators in scapegoating Keating.

Keating's Failure

Ultimately, and with Keating's assistance, the students fail to bridge Bacchic revelry with Bakhtinian transgression. They lack the ability to articulate a political project that extends beyond the celebration of self to include the transformation of their social conditions. Keating's concept of agency is ultimately naive. He seems unable to grasp the idea that real relations declare their own meanings unambiguously within the regime of the "taken-for-granted" yet are still ideological because they can only be understood within certain systems of representation. Had Keating been able to engage his students in ideology critique, he would have been able to assist them in understanding their misrecognition of themselves. Keating retains an exaggerated belief in autonomous agency and in the novelty and ludic power of personalistic transgression. In doing so, Keating simply enacts one of the most recurring *topoi* of modern education, the rejection of sameness and routine, and the celebration of the new.

Keating fails to consider how individuals are differentially enabled to act by virtue of the economic and cultural constraints they face, and by virtue of the privileging hierarchies constructed out of the discourses of race, ethnicity, class, gender, and sexual orientation. Furthermore, he fails to recognize how knowledge is socially and historically constructed, and how individuals are synechochically related to the wider society through asymmetrical relations of power and privilege. Keating's position denies and obscures the politics of difference. While Keating rightly and admirably seeks to imperil the familiar, to unsettle the certainty of Welton's sovereign regime of truth, and to render problematic the regulatory apparatuses within which proper behavior and comportment and social interactions are analyzed, he is unable to analyze how student subjectivities are rationalized and accommodated to existing regimes of truth and social divisions of labor. Because Keating appears to adopt a quasi-Durkheimian view according to which the social order is integrated by way of an organic solidarity, he fails to consider sufficiently how individuals are formed out of competing solidarities that overlap and are conflictual. Keating's resistance is just another way of rewriting ethnocentrism as a defense of Western civilization. He subsumes and simplifies diverse political and cultural forms of resistance and celebrates unwittingly the ideology of individualistic transgression that reinforces the very traditionalism and ethical quietism that he is trying to subvert.

We are not arguing that personal responsibility be erased by collective responsibility. Critical pedagogy requires the cultivation of a receptivity toward a dialogue that is rooted in everyday sensuous existence in the communal world. Such a dialogue is not rooted in collectivism nor a Nietzschean act of individual self-realization but rather in a community of learners that is fundamentally *dialogic*. While Keating recognizes that the school requires atomized individuals but cannot tolerate interpersonal relations based on free association, he is unable to create a genuine community based on an openness to the other. This is because his pedagogical dialogism is still trapped in the idea of the self-sufficient, Cartesian cogito. He fails to notice the necessity of the presence of the other in the self. His assertion of "seize the day" is ultimately an arrogant conceit, a dogmatic postulate premised on the autonomous, self-centered ego. Peak experiencing by "sucking the marrow out of life" is constituted dialogically, accompanied by the multiple consciousness of a self-other relation. For Keating, "seize the day" becomes an enunciative act celebrating the single consciousness and monologic desire that suppresses an understanding of the ethical power of the self-other relation.

In fact, Keating's "essence of man" humanism ultimately betrays the boys. His pedagogy embodies a notion of liberation that ends with the self that merely needs to be recovered and not with the continuous transformation of material conditions (Althusser, 1965). Humanism is limited by its reduction of people as free and rational. It purports that through the law of reason, liberation is realized as a fact of human nature and is an anticipated yet preexisting essence. Humanism, to Althusser, involves a fallacious double move characterized by an empiricist-idealist epistemology. It assumes, in one move, that if human essence is universal, then it necessitates a given that individuals are concrete subjects: hence an *empiricism of the subject*. In another move, humanism locates the essence of humanity in every individual: hence an *idealism of the essence*. Both moves affirm the individual at the cost of the collective. However, a negation of humanistic universals is not the same thing as a rejection of the conditions of its historical necessity as a discourse with material consequences. Humanism is a symptom of the overall social formation and its determinations.

As a result of the film's classical humanism, resistances are isolated from one another. For instance, Charlie invites two women, Gloria and Tina, to the Dead Poets' cave meetings without consulting his comrades, let alone self-reflecting on his motives. He also informs the boys of an anonymous letter he wrote to the Welton administration asking that girls be admitted to the school. Despite the boys' objections, Charlie implicates the group during his "God is on the phone" antics in the chapel. He never fully negotiates his position with others toward a collective solidarity; resistance becomes a private decision. Consequently, it is relatively easy for administrators, teachers, and parents to "divide and conquer" the Dead Poets Society II. Also, we empathize with Neil as an individual in anguish without connecting him with Charlie or with the others. Neil seems to suffer alone. As a group, the students never fully shatter the microtechnological gaze that Welton's sentinels of truth and custodians of tradition use to discipline the students. This is best illustrated when Nolan, announces that he aims to indict the culprits responsible for inserting an "unauthorized article" in the school newspaper. He warns, "Rather than spending my valuable time, ferreting out the guilty persons, . . . and let me assure you I will find them . . . I'm asking any or all students who know about this article to make themselves known now." Isolated from one another, the subversives are cut off from each other, depotentiated as a body politic. Their resistance is regulated under the supervision of Nolan and company.

The film leaves unproblematized the different faces of oppression by isolating one type: student oppression. The discourse on students lacking a voice in school is emphasized at the expense of gender oppression. Indeed, the film's portrayal of women during a cave meeting does not transcend their stereotypical role as sexual objects. Kris is in constant fear that her boyfriend-protector, Chet, will discover Knox's persistent effort to steal her from him. Kris is caricatured as Chet's possession. Kris is seen as morally powerless to judge Knox's actions according to her own ethical standards; she must look to Chet for accountability. Charlie contradicts his own wishes for emancipation when he attempts to seduce Gloria and Tina with the very same (Shakespearean) sonnets that the group recites during cave meetings in order to feel liberated from their teachers. This *dialectic of consciousness raising* points out the contradictions inherent in what we see as a discourse lacking a self-reflective apparatus.

The Romantic Pedagogy of Individual Expression

As McLaren has said elsewhere (1991), compared to the dictatorial approach involving rote learning and severe military-style discipline that is used by most teachers at Welton, the classroom approach used by Keating is very innovative—you could call it "liberal" and not be wrong—and amounts to shattering mainstream conventions in the school. The students find Keating to be a charismatic leader, if not a liberating one. One of the problems that we have with this form of pedagogy is that it suggests that self-empowerment can exist without calling the existing capitalist social order into question. Issues of class, gender, and ethnic inequality are never raised. In fact, we would go so far as to claim that this form of liberal, humanist pedagogy serves to contain the political, to discursively police revolt, to equate liberation with the personal over the social, and to mask forms of domination. It is a pedagogy steeped in the romance of the word at the expense of the world. This is revealed in the sexism of Keating, who claims that poetry was invented to "woo women." The students are conspicuously not invited to problematize the relationship among the authoritarianism in the school, the way power works in the larger society to silence certain groups, and its entanglements in social practices that serve the rich and the powerful.

Berlin would refer to this as a form of "expressionistic rhetoric": (1987) although it includes a denunciation of economic, political, and social pressures to conform—to resist the institutionally sponsored production of desire, attitude, and behavior—it is resistance in the service of the privatized ego, and the privatized male ego at that. As Berlin notes, expressionistic rhetoric reinforces the entrepreneurial virtues of individualism, private initiative, risk-taking, and subversion of authority. It is the ideology of the unique, private vision of a Donald Trump buried in the tropes of Walt Whitman, devoid of a concern with how material and social constraints prohibit other, less fortunate groups from realizing their private vision. It is as if consciousness were somehow not connected to the workings of power or as if hierarchies of power and privilege were natural hierarchies. As a teacher, Keating attempts to defamiliarize the experience that the students have of rote learning and blind obedience to adult authority and the ruling-class economies of power and privilege, and while he is intent, perhaps even insistent, on getting beyond the deformation of the individual as authorized by the discourses of tradition and the prevailing regimes of truth of the time, the result is a struggle for uniqueness—perhaps even eccentricity—of individual expression. Berlin describes this kind of subversiveness as more apparent than real. It is debilitatingly divisive of political protest because it encourages individuals to achieve unique personhood in antiseptic isolation from any sense of collective struggle around the referent of difference and otherness. It is a pedagogy that operates without consideration of how power works to privilege certain groups over others on the basis of race, class, and gender, and Keating takes no pains to narrate the contingency of his own and the students' race, class, and gender privilege.

This is a soft mode of resistance easily co-opted by those forces it seeks to delegitimate; a form of resistance that actually complements the capitalist ethos of possessive individualism. In Eagleton's terms (1990), Keating's pedagogy is a form of moral technology that structures modes of desire that the society needs in order to promote capitalist social relations and the international division of labor. It teaches what he terms a *bourgeois mode of subjectivity* precisely in the way it celebrates learning for the sake of learning, and creativity for its own sake, which is a mistaken virtue we believe, because creative learning never speaks for itself and is always inscribed by political interests and supported by relations of power. There is a certain creativity to the Nazis' "final solution" that we dare say no teacher would ever want her students to emulate. We are not arguing that liberal humanism was responsible for the Holocaust, but we are arguing that freedom and creativity should always be understood in relation to the social context in which they are engendered and put to use. Critical pedagogy poses a crucial question, Freedom and creativity for what?

Zavaradeh's critique of the liberal humanist classroom can be appropriately applied to the pedagogy of *Dead Poets Society*. Keating's pedagogy reveals itself as one of "fancy"—what Zavaradeh's calls a "pedagogy of pleasure" (1994). Keating's notion of liberation is personal and eminently ahistorical, and has little to do with emancipation. It is a pedagogy formally "at odds" with the "serious" workaday bourgeois world but that does not seriously question the underlying assumptions or relations of power that inform it. Questions involving power/knowledge relations are suspended, and dangerous memories of human suffering and rebellion are never raised.

Dead Poets Society inspires its viewers to resist oppression in schools. Through Keating, the power of a transgressive pedagogy offers alternative ways of looking at education. Keating encourages the viewer to stand within different planes of vision in order to look at the familiar from new frames of reference, or in Rorty's terms, to search for more "edifying" (1979) ways to tell stories about the world. However, the film falls short of moving beyond bourgeois forms of resistance and into a political project. The students experience moments of *jouissance*. By the end, one senses that some aspects of the school's culture have changed without transforming the culture of power. This is not an altogether hopeless state of affairs. Sporadic jolts to the system may give rise to larger political movements (Bottomore, 1993). However, without a critique of language and a language of critique, Welton students lack a powerful tool for cultural emancipation and social liberation. They are limited by the structures of signification within the discourses that they occupy.

At the film's conclusion, the viewer witnesses a triumphalistic moment as the students stand proudly atop their desks and hail their leader, Keating: "Oh captain, my captain." In solidarity, the subversives stand side-by-side. Yet if we slice through the cloud of emotions, we are left hopeful but ambivalent about their plight. A collective oppositional discourse offers hope for social justice. We can only wish that these individual strands of disenchantment and resentment gradually entwine themselves into a collective struggle. Without a public, counterhegemonic coalition, students do not muster enough power to challenge the dominant discourses of their school. What may result is their heightened marginalization.

Viewing the Film in the Classroom

We leave our students with the following questions in relation to the pedagogy represented in the film: What vision of the future inheres in the pedagogy of *Dead Poets Society*? What vision of social justice? What model of the individual subject? What suppositions involving democracy? We believe that the more we attempt to clarify what we mean by "critical pedagogy," the more we will be given opportunities for discussing and elaborating the values, suppositions, and basis for practice that inform our teaching, learning, research practices, and, perhaps most important of all, the vision of the future that inheres in them.

Students who viewed *Dead Poets Society* with us were initially enthusiastic about the film. Some saw it as a definitive representation of an embodied critical pedagogy. Virtually no students were able to discern the distinction between critical pedagogy as articulated by Freire and by other criticalists, and liberal bourgeois pedagogy as practiced by Keating. We began discussions of the film by asking students to compare their own experiences as high school students with those of the students in the film. We also asked our students to evaluate Keating's pedagogical practices in light of their pedagogical imperatives and characteristics that they would like to embody in their own teaching practices. We found that the charismatic portrayal of Keating by Williams made it difficult to separate Keating's engaging personality from the pedagogical philosophy he appeared to embrace in the film. Students admired Keating's nonconformist teaching practices and described them as desirable attributes for a teacher to possess. Our attempts to contrast Keating's pedagogy with what we had been reading about critical pedagogy was described as an expression of "militant Marxism" or "dogmatic social viewpoints" by some students. Other students reacted by saying that a single teacher "can do little more than reach out to help students on an individual basis." This was followed by a reaction that stressed the vulnerability of the critical pedagogue in terms of sanctions by the administration for supporting "biased political viewpoints." In short, we found that our students reacted to our pedagogy in much the same way as Keating's students in the film did to him: they were initially hesitant, cautious, and skeptical.

After discussing with students various readings in critical pedagogy and developing with them a working vocabulary of critical terminology, students were able to point to many of the limitations in Keating's pedagogical philosophy and praxis. Critical pedagogy was identified in the final instance as the production of a pedagogical locality that can be characterized as a situated community of dialogic learners committed to the development of a socialist imaginary. Such a community is dedicated to generating the *context* for dialogic praxis whereas in mainstream pedagogies, schooling is produced or driven by the already existing context provided by the nation-state. That the students were able make this distinction is, in our minds, one of the most essential steps in understanding both the perils and the promise of critical pedagogy.

Dead Poets Society belongs to a genre of film about pedagogy where a teacher enters an oppressive school condition and attempts to liberate the students. Other films with similar themes, though different content, include *Stand and Deliver, Lean on Me, Dangerous Minds, Sunset Park,* and *The Substitute*. These films are helpful in pointing out the oppressive structures in schools, especially inner-city schools. They have a seductive appeal for the mainstream audience because learning and liberation are usually overt themes. Liberatory teaching become commonsensical goods-in-themselves. But because the films usually construct learning in a technicist way, knowledge through a naturalistic (i.e., uncommodified) framework, and schooling in a typically unsocial manner, they also become quickly problematic. This has been our position with respect to *Dead Poets Society*. Although the director has constructed an arch of hope for his viewers, in the film's problems with resistance for pleasure, un-self-reflexive discourses, and lack of attention to social contradictions that are traceable to capital, he undoes his otherwise progressive message.

As part of an alternative, and usually illegitimized, form of literacy, popular culture is a valuable terrain for a critical study of race, class, gender, and sexual relations. Watching *Dead Poets Society* enables students to read how the body is schooled to produce docile students. This move is also instructive for a strategic problematization of the issues behind nonmaterialist pedagogies, even those that appear, on the surface, to be liberating. A study of pop culture is central to an understanding of the larger, material totality that informs schooling and how this is understood and mediated by students through discourse. Through critical interventions, popular culture pedagogies offer students an education for a more complete understanding of everyday life. Moreover, a materialist discourse helps students understand that film images are inscribed by the social relations of production and the division of labor.

References

Althusser, L. (1965). *For Marx*. London and New York: Verso.

Appadurai, A. (1996). *Modernity at large: Cultural dimensions of globalization*. Minneapolis: University of Minnesota Press.

Bakhtin, M. (1981). *The dialogic imagination*. (M. Holquist, Ed.) (C. Emerson & M. Holquist, Trans.). Austin: University of Texas Press.

Baudrillard, J. (1983). *Simulations*. New York: Semiotext.

Baudrillard, J. (1990). *Fatal strategies*. New York: Semiotext.

Berlin, J. A. (1987). *Rhetoric and reality: Writing instruction in American colleges, 1900-1985*. Carbondale and Edwardsville: Southern Illinois University Press.

Blacker, D. (1996). Teaching in troubled times: Democratic education and the problem of "extra people?", *The Teacher Educator, 32*(1), 62-72.

Bottomore, T. (1993). *Political sociology*. (2nd edition). Minneapolis: University of Minnesota Press.

Calhoun, C. (1994). Social theory and the politics of identity. In C. Calhoun (Ed.), *Social theory and the politics of identity* (pp. 9-36). Cambridge, MA: Blackwell.

Cohen, S. (1996). Postmodernism, the new cultural history, film: Resisting images of education, *Pedagogica Historica: International Journal of the History of Education,* 32(2), 395-420.

De Certeau, M. (1984). *The practice of everyday life.* Berkeley: University of California Press.

Deleuze, G., and Guattari, F. (1983). *Anti-Oedipus: Capitalism and schizophrenia.* Minneapolis: University of Minnesota Press.

Durkheim, E. (1961). *Moral Education.* New York and London: Free Press.

Eagleton, T. (1990). *The ideology of the aesthetic.* Cambridge: Basil Blackwell.

Fiske, J. (1992). The culture of everyday life. In L. Grossberg, C. Nelson, & P. Treichler (Eds.), *Cultural studies* (pp. 154-173). New York and London: Routledge Publishers.

Foucault, M. (1977). *Discipline and Punish.* New York: Vintage Books.

Freire, P. (1993). *Pedagogy of the oppressed.* New York: Continuum.

Giroux, H., & Simon, R. (1989). Popular culture as a pedagogy of pleasure and meaning. In H. Giroux & R. Simon (Eds.), *Popular culture: schooling & everyday life* (pp. 1–29). New York, Westport, and London: Bergin & Garvey.

Giroux, H., & Simon, R. (1994). Popular culture and critical pedagogy: everyday life as a basis for curriculum knowledge. In H. Giroux & P. McLaren (Eds.), *Critical pedagogy, the state, and cultural struggle* (pp. 236-252). Albany: State University of New York Press.

Goodman, N. (1978). *Ways of worldmaking.* Indianapolis: Hackett Publishing Company.

Haft, S., Witt, P., and Thomas, T. (Producers), & Weir, P. (Director). (1989). *Dead poets society* (Film). Burbank, CA: Touchstone Home Video.

Kant, I. (1970). Critique of judgment: First book "analytic of the beautiful." In H. Adams (Ed.), *Critical theory since Plato* (pp. 379-390). San Diego; New York; Chicago; Atlanta; Washington, DC; London; Sydney; and Toronto: Harcourt.

Kerkvliet, B. (1990). *Everyday politics in the Philippines.* Berkeley, Los Angeles, and Oxford: University of California Press.

McLaren, P. (1991). Critical pedagogy: Constructing an arch of social dreaming and a doorway to hope, *Sociology of Education in Canada, 173*(1), 137-160.

McLaren, P. (1993). *Schooling as a ritual performance: Towards a political economy of educational symbols and gestures*. London and New York: Routledge.

McLaren, P. (1994). Postmodernism and the death of politics: A Brazilian reprieve. In P. McLaren & C. Lankshear (Eds.), *Politics of Liberation* (pp. 193-215). London and New York: Routledge.

McNally, D. (2001). *Bodies of Meaning: Studies on Language, Labor, and Liberation*. Albany: State University of New York Press.

Montag, W. (1988). What is at stake in the debate on postmodernism?. In E. Kaplan (Ed.), *Postmodernism and its discontents* (pp. 88-103). London and New York: Verso.

Pagano, J. (1995). Matters of the mind. In W. Kohli (Ed.), *Critical conversations in philosophy of education* (pp. 340-354). London and New York: Routledge.

Rorty, R. (1979). *Philosophy and the mirror of nature*. Princeton, NJ: Princeton University Press.

San Juan Jr., E. (1992). *Articulations of power in ethnic and racial studies in the United States*. New Jersey and London: Humanities Press.

Shumway, D. (1989). Reading rock 'n' roll in the classroom: A critical pedagogy. In H. Giroux & P. McLaren (Eds.), *Critical pedagogy, the state, and cultural struggle* (pp. 222-235). Albany: State University of New York Press.

Sleeter, C., & McLaren, P. (1995). Introduction: Exploring connections to build a critical multiculturalism. In C. Sleeter & P. McLaren (Eds.), *Multicultural education, critical pedagogy, and the politics of difference* (pp. 5–32). Albany: State University of New York Press.

Stam, R. (1988). Mikhail Bakhtin and left cultural critique. In E. Kaplan (Ed.), *Postmodernism and its discontents* (pp. 116-145). London and New York: Verso.

Storey, J. (1993). *Cultural theory and popular culture*. Athens: University of Georgia Press.

Thoreau, H. D. Zavaradeh, M. (1994). *Theory as resistance: Politics and culture after (post)structuralism*. New York and London: Guilford Press.

Contributors

Katherine Brown is interested in organizational communication and the adult learning workplace. As a postdoctoral researcher affiliated with the Laboratory of Comparative Human Cognition, she coauthored several progress reports, monographs, and articles and contributed to the production of a CD and two television programs about the history of the Fifth Dimension model and its widespread dissemination. Topics of her joint work with Michael Cole include adult learning and conceptual development, organizing collaborative research, and the long-term sustainability of Fifth Dimension model adaptations.

Lyn Mikel Brown is Associate Professor of Education, Human Development, and Women's Studies at Colby College. She received her doctorate in Human Development and Psychology from Harvard University. She has also taught at the Harvard Graduate School of Education. She is the author of *Raising Their Voices: The Politics of Girls' Anger* (Harvard),coauthor (with Carol Gilligan)of *Meeting at the Crossroads: Women's Psychology and Girls' Development* (Harvard), as well as numerous articles on girls' and women's psychological development, girls' education, and feminist research methods.

Michael Cole is Professor of Communication and Psychology at the University of California, San Diego and Director of the Laboratory of Comparative Human Cognition. He has conducted studies on the role of culture in human development, particularly in schools. He is the author of *Cultural Psychology* (Harvard) and coauthor, with his wife Sheila, of *The Development of Children* (Freeman), as well as a number of more specialized texts and monographs. His current research focuses on the design, implementation, and sustainability of new cultural forms of development-enhancing activity.

Elizabeth Debold is a founding member of the Harvard Project on Women's Psychology and Girls' Development. She received her doctorate in Human Development and Psychology from Harvard University. She is coauthor (with Marie Wilson and Idelisse Malave) of *Mother-Daughter*

Revolution (Addison-Wesley), and she is currently working on a new book, *Beyond Gender* (forthcoming from Pantheon). She is a consultant to the Ms. Foundation for Women, and the foundation's Director of Evaluation to the Healthy Girls—Healthy Women Collaborative Fund.

Robin L. Leavitt is Associate Professor and Chair of the Educational Studies Department at Illinois Wesleyan University. She received her graduate degrees in Early Childhood Education and Educational Policy Studies from the University of Illinois, Urbana-Champaign. Her scholarship has focused on interpretive and ethnographic studies of children in early childhood settings, with a focus on their emotional and moral socialization. She is the author of numerous articles; her most recent book is *Power and Emotion in Infant-Toddler Day Care* (State University of New York Press).

Zeus Leonardo is Assistant Professor in the Division of Social and Multicultural Foundations of Education at the California State University, Long Beach. He earned his doctorate at Univeristy of California at Los Angeles's Graduate School of Education and Information Studies, and has also taught at the University of St. Thomas, Minneapolis. His work can best be described as the intersection between ideology, discourse, and school reform. He is coeditor (with Tejeda Martinez) of *Charting New Terrains in Chicano(a)/Latino(a) Education* (forthcoming from Hampton Press). He has also published several articles on critical educational theory.

Peter McLaren, a former elementary schoolteacher and union journalist, is currently Professor at the Graduate School of Education and Information Studies, University of California, Los Angeles. Active as a critical social theorist and in local, national, and international political reform efforts, he has published over thirty books and monographs in a variety of fields including anthropology, cultural studies, critical literacy, sociology, critical pedagogy, and multicultural education. He also lectures worldwide on the politics of liberation. His most recent books include *Critical Pedagogy and Predatory Culture* (Routledge), *Revolutionary Multiculturalism* (Westview Press), *Schooling as a Ritual Performance* (3rd edition, Rowman and Littlefield), *Life in Schools* (3rd edition, Longman), and *Che Guevara, Paulo Freire, and the Pedagogy of Revolution* (Rowman and Littlefield). His books and articles have been translated into twelve languages.

Usha Menon is Assistant Professor of Anthropology at Drexel University. Her research site has been the temple town of Bhubaneswar in Orissa, India. She writes on popular, contemporary understandings of the goddess Kali, on family dynamics and gender relations in Oriya Hindu society, and on Hindu morality. She is currently studying the supposed militancy of Hindu women vis-à-vis Muslims—a relatively recent phenomenon on the subcontinent and one that is potentially troubling. She is also completing a book on the life experiences of Oriya Hindu women and the relevance of Western feminist thought to their lives and experiences.

Martin J. Packer is Associate Professor of Psychology at Duquesne University, where the Department of Psychology takes an existential-phenomenological stance. He has also taught at the University of California, Berkeley, and at the University of Michigan. His research focuses on the practical and situated character of learning and development, and he currently teaches developmental psychology and interpretive research methodology. He is the author of *Changing Classes: School Reform and the New Economy* (Cambridge University Press), *The Structure of Moral Action: A Hermeneutic Study of Moral Conflict* (Karger), and coeditor (with Richard Addison) of *Entering the Circle: Hermeneutic Investigation in Psychology* (State University of New York Press), and (with Mark Tappan) of *Narrative and Storytelling: Implications for Understanding Moral Development* (Jossey-Bass).

Linda J. Rogers is Professor of Educational Psychology at California State University-Monterey, and the Executive Director of the Semiotic Society of America. She is the author of *Wish I Were: Feltpathways to the Self* (Atwood Publishing), *Semiotic Framings of Third Space Across the Disciplines* (forthcoming from Atwood Publishing), *Semiotics and Dis/Ability* (forthcoming from State University of New York Press), and coauthor (with Susan Tucker) of *Semiotic Methods for Evaluation and Qualitative Research* (forthcoming from Sage). She has also worked with children and teachers in Northern Ireland, Australia, and Cleveland.

Richard A. Shweder is a cultural anthropologist and Professor of Human Development at the University of Chicago. He received his doctorate in Social Anthropology from Harvard University. He is the author of *Thinking Through Cultures: Expeditions in Cultural Psychology* (Harvard) and editor or coeditor of several books in the areas of cultural psychology, psychological anthropology, and comparative human development. For the past thirty years he has been conducting research on moral reasoning, emotional functioning, gender roles, and the moral foundations of family life practices in the Hindu temple town of Bhubaneswar, India.

Mark B. Tappan is Associate Professor and Chair of the Education and Human Development Program at Colby College. He received his doctorate in Human Development from Harvard University. He has also taught at the University of Massachusetts, Boston, Trinity College, Clark University, and the Harvard Graduate School of Education. He has published numerous articles on moral development, moral education, narrative, hermeneutics, gender differences, and adult development.

Index